Core of my heart...

The love of field and coppice
Of green and shaded lanes
Of ordered woods and
                    gardens
Is running in your veins —
Strong love of grey-blue dies:
                    : Fance
Brown streams and soft
                    dim skies ----
I know but cannot share it,
My love is otherwise.

I love a sunburnt country,
A land of sweeping plains
Of ragged mountain-ranges
Of droughts and flooding
                    rains.
I love her far horizons
I love her jewel-sea,
Her beauty and her terrors —
The wide brown land for
                    me!

Her Sunburnt Country

The Extraordinary Literary Life of Dorothea Mackellar

DEBORAH FITZGERALD

SIMON &
SCHUSTER

HER SUNBURNT COUNTRY: THE EXTRAORDINARY LITERARY LIFE
OF DOROTHEA MACKELLAR
First published in Australia in 2023 by
Simon & Schuster (Australia) Pty Limited
Suite 19A, Level 1, Building C, 450 Miller Street, Cammeray, NSW 2062

10 9 8 7 6 5 4 3 2 1

Sydney New York London Toronto New Delhi
Visit our website at www.simonandschuster.com.au

© Deborah FitzGerald 2023

All rights reserved. No part of this publication may be reproduced, stored in a
retrieval system, or transmitted in any form or by any means, electronic, mechanical,
photocopying, recording or otherwise, without prior permission of the publisher.

The trustees of the Dorothea Mackellar estate (Jennifer Stiller, Kathleen Sue Kruger,
Anne Coffison) endorse this biography, noting that some cultural attitudes have shifted
since the historical period depicted, which has been referenced in the text.

All images, unless otherwise credited, are courtesy of the Mitchell Library and printed
with permission of the estate of Dorothea Mackellar.

 A catalogue record for this book is available from the National Library of Australia

ISBN: 9781760855406

Cover design: Christa Moffitt, Christabella Designs
Cover images: Portrait of Dorothea, courtesy of Jennifer Stiller; View from Tarrangaua,
courtesy of Mitchell Library and the estate of Dorothea Mackellar/Curtis Brown.
Endpaper image: Pages from 'Core of My Heart' from Dorothea Mackellar's 1907
verse book, courtesy of Mitchell Library, State Library of New South Wales.
Typeset by Midland Typesetters, Australia
Printed and bound in Australia by Griffin Press

 The paper this book is printed on is certified against the
Forest Stewardship Council® Standards. Griffin Press holds
chain of custody certification SCS-COC-001185. FSC®
promotes environmentally responsible, socially beneficial
and economically viable management of the world's forests.

Contents

Introduction   vii
Prologue   1

PART I

'MY COUNTRY'   9

Chapter 1	Young Dorothea	11
Chapter 2	The Mackellars	19
Chapter 3	Brother in Arms	27
Chapter 4	New Woman	41
Chapter 5	Core of My Heart	63
Chapter 6	A Rising Star	83
Chapter 7	Mr Dods	97
Chapter 8	The Closed Door	111

| Chapter 9 | The Grand Tour | 133 |
| Chapter 10 | Two's Company | 157 |

PART II
'COLOUR' — 171

Chapter 11	A Storm Brewing	173
Chapter 12	Theatre of War	191
Chapter 13	Armistice	203
Chapter 14	Wanderlust	215
Chapter 15	The Literary Life	229
Chapter 16	Sorrow and Sanctuary	241
Chapter 17	Of Kings and Trolls	259
Chapter 18	A Changed Country	275
Chapter 19	Out of Reach	291

Acknowledgements — 311

Notes — 313

To my beautiful mother Jean Lenehan, who was the brilliant storyteller in our family.

To the men in my life, my husband Mark Waugh and my sons Mac and Finn. You are everything.

Introduction

When I was first asked to write the official biography of Dorothea Mackellar by her cousin Jennifer Stiller, on behalf of the Mackellar Family Estate, I was immediately excited and intrigued. I had grown up reciting her famous poem 'My Country', along with generations of Australian children, as it was part of the school curriculum for decades. It was a cultural touchstone that captured a breathtakingly beautiful and sometimes frightening continent. But I soon realised that, like many Australians, I knew very little about the life of its author. I expected there would be a wealth of material documenting the life and times of a woman who gave us such an iconic poem. Checking online in the first instance, I was surprised to find there was a plethora of information about her most famous work, but very little written about Dorothea's life.

By far the most useful resource was the Mackellar Papers held at the Mitchell Library in the State Library of New South Wales. These included Dorothea's diaries from 1907, when she was twenty-one years old. Her earlier diaries are lost to time.

The surviving diaries, many of them unpublished until now, stretch through to the 1930s, albeit with some fragments missing. The collection also includes verse books with drafts of her poems, letters, family mementos, and manuscripts of plays she wrote with her friend and collaborator Ruth Bedford. To be granted permission to open the boxes and folders, to hold her diaries and verse books – and even a lock of her hair from the late 1880s – was a rare and thrilling privilege.

Dorothea's diaries were my primary resource, along with newspaper articles that documented her every move once she became famous. From her world travels to her social commitments, from her clothing to her political and literary views, she truly was a celebrity of her time.

Besides Dorothea's own collections of poetry and several novels, Jyoti Brunsdon's *I Love a Sunburnt Country: The Edited Diaries of Dorothea Mackellar*, a collection of extracts from her diaries from 1910 to 1918, was also invaluable. I am indebted to Brunsdon for cracking a secret code Dorothea used to protect the privacy of her diaries. Dorothea used a series of symbols to represent letters in the hope of preventing prying eyes from discovering her secrets, particularly in relation to her romantic life. Applying the code also allowed me to access diary entries which had never been published.

Another key resource was a slim volume, *My Heart, My Country*, by Adrienne Howley, a woman who nursed Dorothea in the last decade of her life and went on to become a Buddhist nun. It sheds light on Dorothea's early life, where diaries are missing, as well as on her final years. However, my research suggests that Dorothea's memories as recounted by Howley are not always reliable. There are some incidents and dates that do not add up.

This is not surprising – after all, who among us can remember our lives in perfect detail? Nonetheless, it was a very welcome resource and Dorothea's character can be glimpsed between the lines.

Dorothea emerged from the archives as sophisticated, intelligent and talented: a renaissance woman who spoke five languages; wrote poetry, plays and novels; sketched and painted; and rode horses, drove motor cars, swam and surfed. She was a woman who led a full and fascinating life despite the limitations placed on women of her time, and all the turmoil of the political and social upheavals she lived through – from Australia's Federation, to the fight for women's suffrage and the First and Second World Wars.

I feel compelled to address the issue of the colonial eye and the invisibility of Indigenous Australians in this work. Dorothea was a product of her time and her class. Casual racism was common but Dorothea's diaries reveal little of this. Rather, it is the fact that they are not seen at all that is telling. For those who argue the poem 'My Country' is about colonial possession, it must be remembered that Dorothea originally called the poem 'Core of my Heart' and it was a later editing decision that arrived at 'My Country'. It was not her intention to claim it but rather to describe it in all its 'beauty and terror' as a place she loved and was proud to call home.

With the help of Dorothea and the estate that has preserved her invaluable diaries and works, this biography will shed new light on the life of the woman who gave Australia one of its best-loved poems, 'My Country'.

In 1922, more than a decade after Dorothea gave us this extraordinary anthem, a group of prominent Australians were gathered in one of New York's finest dining rooms at the invitation of the Home Minister, George Pearce. Following a recitation of 'My Country', they rose as one to applaud. It was a public show of patriotism which also revealed how much the poem had captured the hearts and minds of Australians, and the depth of the affection they felt for its author. Meanwhile, the creator of this famous ode to Australia – by that time a spirited, independent woman in her thirties – was travelling, writing and cementing her reputation as one of the country's great poets.

In the interests of readability, I have reimagined some scenes based on details from her diaries, manuscripts and novels. Wherever possible, I have endeavoured to capture Dorothea's voice to describe places and events. Her lyrical and colourful prose takes the reader on exotic journeys that make you feel you are there looking over her shoulder. It was a joy to share her journey and I hope readers of this biography will take as much delight as I have in her amazing story.

Prologue

Dorothea sat on one of the wide peacock chairs on the verandah at Torryburn station, stockinged legs tucked beneath her, head bowed. She was writing, her pen moving hurriedly across notepaper resting on a book. She often wrote like this: in a rush, as though she could not get the words down fast enough, afraid the images in her head might disappear if she did not capture them on the page.

The late morning was impossibly hot. The kind of heat that burned your lungs and left you listless. The teenage girl had a vivid imagination, and if she closed her eyes she could picture herself diving down, down into a deep billabong. She could imagine touching the bottom, her lungs fit to burst, before turning and pushing back up through the glorious icy water, the movement displacing and replacing droplets all over her body like the pricking of a thousand needles.

Would she ever experience that thrill again? The billabongs were dry, along with the rivers and the creeks. The year was 1899 and a parched landscape stretched out before her. An obstinate drought had scarred the once verdant countryside.

Fourteen-year-old Dorothea had travelled 175 miles from Sydney with her parents, three siblings – older brothers Keith and Eric and younger brother Malcolm – and the family's servants. The convoy of horse-drawn carriages had bumped over rough and winding roads to their own version of the promised land at Torryburn station in the Hunter Valley, New South Wales. Owing to the drought, though, the family's country retreat was now less Garden of Eden and more Dante's 'Inferno'. The Big Dry had been stretching on for months and even the restrained Protestantism practised by the Mackellar family was being tested as they, along with everyone else, were urged to pray for rain.

Dorothea loved this piece of paradise that her father, Charles Mackellar, had acquired in 1898 for the express purpose of giving his offspring a healthy alternative to the polluted air of the city. A family history of asthma had spurred the decision to find a country property where they might enjoy some fresh air. Dorothea may have been a city girl by birth, but she felt completely at home at the homestead and surrounding property at Torryburn, where she spent hours walking in the bush, exploring and writing down the names of native plants, animals and birds in her ever-present notebooks.

But the drought had forced the wildlife to retreat to places unknown, presumably north where the rivers had not yet been reduced to the dry beds of clay Dorothea saw before her. The kangaroos, koalas, goannas, blue-tongued lizards, kingfishers and sulphur-crested cockatoos had fled. Countless sheep and cattle had died and those remaining were so emaciated that their rib cages showed through. Her deep affinity with animals meant that

Dorothea hated to see any creature suffer, so these sights broke her heart. Even her mother Marion's prized garden, once full of English roses thriving alongside flowering natives, had shrivelled in the heat. There was a heavy, leaden atmosphere that oppressed Dorothea's spirit.

Dorothea was trying to describe the desolate setting before her in a letter to her cousins in England, the Faithfull sisters: Pearl, Hope and Clare. The sweeping plains with their earthy colours were a stark contrast to the green fields of England. She wanted to describe how the scene impacted her in a visceral way, to convey why she loved the land *because* of its extremes and ambiguities not despite them. There was a grandeur to this country, but it came with a sense of foreboding – something Dorothea wanted to capture in her poetry. It was an inexplicable quality that could be both mystifying and terrifying at the same time. And there was something biblical about the chaos it unleashed: droughts and floods and plagues, the land throwing everything at those who sought to tame it – people who often lost the battle and sometimes their lives.

Dorothea's older brothers, Keith and Eric, considered time spent outdoors preferable to just about any other pursuit and longed to take their horses out for a ride, but even they had to concede defeat. The thick air was too hot and stifling and their horses were likely to keel over from heat exhaustion. Ten-year-old Malcolm – known to all as 'Mac' – would complain whenever the older boys insisted he could not join them on rides, but for now heat and lethargy made it a moot point.

Keith, the eldest of the Mackellar children and Dorothea's favoured childhood playmate, had grown into a handsome young man. Despite being almost six feet tall, his thin frame gave him a look of fragility, as though he might break. It was a trick of the eye, of course, because Keith was strong. Horseriding, polo, swimming, fencing and military training had developed his fine physical shape. His fair hair was combed straight back from his face and a ripple of sunlight revealed the beginnings of a moustache.

Five years older than Dorothea, Keith doted on her. He wanted to protect her from all manner of threat, real or imagined. There was duty, certainly, behind his devotion – he was the oldest and she was his only sister – but there was something more between the two of them: a deeply felt understanding that forged an unbreakable bond. Of course, Dorothea loved all three of her brothers. Eric was sweet and sensitive and Mac was confident and funny, but it was Keith's company she craved most, along with his approval. He didn't have all the answers but he was patient and listened carefully. From an early age, Dorothea and Keith wrote letters to each other whenever one of them was away. Keith wrote affectionately about everyday things:

> My dear Dorothea,
> I hope you are quite well. How are the kittens, there are three down here. I have planted a little oak tree . . . I cannot think of anymore to say so with love,
> I am your loving brother Keith.

But his clever little sister often used her letters to Keith to practise her French:

> *Mon cher* Keith,
> *J'espere que tu recevras cette letter vendredi avant tu partis pour l'ecole, parce qu'a moins ce c'est aucun profit pour toi et moi.*

(My dear Keith, I hope you get this letter Friday before you leave for school, otherwise there is no benefit to us.)

With rumours swirling about war in South Africa, Dorothea worried for her brother, who was seeking a commission with a New South Wales regiment to expedite his chances of fighting with his countrymen on behalf of the British Empire. She knew he was brave and capable but she had read enough books set in wartime to know it could change him forever even if he made it home alive.

But there would be time to worry about war later. Dorothea returned to her letter, trying to describe the relentless blue sky that seemed to stretch on forever. When she looked up again, she saw something shivering on the horizon; a blue-grey, undulating cloud that seemed to be moving towards her. At first, she thought it might be a dense flock of birds, but no, she knew the birds had long gone. After a moment, she realised it was rain. Sheets of shimmering drops were racing towards her, yet she saw the rain in slow motion, the filmy mist saturating the countryside one field at a time.

Dorothea leapt up, dropping the letter in which she would later describe this moment. She rushed towards the sheets of rain, lifting her skirt to keep the hem from brushing the ground. Bolting through the garden gate, she ran into the middle of the first paddock where the shower caught her, soaking her shirt, curling her hair and sending rivulets of water down her face. She opened her mouth and allowed the rain to rush in, blinking stinging drops from her eyes. Then she began to dance in delight, twirling around as if possessed, her arms open wide. When she finally slowed, dizzy, Dorothea staggered and looked down to see her stockinged feet caked in clay and the bottom of her skirt heavy with mud. Raising her eyes, she saw her parents and brothers standing on the verandah watching her with bemused affection. Later, as she described the scene in detail in the letter to her cousins, she also filed it away in her mind, hoping that one day she might find the perfect words to capture it in verse.

PART I

PART I

'MY COUNTRY'

The love of field and coppice
Of green and shaded lanes,
Of ordered woods and gardens
Is running in your veins.
Strong love of grey-blue distance,
Brown streams and soft, dim skies
I know, but cannot share it,
My love is otherwise.

I love a sunburnt country,
A land of sweeping plains,
Of ragged mountain ranges,
Of droughts and flooding rains.
I love her far horizons,
I love her jewel-sea,
Her beauty and her terror
The wide brown land for me!

The stark white ring-barked forests,
All tragic to the moon,

Deborah FitzGerald

The sapphire-misted mountains,
The hot gold hush of noon,
Green tangle of the brushes
Where lithe lianas coil,
And orchids deck the tree-tops,
And ferns the crimson soil.

Core of my heart, my country!
Her pitiless blue sky
When, sick at heart, around us
We see the cattle die
But then the grey clouds gather,
And we can bless again
The drumming of an army,
The steady soaking rain.

Core of my heart, my country!
Land of the rainbow gold,
For flood and fire and famine
She pays us back threefold.
Over the thirsty paddocks,
Watch, after many days,
The filmy veil of greenness
That thickens as we gaze . . .

An opal-hearted country,
A wilful, lavish land
All you who have not loved her,
You will not understand
though Earth holds many splendours,
Wherever I may die,
I know to what brown country
My homing thoughts will fly.

Chapter 1

Young Dorothea

When Dorothea looked out her bedroom window, the view was as magical as any child could wish for. From her room on the first floor, she had the perfect vantage point from which to view the exotic gardens surrounding the Mackellar family home, Dunara. The land at Point Piper ran all the way to the edge of Sydney Harbour, which dazzled and quivered, reflecting light with glorious abandon. The horizon beckoned Dorothea with the promise of adventure on the high seas, and the garden was a masterpiece of contradiction sprawling across five acres, with native plants like grevilleas, kangaroo paws, jumping-jack wattles and billy buttons clustered alongside imported roses, lilies and daffodils. There were succulents and ferns including magnificent staghorns that Dorothea must have viewed with great trepidation, fearing the limb-like fronds might reach down and catch her up. There were secret pathways and pockets of darkness where her secret imaginary world came to life, wriggling and fluttering unseen. Above it all, towering trees – the grand Sydney blue and the elegant Queensland black bean – stood guard with great solemnity.

Dunara was the only home Dorothea knew as a small child. She was born on 1 July 1885 after the Mackellars had moved there from their first home in Macquarie Street in the city – an apartment above Charles's medical practice and consulting rooms. The house at Dunara was a Victorian-style two-storey stuccoed brick building featuring a fine cast-iron verandah and balcony, with city views on one side and spectacular harbour views on the other. A camphor laurel-lined driveway swept around a fishpond and fountain and up to the main entrance. The house was surrounded by servants' quarters, stables, a coach house and numerous outbuildings. The Mackellar family had a host of servants, including a cook, kitchen maid, parlour-maid, two housemaids, a groom, a gardener and a coachman. To Dorothea, the servants were all part of the fabric of things, part of the family.

Dunara's extensive gardens were paradise for all the lively, inquisitive Mackellar children. They nurtured young Dorothea's enthusiasm for native animals and flowers, and her love of the water with the harbour and the nearby beaches on her doorstep. It was here the twin aspects of Dorothea's character were shaped – the well-mannered, accomplished society maiden and the strong, active tomboy who loved to bushwalk, swim, ride horses and climb trees.

The acres of grounds allowed the children to wander freely, climb trees and explore away from adults. Dorothea was determined to keep up with her brothers, and this instilled in her a sense of confidence, a competitive streak and a physicality which was unusual in upper-class girls in the late nineteenth century. Dorothea was only five years old when she took her first riding lesson, sitting side-saddle and learning to hold the reins under strict supervision. Keith and Eric were already riding and Dorothea was eager to join her brothers. Soon after her first lesson, she was called to the driveway at Dunara, the whole family in tow, to find a small pony standing patiently in the twilight. The gentle pony was perfect for the new student to learn to ride on, and this was the beginning of her deep affection for horses. Even after she learned to ride alone, Charles sometimes took Dorothea up in front of him on his black stallion, Rioter, and they would ride out to Watsons Bay or Bondi Beach and gallop along the wet sand at the water's edge, a thrill Dorothea never forgot. Riding home, they would pass a desolate cottage at Rose Bay, the sight of which made Dorothea shiver involuntarily. She later discovered it was the house of the public hangman.[1]

The house and grounds of Dunara were an idyllic place to grow up. Dorothea particularly adored her bedroom with its balcony overlooking the garden. She spent many happy hours writing and imagining the fairies, nymphs and dryads that lived below. For her, the garden was a place to create her own world where fairies and witches appeared and disappeared in a heartbeat. Later in life, she recalled her many adventures in the garden, fuelled by real and imaginary creatures she encountered or conjured there. It is easy to imagine her slipping out of bed on a summer's night and silently making her way downstairs, being careful not to wake the household as she opened the heavy front door. She would have needed to lift the hem of her long white nightdress as she ran across the verandah and onto the lawn, enjoying the feel of the soft grass under her bare feet. Navigating her way through the garden, along the well-worn pathways lit by the moonlight, she would soon have found herself close to the water's edge. The view was magnificent. Although it was familiar to her in daylight hours, the midnight blue of the seawater sparkled mysteriously, rising until it met the night sky on the far horizon where the stars mirrored the silver-shot cloth of the harbour. With the moon spilling a luminous ribbon across the water and the ancient native trees flecked with silver in its outfall, she may have felt something like what she later expressed in her poem, 'In a Southern Garden':

> And a chorus rises valiantly from where the crickets hide.
> Close shaded by the balsams drooping down
> It is evening in a garden by the kindly waterside,
> A garden near the lights of Sydney town![2]

On those Sydney summer nights, the air stayed warm with the day's heat and a faint hum could be heard in the distance – as though the insects were vibrating with outrage. Every murmur of the leaves and rustle in the bushes would have been audible in the quiet grounds of Dunara, stirring young Dorothea's imagination. Was that the Roman goddess Diana 'glistening silver-limbed and crescent-crowned' in the tangled scrub, watching her?[3] More likely a low-flying tawny frogmouth flashing past to settle on a branch nearby. She would have recognised the small owl, grim in its beauty, from previous encounters and she relished any opportunity to commune with the creatures she found in the garden.

She might have admired the bird's restraint, all things considered, as she often felt she was the one trespassing.

Dorothea was herself a night owl, often lying awake for hours fighting sleep. In later years, she recalled how, as a girl, she had tried to avoid sleep at any cost, viewing it as a waste of time. She didn't want to miss a moment of her life. Her bedroom faced east, and even with the shutters closed the flash from the Macquarie Lighthouse would illuminate the room for a second before darkness returned. Dorothea would wait for each wash of light with anticipation, counting the time between the flashes, desperately clinging to wakefulness.[4] Only much later – when she was a grown woman and the awful uncertainties of life came to visit in the darkness – did she long for sleep and its sweet relief.

Dorothea was a pretty child whose dark hair was usually fashioned into tight ringlets. Her beautiful hazel eyes were quick to register curiosity or delight as her magical childhood unfolded. Having begun to read at the age of four, she was bright, quick-witted and had an enviable vocabulary. She liked to recite nursery rhymes and other verses, fostering a formidable memory. But there was also something innate in her fierce intellect, as her father Charles discovered when he arrived home one evening and stopped by the nursery to check on little Dorothea. According to family lore, he found her lying on her stomach on a rug, playing with blocks with letters on them, her nurse sitting in a corner, sewing. As he watched, Dorothea arranged the blocks in lines and Charles saw she had spelled out the names of her brothers Keith and Eric. He suddenly grew angry.

'What are you doing to the child?' he demanded of the nurse. 'You are forcing her beyond her years!'

The nurse looked up, incredulous. She'd had nothing to do with the exercise – the child had taught herself![5]

When Dorothea was four, her parents arranged for her to attend a kindergarten class organised by Lady Cecilia Carrington, wife of Governor Charles Carrington, who had several young children of her own. With Keith and Eric both at school by 1889, Charles and Marion had worried Dorothea might feel isolated and lonely at home. Lady Carrington invited some of her friends' children to join the classes run by her governess at Government House, a stunning Gothic revivalist-style building overlooking Sydney Harbour in the Royal Botanic Gardens. Dorothea was dropped at the grand home by horse-drawn carriage, and spent several hours having lessons before being delivered home.

But Dorothea outgrew the kindergarten lessons after a year, and since formal schooling was not considered necessary for girls at the time, she was taught at home by a governess, Miss Ridley. She threw herself into her schoolwork, especially reading, but despite baby Mac's presence, Dorothea was lonely and counted the hours until her older brothers returned from school every afternoon.

When Dorothea turned eight, her parents decided she had outgrown even Miss Ridley, and she continued her schooling at Rona, the Bellevue Hill home of the Mackellars' friends, Edward and Edith Knox. She joined their daughters Marjorie, Barbara and Janet – along with assorted cousins and the children of other friends – in being educated by a governess there. Mac would accompany Dorothea at Rona for the best part of a year, until he joined his brothers in formal schooling. Though the Knox sisters were bright, cheerful girls, Dorothea found them condescending and felt she had little in common with them, and only Mac's presence made the arrangement tolerable.[6]

∽

By the age of ten, Dorothea was already searching beyond the classroom at Rona in her quest for knowledge. After starting French lessons and showing an aptitude for the language, Dorothea's parents arranged for her to spend the summer of 1895 with a French couple, Mr and Mrs Joubert, who lived in Minto on the outskirts of Sydney. Only French was spoken in their household, making it the perfect environment for improving her accent.

Dorothea was speaking fluently by the time she returned to formal lessons. A young Frenchwoman was hired to teach the group at Rona, but Dorothea's almost flawless accent was resented by the Knox girls, who thought it was ostentatious to 'speak like a native'.[7] Dorothea's excellent ear for languages, along with her lively intelligence, seemed to irritate Marjorie, Barbara and Janet Knox, who teased her. They found Dorothea's enthusiasm for learning rather excessive, and thought she was too serious for her own good. Dorothea, for her part, would later privately call the two younger girls, Barbara and Janet, 'Barbed wire' and 'Granite' because of what she considered were their prickly and inflexible personalities. Although she sometimes felt lonely and disconnected when the Knox girls ignored her over some perceived slight, Dorothea would not bow to peer pressure – she would not be frivolous or superficial to gain favour with the other girls.

One of the games the girls played when taking a break from study was dubbed 'The Bush Telegraph'. Someone from 'head office' would call each of the girls by name and ask for a report from a region of New South Wales. The Knox sisters would each insist there was nothing of note happening in their areas and sign off quickly, as though the game was beneath them. Dorothea, however, loved playing the game as it gave her an opportunity to use her imagination, conjuring all manner of incidents that she knew might very well be happening out in the bush. While not oblivious to the impatience of the Knox girls, she ignored them to focus on her intricately detailed tales of bushfires and droughts, stampedes and floods.

When she was twelve, Dorothea told her parents that school with the Knox sisters was a hellish experience she could no longer tolerate, and a young governess called Lilian Anderson was hired to supervise Dorothea's lessons at home. The accomplished Miss Anderson was like a breath of fresh air. She encouraged Dorothea's curious mind and her imagination, bolstering the increasingly important role of play-acting in her creative life. During this period, Dorothea became deeply immersed in a pretend life as a girl in medieval times – a role that the family indulged with good humour. While her brothers Eric and Mac teased her, Keith encouraged her, understanding that her play-acting was a creative outlet. While staying with friends in the country in July 1899, Keith even sent his sister a letter addressed to 'Mifs' Dorothea Mackellar, embracing the typography of the period. 'What a splendid game this one of yours of talking, thinking and living in the Middle Ages must be,' he wrote.[8] Whatever slights she might suffer at the hands of others, Dorothea could always bask in the approval of her eldest brother, Keith.

Chapter 2

The Mackellars

Charles and Marion Mackellar, while traditional in many ways, were open and loving parents who gave their children more freedom to speak their minds and ask questions than many of their contemporaries. Rather than insisting on children being 'seen and not heard' they encouraged an active curiosity and enjoyed their children's company. Most nights after dinner, Dorothea would go quietly into the library and climb into the big armchair near her father's desk. While he worked diligently at paperwork by the light of a gas lamp, she would take a book from one of the shelves and read until her nurse came to take her to bed. This easy, silent camaraderie created a special relationship between father and daughter, and also accelerated Dorothea's love of reading. When she said good night, Charles would take her into his arms and swing her up in the air, her feet nearly touching the ceiling before he caught her and gently set her down. It was their ritual.

Perhaps losing his own father at the age of seventeen had instilled a warmth in Charles that might not have been cultivated in his Scottish ancestors. The death of young Charlie's father thrust him into adulthood. The decision was made that he should attend the University of Glasgow, where he followed in his father's footsteps, and graduated with a medical degree in 1871. On his return to Sydney, Charles worked as a physician and, in 1873, became a surgeon at the Sydney Infirmary and Dispensary – renamed Sydney Hospital in 1881 – where his father had worked before him. Hard work, civil duty and loyalty were attributes that had been imbued in Charles. However, it was his compassion as well as family influence that led him into medicine and eventually public service.

When Charles met the beautiful and confident Marion Buckland, he felt they were perfectly suited. Marion was the second daughter of Thomas Buckland, who had emigrated to Sydney from Kent in 1830 at the age of sixteen, working his way up to eventually become a wealthy merchant and pastoralist. He would ultimately become the president of the Bank of New South Wales and a director of the influential Colonial Sugar Refining Company.

When Charles and Marion married on 9 August 1877 at St Paul's Anglican Church in Redfern, it was considered a powerful union that brought together two formidable families who had staked their claim as part of the political and business elite of the rapidly growing colony. Dorothea's father was handsome, if a little serious, and her mother was elegant, poised and kind. And they clearly adored each other. By the time Dorothea was born, in 1885, Charles had been elected to the New South Wales Legislative Council and would go on to contribute to many areas of public health over several decades, proving himself a skilful and progressive legislator.

Charles was also an accommodating husband who was proud of his wife's considerable intellect. Marion was articulate and forthright while always putting others at ease. She counselled her husband and ran the household with a cheerful disposition. Her servants seemed devoted, their tenure lasting much longer than those in the houses of others.

Dorothea loved to hear the story of her parent's engagement – in her eyes, theirs was a grand love story. But it almost didn't happen. Although being courted by a handsome young doctor was everything Marion could have hoped for, she resisted his early attempts to propose, fearing that she might not be the kind of wife such an ambitious man required. Marion had inherited a hearing problem and had been told her hearing would deteriorate over time until she was completely deaf. She did not want to be a burden. Charles's kindness and patience convinced her that her 'flaw' – for that was how she saw it – was something they could manage together, and she eventually consented. Marion's formal acceptance of Charles's proposal did not betray her deep feelings for the young surgeon: 'I have decided that the answer to the question you asked yesterday is yes. May God keep you.'[1]

Another chapter of the family history that Dorothea loved to hear about were the stories her father told of their Scottish ancestors. Charles's grandparents, John Mackellar and Euphemia Jackson, were married in the early 1800s and settled in Dundee, Scotland. Loving but sensible parents, they had made the ultimate sacrifice in sending their three sons, Keith, Frederick and Charles, to the other side of the world, knowing they might never see their boys again. Their youngest son Charles's diagnosis of a weak heart was reason enough for the Mackellars to encourage their sons to emigrate to Australia in the 1830s, in the hope a warmer climate might improve his health.

In Australia, middle brother Frederick met and fell in love with a beautiful widow, Isabella McGarvie. Her late husband, William McGarvie, had been a journalist and a founding partner of the *Sydney Morning Herald*. McGarvie died in 1841, leaving behind his young wife and their son, John. Isabella inherited 320 acres of land at Port Macquarie known as Mount Pleasant, which fortuitously neighboured a property owned by the Mackellar brothers. Frederick and Isabella married in 1844 and soon after had a son, Charles Kinnaird Mackellar, Dorothea's father, who was followed two years later by a daughter, named Euphemia after her grandmother.

Dorothea was fascinated by history and the lives of her Scottish ancestors, and how their stories layered her own. By reputation, her late paternal grandmother, Isabella, and great-grandmother Euphemia were strong and resolute women who faced adversity with good grace and were ambitious for their children. She was no doubt thinking of them when she wrote of 'All the dead women in my soul / stirred in their shrouded sleep'.[2]

She was also proud of her Scottish heritage and her father's homeland. The Scots had seen off the Celts, the Romans and the English and they would take on any new oppressors. They had earned their stoicism. Dorothea wrote of her strong connection to her ancestors and a very different landscape, even romanticising the Scottish weather, in her poem 'Another Heritage':

Not long ago, only three lives ago,
Half of my blood ran warm in northern weather

On a far strand, in a grim lovely land
Shrouded with mist and glorious with heather.³

༄

The Mackellars were a close family who enjoyed each other's company, but they were also very sociable. Weekend outings often meant carriage rides to visit Marion's parents, Thomas and Marion Buckland, at Belvoir – their home in Strawberry Hills – or to spend time with her sister Emily Rose at Elizabeth Bay. Some Sundays the family took the carriage to the fledgling Centennial Park, Charles riding alongside on horseback and the children tucked up inside with blankets to keep out the cold as they marvelled at the newly laid driving circles and all the wonderful new plantings.

The family also socialised with a tight-knit group of friends that included the Knoxes, who were among the most prominent families in Sydney. Edward Knox, known as Ned, was a close friend of Charles's. His father, Edward Senior, had founded the Colonial Sugar Refinery Company in the 1850s and his brother, Adrian, was a leading barrister who went on to become Chief Justice of the High Court. Ned and his wife, Edith, entertained the Mackellars at Rona, the gabled stone house at Bellevue Hill where Dorothea received her early schooling, and Charles and Ned often competed against each other in sailing races on the harbour. Charles had a fifteen-ton black-hulled cutter called *Oithona*, meaning 'Maid of the Waves', which was managed by Sam Miller, a white-haired former navy man. Sam was a knockabout bloke – an excellent sailor, a good fisherman and a strong swimmer – and he taught the Mackellar children many skills.

He showed them how to tie knots, chop wood, swim and sail. For Dorothea, all these lessons meant she was well prepared when, in later years, she chose to wander the bush alone.

The Mackellars and their friends enjoyed family picnics during summer, and would sail their yachts around the harbour, exploring the inlets and islets before dropping anchor to ferry everyone across to a welcoming beach. The two families also often took holidays together, and Dorothea's love of the country was cemented in the 1890s when the Mackellars began to join relatives and other well-to-do families on summer holidays at Burradoo – a village near Bowral in the Southern Highlands about seventy miles from Sydney. They all rented charming farmhouses close to each other so they could spend their days together.

The Mackellar children relished these holidays as they provided an opportunity to spend time with their cousins. Marion's brother, Tom, had a daughter, Vera, who had always been close to her cousin Dorothea despite a four-year age difference. But Dorothea's favourite companions were her cousins Pearl, Hope and Clare, the daughters of Marion's sister Emily Rose, better known to the children as 'Aunty Bee' on account of her effervescent personality. Aunty Bee's swashbuckling husband, Henry Montague Faithfull, or 'Monty', was a solicitor as well as an accomplished cricketer. Dorothea was not the only one who loved to be in the company of Bee and Monty, and family cricket games would have allowed for much playfulness and laughter amid the fierce competition.

The house at Burradoo was much older than Dunara, but the children loved it for all its creaks and sighs. By day, the children followed the farmhands and grooms about the farm and witnessed the births and deaths of various farms animals, learning the natural way of things. Many years later Dorothea still remembered scrumping peaches in the nearby orchards, and enjoying cream from the house cow and delicious butter churned by hand. At night, the children went to bed by candlelight with hot bricks sewn into flannel to warm the beds.[4]

But in 1894, the Mackellars returned from their idyllic stay at Buradoo to meet with tragedy in Sydney. A group of Dorothea's cousins and friends had been invited to a birthday party and, though she desperately wanted to join them, Dorothea had a minor sniffle and was ordered to stay in bed. Forty passengers headed for the party were travelling by launch near Chowder Bay on Sydney Harbour to a picnic spot on a sheltered beach when their vessel was struck by a tugboat. The *Sydney Morning Herald* reported on 19 December 1894 that up to twenty people on board the *Princess* were thrown into the water as the vessel almost capsized. Two children drowned that day, including Dorothea's beloved cousin Vera Buckland, who was just five years old. Dorothea never forgot the terrible whispered detail that Vera's body was not recovered for some days and could only be identified by the brightly coloured clothes she had been wearing on her way to the birthday party.

Only a few years later, another holiday would end in doom. Beloved Aunty Bee was convalescing at Buradoo following an unidentified illness – it was hoped that the country air would help her recover. But in a devastating twist, her health took a turn for the worse and she died suddenly, leaving the family bereft. Bee had been so full of life; someone who reverberated with energy and joie de vivre.

Two tragedies had befallen Dorothea's family in just a few short years – and there were more to come.

Chapter 3

Brother in Arms

During the last years of the nineteenth century – and well into the twentieth – the Mackellars divided their time between Dunara and their new property, Torryburn, in the Hunter Valley region north of Sydney. Torryburn had a chequered history which fired Dorothea's imagination. In 1825, Scotsman John McIntyre arrived in Australia from England on the *Hugh Crawford* and was granted 2,000 acres in the region. He named the property after his home back in Fife, which was on Torry Bay, an inlet of Scotland's Forth River.[1]

The new Torryburn had access to water through a long river frontage which would run dry in drought and flood in the wet. A three-room house was built, and huts for the workers McIntyre hired. In September 1830, however, McIntyre went missing, and convict workers were eventually convicted of the murder. The simple cottage built by McIntyre eventually made way for a grander building and additions as it passed through several owners. By the time Charles Mackellar bought Torryburn station in early

1898, there was a substantial brick and slate homestead wrapped on three sides by a wide verandah. It was enclosed by a garden and orchard and sat on more than 4,000 acres of land, with some paddocks cleared of timber.

For the Mackellars, Torryburn was a refuge from the hectic pace and pollution of the city. During holidays, the family and assorted servants would make the trek in a convoy of horses and carriages from the city to the farm, where the three teenaged Mackellars and their youngest brother, nine-year-old Mac, enjoyed the freedom to ride, swim and walk in the bush. From the beginning, Dorothea felt at home at Torryburn. Taking a favourite book, she would spend hours beside the creek, hoping that if she kept quiet and still enough, the hidden creatures would show themselves. In the early days, the bush was teeming with native animals and Dorothea documented her sightings in her notebook, listing species including rock wallabies, bandicoots, pademelons, blue-tongue lizards, kingfishers and sulphur-crested cockatoos.

When the Mackellars first bought the property in 1898, it had rolling green hills, spectacular vistas and a rich array of native flora and fauna, but by late 1899 the protracted drought had left the land parched and lifeless. The big dry had cast a pall over one of their favourite places, and soon news of war in South Africa would add to the Mackellars' worries.

Having completed his education at Sydney Grammar School, the now eighteen-year-old Keith Mackellar had chosen to pursue a military career. He received a commission to become a junior officer as part of the 5th Infantry Regiment, also known as the Scottish Rifles. A photo shows him standing proudly in his army uniform, complete with a traditional Scottish kilt. He is dark and handsome, tall with a fine physique, and his expression is one of expectation, as if impatient to make his way in the world.

As a volunteer soldier, Keith undertook training and other duties on a part-time basis which allowed him to begin an Arts degree at the University of Sydney in 1899. Keith was a good student and showed creative talent, taking drawing lessons from the Italian artist Antonio Dattilo Rubbo, who was lauded as a mentor to Sydney's first generation of modernist painters and who was also, for a time, Dorothea's art teacher. Both she and Keith were gifted artists; they were the quintessential renaissance man and woman who pursued languages, literature and aestheticism, but also enjoyed horseriding, surfing, fencing and bushwalking as a counterbalance to their intellectual pursuits. Interspersed in Dorothea's verse books and diaries are sketches and watercolours. The surviving paintings among her papers reveal intricate drawings of insects – beetles and butterflies – and, later, scenes from her travels: delicate Japanese parasols or pastoral scenes of Chinese peasants at work.

Keith understood Dorothea's love for books, poetry, play-acting and the arts, and encouraged her. He could see her talent even if it hadn't yet quite revealed itself to her. When they took their books and sketching pads to the clearing by the creek at Torryburn, the easy silence between them was all they needed. While his sister preferred to watch for animals or draw the trees and flowering plants nearby, Keith was more likely to be studying his copy of *Company Drill Made Easy* or sketching the trajectory of a volley of bullets released from a Martini-Henry rifle.

When Britain had declared war on the Boers in South Africa on 11 October 1899, there was initially uncertainty about the role Australian troops might play. Dorothea was concerned about what it might mean for Keith. He had originally applied for a commission with the Gordon Highlanders – a Scottish battalion based in the Punjab region of India – but word reached him that the troop had already left for South Africa. Undeterred, Keith applied for a commission with British 7th Dragoon Guards based in Kent, England, and was now awaiting his orders. Dorothea was proud of her brother but did not understand the rush to apply for a commission with an overseas battalion in the hope of going to war sooner. She understood his ambition, the opportunity for advancement as an officer, but the idea of him fighting on the other side of the world frightened her.

There was a story in Mackellar family folklore surrounding the fate of Keith's namesake, Great Uncle Keith, that would have caused Dorothea to wonder if her brother might have inherited some of their ancestor's desire for adventure. Great Uncle Keith had abandoned his brothers' initial farming interests in wheat and cattle in New South Wales for a more exciting life at sea. He bought a trading schooner that he sailed around the Pacific Islands, and it was not unusual for Keith to be away from home for months at a time. But in the early 1840s, he failed to return home at all.

It was not until several years after his disappearance that the Mackellars got answers about Keith, when a small, white-haired Chinese woman turned up at the family home several years later to tell a tale of treachery on the high seas. She had worked on Keith's schooner as a cook, and they had been sailing close to Java in Indonesia when local traders asked to come aboard to trade fruit and vegetables. When a crewman went to inspect the wares, one of the traders pulled out a hidden blade and slashed his throat, killing him instantly. Coming up from below deck to investigate, Keith managed to put a bullet through the head of the intruder, but an invading crew had followed the pirate on board and eventually Keith was overwhelmed. He suffered the same bloody end as the rest of his crew. Only the cook was spared, and she had continued to work on the schooner until they reached Thursday Island, where she eventually managed to escape.

Dorothea thought it was a thrilling story, and there was something epic about Great Uncle Keith's life, all adventure and high risk. As a child, she was both horrified and fascinated by his fate. She had encountered death among the farm animals at Burradoo, and in the garden, where she witnessed all sorts of creatures consumed, squashed or pecked to death, playing their part in the circle of life. But poor Great Uncle Keith bleeding to death on the deck of his boat far from home was an image she found hard to shake. She could not imagine such an ignominious and violent death for her beloved brother.

But Keith was about to be tested in the theatre of war a long way from home. He had been commissioned temporarily as a lieutenant in the 1st Australian Horse squadron – part of the Mounted Infantry unit – while he waited for his commission with the Dragoon Guards, which he hoped would be gazetted by the time he arrived in South Africa. On hearing that Keith had been called up, the family gathered to pray, quoting aloud from the Old Testament's twenty-fourth psalm which promised, 'he that hath clean hands, and a pure heart . . . shall receive the blessing from the Lord, and righteousness from the God of his salvation.'[2]

As the Mackellars farewelled him, they were sad but proud of their handsome, spirited boy. They firmly believed that the British

Army would prevail, the war would wrap up quickly and their beloved firstborn son and brother would meet them in London midyear. In fact, Charles decided to take the family to England on an extended visit so they could see Keith when he was on leave from the Dragoons, which were based in Kent. And, when the war was over, they could be reunited with Keith much sooner.

Keith was just nineteen and full of potential when he sailed on the *Surrey* on 17 January 1900. As an officer, he took his own horse and a groom with him. His ship sailed into Cape Town where the soldiers and their horses disembarked and travelled inland to meet up with the British Army. According to Keith's letters to Dorothea, South Africa appeared a 'strange and wonderful land with its wide stretches of treeless though fertile "veld" broken only by rugged steep and barren "kopjes" sometimes in ranges, sometimes solitary, and its steep banked rivers, unabridged and impossible to cross except at certain "drifts" or fords'.

In one letter, Keith seemed a little embarrassed that at the raw age of nineteen he was in charge of men much older, writing that it felt strange but he was finding his feet: 'Much as I miss you all I am enjoying this life above everything I have ever experienced and feel sure that it is what I will do best at and while not a Napoleon just yet, though in future time I may be one, and in everything else I am an awful duffer.'

Keith's letters were frequent and for the most part cheerful during his first few months in South Africa. Even when he saw action, he spared Dorothea the detail, not wanting her to worry. His squadron first came under fire when the Boers tried to stop the British army at Poplar Grove on the Eastern Cape of South Africa. But the Boers were overwhelmed and forced to retreat, allowing Keith to experience live action without any serious threat to his life. The British army took the capital of Bloemfontein on 13 March and for the next seven weeks the regiments rested and restocked. Keith wrote to Dorothea that typhoid and dysentery were the more immediate enemies. 'We have on the whole lost few men in action though the fever has made rather large gaps in our ranks.'

They rode north in May 1900 to the other Boer capital, Pretoria. About a week away from their destination, Keith's squadron was caught out in the open by a Boer police unit. Keith was unhurt but was suffering, along with his men, from exhaustion. After fighting at Diamond Hill to the east of Pretoria, the squadron enjoyed proper sleeping quarters for the first time in months. Although sentiment back home in Australia had started to turn in favour of the Boers owing to reports of atrocities the British had committed against civilians, Keith found the English soldiers to be courageous and upstanding men, and felt they were being unfairly judged for the sins of their commanders. He was full of praise for his British counterparts, describing to Dorothea how a British naval artillery sent shells over their heads while they were under heavy fire, scattering the Boers.

After entering Pretoria, the news arrived that Keith had been accepted into the 7th Dragoon Guards, 4th Cavalry Brigade. The Mackellars were already in London – hoping that a swift end to the war would allow Keith to join them there – and when Dorothea heard of her brother's commission, she rushed out and bought a print of a soldier in the Guards uniform of red coat, blue breeches and steel helmet with black and white feathers.[3]

By May 1900, Keith's letters had begun to reveal a growing impatience with the war: 'I expect you are all enjoying England very much. I know that I shall be glad enough when this war is over – I'm pretty sick of it now, especially that we get heavy frosts every night, they make sleeping in the open hardly what one might call fun. However, it can't last much longer.' A further letter from Keith on 18 June complained that he had not received any letters from Dorothea since she had left for England, because the Boers had captured and burnt all their mail. It revealed the extent of his deepening disillusionment: 'Nearly all the men are now heartily sick of the war and wish they could finish the Boers off at one fell swoop and get home.' By the end of June, the Mackellar family held great hope the war would soon be over and Keith would be reunited with them.

But at dawn on 11 July 1900, a squadron was ordered to attend a farm about fifteen kilometres north of Pretoria after reports of Boer movement in the area, and Keith – having been to the property before – volunteered to act as a guide. His decision to aid another squadron would prove to be a fateful one. Another Australian and friend of Keith's, Arthur Onslow, had joined the same British regiment and decided to join the sortie. Together they rode out as a pale sun broke the horizon and began its slow ascent. The plains stretched out endlessly in the half light and there was a coolness in the air which stalled the heat they all knew was coming.

Keith rode alongside Arthur in comfortable silence. He had visited the farm several times to check if there were enemy soldiers being sheltered there, and he knew the approach well – there were good sightlines and he did not believe there would be enough enemy troops in the area to take on the squadron. If there were soldiers nearby, they were likely to remain hidden.

As the advance patrols approached the farm, they saw that the area was full of horsemen wearing their own field uniform of khaki helmets and jackets. Keith was surprised to see what seemed to be another British squadron waiting for them as they urged their horses towards the farm buildings. The patrol was within fifty yards of these unexpected compatriots when suddenly the British soldiers opened fire on them, catching them off guard. It was the Boers, dressed in British uniforms to lure their enemy closer, and now Keith and the other men were in serious peril.

Keith responded quickly, leaping from his horse and rolling into a 'donga' or shallow gully that afforded him and some of the other members of his squadron, including Arthur Onslow, a little protection as they returned fire. But the enemy was working its way around their flank. Arthur heard the crack of rifle fire before he saw it. Keith had raised his head to fire when an enemy bullet hit him in the forehead, killing him instantly. He was not quite twenty years old.[4]

The men carried his body back to camp that night, and the next day laid him to rest in Pretoria cemetery at the foot of a gum tree.[5] Eucalyptus trees had been introduced to South Africa in the 1870s, and the great gum served as a fitting resting place for the fallen Australian.

Major Robert Thompson, who had been in command of the Australian Horse regiment when Keith left Australia, wrote from the Military Governor's Office in Pretoria: 'Just before the funeral I met Wilkinson, of the Australian Horse, and he at once went off and got all his men, who followed the hearse. The coffin was carried to its resting place by three of the 7th Dragoon Guards and three of the Australian Horse.'[6]

When news of Keith's death reached the Mackellars in London, the loss was devastating. The telegram read: 'Your gallant son lies in Pretoria Cemetery. He died at his post – bravely.' Dorothea was heartbroken over the brutal death of her brother. Something fundamental in the tight-knit family broke, and would never quite be mended. Compounding the family's grief was the realisation that Keith was not attached to the squadron that came under attack but had volunteered to join them on patrol – it was his willingness to aid others that had ultimately led to his death. Dorothea watched as her mother crumpled under the weight of the news, folding in on herself, pain etched across her face, while her husband – pale but steadfast – tried to hold the family together.

Although friends of the Mackellars were quick to remind them in dozens of letters and telegrams how proud they should be of Keith – who had fought and died bravely – it is hard to believe that such remarks would have been much consolation to the grieving Dorothea. At just fifteen years old, losing her favourite brother and closest confidant would have utterly shattered the young woman. What did courage and country matter when his body was still and lifeless in a wasteland far from everyone and everything he loved? He had been fighting with a British squadron in South Africa – what did any of that have to do with his life in Australia? Though politeness prevented Dorothea sharing the true extent of her outrage and despair with others, it is clear that she felt Keith's loss deeply.

A sympathy letter sent to the Mackellars on 14 July 1900 from Keith's friend Arthur Onslow showed the high regard in which Keith was held:

> His loss is felt keenly in the regiment for though he had only just joined he had made himself a general favourite and we all feel that he met his death as a gallant and true son of the Empire.

Another tribute from family friend Dr Robert Scot Skirving expressed the deep affection he had for the Mackellars' eldest son:

> I wish to tell you how deeply and lastingly I must always think on dear Keith – I liked the boy very, very much. A finer, pluckier lad I have never known. We all liked and respected him – brave, good-looking, wholesome-minded and honourable . . .

A report in the *Australian Star* less than a week later described Keith as 'a splendid specimen of rising manhood. Though only about 19 years of age he had reached a stature of 6ft, was splendidly built, and was full of heart.'[7] And in the *Sydney Morning Herald,* an article laid out the enormous loss of a young man full of potential:

> He was highly regarded amongst his brother officers of the Sydney Scottish, and besides being a clever amateur boxer and fencer, he was a good rider and excelled in outdoor sports. His prospects were bright, as he made a good and popular officer, and had thrown all his energies into his military work. Had his career not been nipped in the bud he would quickly have made a name for himself.[8]

In August, with the Mackellars still half a world away in Europe, a memorial service was held in Sydney at the All Saints' Church, Woollahra, which was so crowded that hundreds of mourners had to remain standing. The *Sydney Morning Herald* report of the service noted:

The Scottish Rifles together with a number of officers and men of other regiments formed up at the Centennial Park gates, Queen Street, Woollahra, and marched to the church ... headed by the regimental band. The military chaplain who addressed the congregation declared Keith was 'a young man full of promise and was beloved by all who knew him for his noble, manly and chivalrous spirit. His was a life full of promise, but it had been cut short on the battlefield.'[9]

Dorothea tried to be stoic as the family eventually continued their travels, heading on to France, which they had always planned to visit when Keith joined them. In truth, she was merely going through the motions for her parents' sake. Unable to express it openly, the teenage girl's grief seeped into her poetry, and it was around this time that she penned the heartbreaking poem, 'When It Comes':

How should I like to die, to die?
Without a cry,
In a hard-fought fight, where blows were dealt,
And the death-strokes less than a girl's kiss felt–
So would I die.

So should I like to die, but where?
On the open plain, in the open air,
Where the red blood soaks in the thirsty grass,
And the wild things tread my grave as they pass,
There would I die.[10]

The Mackellars finally returned to Sydney in December 1900. The family had leased out Dunara while they were overseas, and as it was still occupied when they returned, the family settled into an apartment over Buckland Chambers in Liverpool Street, overlooking Hyde Park. Originally Marion's father's offices, the top two storeys of the chambers in the Sydney CBD were residential. Given the memories that Dunara held of Keith, the family – and especially Marion – was in no hurry to return to a home which would remind them of him at every turn.

Dorothea was trying to come to terms with the brutal consequences of war and the unbearable realisation that her brother would never be coming home. In an attempt to escape the pain she was experiencing in the real world, Dorothea, now fifteen, returned to playing the characters she had developed in childhood. One such character she began to flesh out in the aftermath of her brother's death was Kid Prevost, a young English renegade who travels to South America, where he becomes a horse thief. Kid would later feature in her first novel, *Outlaw's Luck*, the opening of which is set in Argentina. Reading between the lines, it seems that Kid's story might have been Dorothea's way of giving Keith the adventurous life that had been stolen from him.

Although he was originally buried in a grave in Pretoria Cemetery, Charles had Keith's body exhumed and moved to Sydney's Waverley Cemetery, to a grave overlooking the ocean. Later, Charles commissioned a stained-glass window in memory of his son and others who had died in the Boer War. In July 1903, the window was installed at St James' Church in Queens Square, Sydney's oldest church, where it remains.[11] A *Sydney Morning Herald* article about the unveiling noted: 'The window represents a striking figure of St George, the patron saint of soldiers.'[12] The face of St George is a likeness of Keith.

Dorothea's deep love for her brother could not have been more poignantly expressed when, decades later, she revealed her wishes for the inscription on her own headstone at Waverley Cemetery in Sydney's Eastern Suburbs, where she would be buried in the same plot as Keith. His epitaph reads:

IN MEMORY OF
KEITH KINNAIRD MACKELLAR,
2ND LIEUTENANT
7TH (*PRINCESS ROYAL'S*) DRAGOON GUARDS,
WHO WAS KILLED IN ACTION
AT ONDERSTEPOORT, SOUTH AFRICA, 11TH JULY
1900, IN THE 20TH YEAR OF HIS AGE.[13]

Beneath, Dorothea's epitaph reads:

HIS SISTER.

Chapter 4

New Woman

Having travelled to Europe as a fifteen-year-old, Dorothea had been exposed to changing political, cultural and literal landscapes, but she was still trying to make sense of her place in the world as a young woman in a young country at the start of a brand-new century. By the time she turned seventeen, in 1902, Dorothea was already an elegant and spirited young woman who had grown into her beauty. She wore her russet hair pulled back in a ponytail tied with a ribbon, as was the fashion for girls up until the age of eighteen, after which they were expected to wear their hair up. On the cusp of womanhood and impatient for some semblance of independence, Dorothea went swimming and horse riding at every opportunity. She was the sort of girl who would have smoked cigarettes when her parents weren't looking, enjoyed the taste of alcohol, and would have likely even worn trousers, imitating many fashionable women in Europe, if her desire to please her parents had not been so strong.

In her late teenage years, just as in her childhood, Dorothea read voraciously, as though words were a life force that she could not do without. She had graduated from Robert Louis Stevenson's *Treasure Island* and *Kidnapped* to more expansive and eclectic reading, from Shakespeare's *Richard III* to Edward Gibbon's *The History of the Decline and Fall of the Roman Empire*. She turned to Greek and French texts when she wanted to challenge herself – and she had very much enjoyed Joseph Conrad's 1899 literary sensation, *Heart of Darkness*. Dorothea's parents were liberal when it came to education and she had been encouraged to read widely from an early age. Her father's office and his considerable library were open to her, with only two books considered out of bounds when she was younger. Lord Byron's *Don Juan* might have been an obvious choice to keep from his daughter, but the perceived sins of the poems of Robert Browning were never revealed to Dorothea. Perhaps the gruesome tale recounted in the poem 'Porphyria's Lover' – in which a man strangles his young mistress to death and proceeds to dance with her corpse – was one that Charles felt unfit for youthful eyes.

Forbidden books aside, Dorothea was permitted to attend classes in English Literature at the University of Sydney to stretch her intellectual capabilities, although she never formally enrolled – her parents deemed a tertiary education unnecessary for such an eminently marriageable young woman. Instead, she slipped into the back of a class and listened intently, thrilled at the passion of the literary discussions, but was ever the outsider. If she could not fully participate in the education on offer, she could at least translate her learning onto the page, dwelling there on the things that obsessed her during the day and kept her awake at night.

And so it was against a backdrop of personal grief and profound social and political change that Dorothea's character, and her poetry, were forged. The colonies had come together on 1 January 1901 to form the Commonwealth of Australia, but for Dorothea, even the excitement of a newly minted Federation was muted by the sorrow of Keith's death. In 1902 the Commonwealth Franchise Act granted the right to vote to white Australian women over twenty-one (while excluding Indigenous, Pacific Islander, African and Asian women). It was also the year one of Australia's most famous suffragettes, Vida Goldstein, made her journey from Portland in Victoria all the way to the White House for an audience with President Theodore Roosevelt. Vida was passionate about women's right to vote and was a skilled and impressive orator. She travelled to America to address the International Woman Suffrage Conference and a committee of the United States Congress, which ultimately led to the audience with the president. It was an impressive resume: a woman from a small country town in Victoria taking tea with the American president! It is more than likely that Dorothea followed the exploits of this singular young Australian, and they may have even had the chance to meet: Vida's sister Elsie married writer and socialist Henry Hyde Champion, who would later become Dorothea's publisher.

In addition to real-life role models like Vida Goldstein, Dorothea found daring young women like herself represented in the fiction of the period. In 1902 Australian journalist and author Louise Mack published *An Australian Girl in London*, an ostensibly fictional work in which the main character, Sylvia Leighton, writes letters home to Australia from London:

> There's the London of shops and carriages, the bright pink London, the very most up-to-date London, Head Office of the Manufacture of Modernity. There's the London of Poets, a grey, mysterious, haunted London, full of souls and spirits, and dead people with long hair; the London that holds fame in its hands and tosses it out sometimes in the strangest places; the London where the writers live, where the publishers are to be seen, the hardest London of all for us to realise.[1]

Dorothea would have admired Sylvia, and recognised her own struggle with national identity represented in fictional form. Sylvia opined: 'Why should it ruffle me, this ignorance of England about us, eating our hearts out to come to her, calling her always 'home'?' Through her young heroine, Mack was asking the same existential questions Dorothea was starting to explore: about nationhood, patriotism, 'otherness' and the interconnectedness of landscape and identity. Sylvia Leighton's questions were also Dorothea's:

> Who would ask London skies to blaze with the gay turquoise that shines upon my sunny country overseas? . . . These vague skies are full of tenderness to their old city. In their dimness they hide her ugliness. For nothing stands out sharp and clear here as in Australia.[2]

Dorothea's workbooks from this time show that she had begun to think seriously about the Australian landscape. In 1902, she wrote 'Drought Time', an unpublished poem likely inspired by the harsh conditions she had witnessed at Torryburn.

Four months and not one drop of rain
The rivers all are dry
And not a cloud has come to stain
The bitter brazen sky
We pray before a week has sped
We all may hear again
The sound of an army's tread
The coming of the rain.³

The poem's final lines contain a striking military metaphor used to describe a sudden downpour, a precursor to the description of the drought breaking that she would use later in her most famous poem, 'My Country': 'The drumming of an army, the steady soaking rain.' Conjuring up the noise of rain on a corrugated iron roof, the image also speaks of rescue – from the long dry, perhaps, or from the horrors of war.

Despite being raised essentially as an urban woman, Dorothea was drawn to nature and revived by the bush. Many of her early poems were about the aesthetics of the bush, the colour, the movement; the mystery lurking within rather than the stories of the drovers, the shearers and the swagmen who take centre stage in the tradition of the bush balladeers. She observed these characters in her travels, but they could not compete with the allure of the landscape when it came to the inspiration for her poetry. Two of the most acclaimed Australian poets of the period, Henry Lawson and A.B. 'Banjo' Paterson – both city-based writers – had become famous for their depictions of the bush figures in their stories and ballads, including 'The Drover's Wife', 'Clancy of the Overflow' and 'The Man from Snowy River'. They had elevated the bushman in the national consciousness as a romantic figure, but Dorothea was more interested in the land itself. She continued to be captivated by its grandeur, its light and colour and sheer extravagance – and she was starting to understand that Australia had a uniqueness that should be celebrated.

Descriptions of the landscapes she encountered became integral to Dorothea's poetry, as can be seen in one of her favourite poems, 'Colour', in which she describes 'almond trees in bloom, and oleanders / Or a wide purple sea, / Of plain-land gorgeous with a lovely poison, / The evil Darling Pea'. The colours and textures of the Australian environment were also at the core of 'Settlers', a poem that would later find its way into her first collection:

> Marble-smooth and marble-pale the blue gums guard the clearing,
> Where the winter fern is gold among the silver grass,
> And the shy bush creatures watching bright-eyed and unfearing,
> See the slender Oreads while we unheeding pass.[4]

Dazzled as she was by the colours of the landscape, Dorothea was also becoming interested in how the land itself might influence the Australian psyche. Was the fledgling national identity tied to the continent's remoteness and its rugged beauty?

On 1 July 1903, Charles marked Dorothea's eighteenth birthday by giving her a substantial bundle of shares, as he had her older brothers. The dividends were intended to cover her expenses as a woman of leisure. This 'pin money' would enable Dorothea to purchase the latest fashion accessories, buy books and attend the theatre. In time, she was expected to marry a suitable man

with similar social status; one who could ensure her comfort and security would be protected.

But it seemed that young Dorothea had her sights set on more than marriage, and she spent her final years as a teenager pursuing two of her most longstanding loves: poetry and travel. Shortly after her birthday, 'When It Comes' – Dorothea's ode to her brother Keith written in the months after his death – was published in the American journal *Harper's Magazine*. It is not clear if Dorothea's family had connections who arranged an introduction to the *Harper's* editor or if she sent the poem unsolicited. While its publication was evidence of her talent and growing confidence, it was a bittersweet experience. The grief she had poured into the poem remained her constant companion. Nevertheless, Dorothea was surprised and grateful for the recognition by the American publication and hoped it signalled the start of a literary reputation in the large North American market.

Already a published poet by the age of eighteen, the year 1904 would prove a momentous one for Dorothea. She was a beautiful young woman, poised, sophisticated and opinionated, and with her parents and younger brother, she was about to embark on a long overseas trip to Japan, North America, London and Europe.

The long journey would be, in part, a work trip for Dr Mackellar, who by this time was a member of the New South Wales Legislative Council and president of the State Children's Board. He was charged with studying the methods used in dealing with neglected and delinquent children in other countries including the United States, Europe and the United Kingdom. The tour was to inform a parliamentary bill which would ultimately lead to the Neglected Children and Juvenile Offenders Act of 1905. The legislation, to be drafted by Charles, would ultimately create children's courts and form the foundations of the probationary system. At this stage, Charles was convinced that wayward children were victims of their environment and deserved compassion alongside policies which would provide support.

In Europe, Dorothea was to act as her father's translator. Having mastered French, Spanish, Italian and German, she would prove invaluable to Charles, who had only a rudimentary grasp of the Romance languages. Her linguistic talents meant that she was given extraordinary access to business and political circles that were almost exclusively male domains. In addition to being her father's voice as far as translation was concerned, Dorothea would also act as her mother's ears on the trip. Marion Mackellar's hearing was now failing, and she was forced to travel with a necessary – but rather alarming-looking – ear trumpet, a precursor to the modern hearing aid. Dorothea sat next to her mother at dinner parties to repeat the conversation in case she misheard. In some ways, she became a stand-in for her mother, who had always feared her increasing deafness might hold her husband back. Charles began to rely on his daughter, not only as a translator but also as a sounding-board, travelling companion and hostess.

In March, the Mackellars sailed aboard the *Empire*. Dorothea's younger brother, Mac, now fourteen, accompanied them. The family first visited Japan as tourists on their way to America and the start of Charles's fact-finding mission. Dorothea fell in love with Japanese culture and purchased the first of many elaborately embroidered silk kimonos which she would wear as housecoats in the years to come.

They then sailed to the Hawaiian islands and on to Canada, where they crossed from Vancouver to Montreal by train, before making their way to St John's in Newfoundland to visit Charles's friend Sir William MacGregor, who was governor there. Sir William and Charles had met as students in Scotland, and when they returned to Australia they had maintained their friendship. After working as a doctor, Sir William had accepted several imperial postings and would eventually become governor of Queensland.

The Mackellars' tour included visits to several American cities, including New York, before they crossed the Atlantic to England on the RMS *Umbria*, arriving in September 1904. Marion decided to stay in London while Charles and Dorothea travelled on to the continent to continue their working tour.

First they travelled to El Borge in the Malaga province of Andalusia in southern Spain. Dorothea loved Spain and was attracted to the passionate sensibility of the people. She had an affinity with Spanish poetry, which she translated into English for the pure pleasure of it. Her first collection of poetry, which was to be published some seven years later, contained several of her Spanish translations, including some dark stories of love and loss, such as 'In the Plague Year':

> This morning on the death-cart
> She passed me in the street—
> One hand outside was hanging,
> By that I knew my Sweet.[5]

And 'The Tearless Girl':

> O man, when I am dead
> And the grave-worms break their fast,
> They will find your name that I dare not say
> Upon my lips at last.[6]

Dorothea enjoyed her relative independence and anonymity in El Borge. She was able to move easily through the plazas, shopping in the *mercado*, her accent so natural that she could have been mistaken for a member of the Spanish upper class. She had an intuitive ear and enjoyed eavesdropping on conversations, especially when people were unaware that she spoke their native tongue. She was amused to discover the Spanish penchant for *piropo*, literally meaning 'dropping the bouquet', the practice of calling out compliments to young women passing by. This behaviour was considered inappropriate and uncouth in English society but Dorothea took it all in her stride. She was no doubt grateful that her father could not understand what was being said, even when it was flattering. At the end of long days punctuated by the mid-afternoon siesta, Dorothea watched the cigarette factory girls come flooding onto the cobbled streets, singing, laughing, arguing and even breaking into the dance of lovers – the flamenco.

Dorothea and Charles moved on to Valencia, where she was able to immerse herself in the regional culture when she wasn't translating for her father, who was visiting local orphanages. Dorothea enjoyed watching the skill and speed of the street sellers flashing their knives as they segmented oranges to make the *mermelada* that was served with her breakfast each morning. She purchased a magnificent black silk *manila* shawl with a long black fringe and intricate hand embroidery and was delighted when the seller showed her how to wear and tie the shawl to signify whether she was a lady or a working girl.[7]

In October 1904, father and daughter arrived in the city of Burgos in the Castile-León region of northern Spain. Excited to explore the city, they took a carriage ride to see the sights, which included the Cartuja de Miraflores, a grand Carthusian monastery that stood on a hill above the city. Dorothea wrote of the visit in her diary with such exacting detail it is possible to share her journey across the sun-soaked Spanish countryside, stepping through the doors of the fifteenth-century monastery and walking with her along its cold stone hallways:

> The . . . carriage pulled up with a flourish before a tall stone gateway. We pulled at the bell rope which hung beside the door and heard a clanging – very far away it seemed – then there was silence except for the flick of the horses' tails as they switched away the flies. The door opened . . . and a small one-eyed man with a villainous face was revealed. He waddled away, leaving us standing in front of another door, most wonderfully carved. The cloister was filled with a hot white light except in the shade of the arches, which were of a grey coolness that rested the eyes. I have never felt so utterly away from the world. Not even a fly stirred in the courtyard; it was impossible to realise that the carriage which brought us from Burgos was only on the other side of the wall. By and by, an old man came all clothed in white, with bare sandaled feet and a girdle of rope about his waist. He had a long beard like spun silver and his eyes were very peaceful. I wondered how old he was, it was impossible to know with any certainty for as he spoke, he seemed first as old as the sea, then oddly innocent and young. I think he was both.

The kindly monk showed the visitors the tomb of Don Juan of Castile and Dona Isabel of Portugal, complete with life-sized statues of the couple fashioned from white marble.

The slender hands were folded in prayer or sleep. The veins showed delicately in them. Dona Isabel wore a high-necked gown with an openwork coif and the lace of the robe looked as if the lightest breeze might stir it. But one could not imagine a breeze in the chapel of Miraflores, though the air was so cool and fresh.

Dorothea was surprised their host said nothing of the history of Juan and Isabel. She made a point of studying the history of any region she visited, and had read about their storied, if brief, reign. The forty-two-year-old Juan had married the nineteen-year-old Isabel in 1447 on the advice of his trusted adviser Álvaro de Luna, who wanted an alliance between Castile and Portugal. But de Luna's control over the king became intolerable to Isabel, who decided he must be eliminated. Dorothea wrote:

> Juan was weak and not ill-natured, the histories say, and yet he ordered the execution of his friend de Luna because the Queen wished it. One cannot help respecting Isabel more, unscrupulous though she may have been.

On their return to London at the end of 1904, Dorothea and Charles joined Marion at the house she had rented in Park Street. The home had once belonged to the notorious, twice-widowed Maria Fitzherbert, an eighteenth-century London socialite who had caught the eye of the future King George IV. The drawing room of the house on Park Street was the scene of their secret, illegal marriage in 1785, which was later deemed invalid.

It was in this house steeped in intrigue that Marion Mackellar hosted a luncheon for some of Charles's political and business contacts. The guests were an eclectic group, ranging from sophisticated raconteurs to – in Dorothea's eyes – bombastic bores. No matter who she conversed with, the young woman always held her own, balancing manners and courtesy with the occasional barb to make her point. As Dorothea later recounted to her biographer Adrienne Howley, a guest at the luncheon was making his position clear on the suffragette movement and the 'abhorrent' notion of women gaining the vote. He felt that the vote would rob women of their femininity. Dorothea glanced over at her mother, fashionable and feminine in a soft grey chiffon and lace dress, and a grey hat trimmed in ostrich feathers. An idea occurred to her:

'I am afraid I must disagree,' she said gently . . . 'By the way, you do know my mother, don't you?'

'Charming lady, quite charming,' he melted into smiles.

Dorothea turned her sternest look on him. 'I'm sorry, sir, that you should consider my mother to be in any way masculine.'

The poor man spluttered an astonished denial.

'No! Absolutely not. Anything but!'

'Well, you see,' said Dorothea, 'my mother has had the vote for nearly two years.'[8]

Her point made, Dorothea changed the subject. She didn't suffer fools and relished her chance to argue a point, but never wished to make a scene.

With her parasol raised against the rare ray of London sunshine, Dorothea would wander the streets of London, pausing occasionally to look in store windows or observe the behaviour of passers-by. Making her way along the Thames Embankment, it would not have been difficult to find a park bench from which to watch the boats glide by. She had been ruminating on the differences between England and her homeland, and what being Australian meant. To Dorothea, England was familiar and yet distant, as though viewed through glass, while Australia's fierce vibrancy was near and tangible to her despite the distance of ten thousand miles that separated her from home.

Dorothea's long, contemplative walks through the streets of London – tinged by homesickness – were the likely inspiration behind a poem called 'September':

> The lamps are lit in London, beneath their searching light
> The smiling anxious faces look strained and very white;
> And over where my heart is, twelve thousand miles away,
> The dewy grass is glinting at the break of day.[9]

Living in the lamplit heart of busy metropolitan London may have made Dorothea homesick, but it also presented her with all kinds of opportunities to explore and socialise. It is hard to imagine anything more welcome than a royal invitation, and there was huge excitement when the Mackellars received invitations to a garden party to be held at Buckingham Palace with *all* the important royals in attendance. King Edward VII and his wife Queen Alexandra would be there, as well as the Prince of Wales, who would later become King George V. It was such a grand occasion that Dorothea would later refuse her parents' offer of a 'coming out' ball in Sydney, reminding them that since she had already attended several society balls *and* a royal party in London, she could hardly consider herself a debutante.[10]

⁓

The Mackellars returned to Sydney in March 1905 on the SS *Moldavia*, and once again stayed at Buckland Chambers until Dunara was ready for them. Dorothea resumed her life in Sydney and caught up with friends, but she was restless. As well as her time in Spain and London, she and Charles had travelled to France, Austria and Germany as part of his investigation into neglected and delinquent children. It was important work, and Dorothea had felt inspired and stimulated when she was translating for her father – sometimes in several different languages at once – when meetings and conferences brought many nationalities together. Now she felt stifled. The usual round of social engagements was a distraction, but not enough to stave off a creeping sense of futility.

In particular, Dorothea disliked the idea of 'coming out', considering the various parties and balls where young women were paraded in front of eligible men as basically a 'marketplace'. She successfully resisted her own parents' attempts to foist such an occasion on her. But while Dorothea never had an official coming out, she did attend several debutante balls. Her attendance was deemed worthy of mention in the *Sydney Morning Herald*'s report of the first ball of the season at the Paddington Town Hall in April 1905:

> The ballroom was prettily decorated with palms and ferns, green ribbons being suspended from corner to corner across

the hall ... the supper tables were artistically arranged with a profusion of cactus dahlias, red being the predominant colour. There were several debutantes, including Miss Dorothea Mackellar, all of whom wore pretty, white dresses and carried bouquets. Quite short dresses were worn by many of the dancers.[11]

Despite her social commitments, Dorothea spent most days working on her poetry. Inspiration seemed to be everywhere – the city, the bush, her travels and even the occasional brush with romance. Her verse books throughout this period reveal a passionate young woman who sometimes had crushes on other young women as well as her male suitors. This was not unusual at a time when romantic friendship with another woman was seen as a normal prelude to marriage.[12] In 'To Her', Dorothea lays out her adoration for an unnamed woman:

There may be others as beautiful as you – I do not know,
There may be other eyes as deep and other mouths as sweet.
But I see none but you, dear love, wherever I may go,
And whatsoever you may do, my heart's beneath your feet.[13]

But even with youthful longing to fill her heart and poetry to occupy her mind, Dorothea's growing restlessness was becoming a chronic condition by the end of 1906. She tried to concentrate on her poetry, but she was finding it hard to focus. Various symptoms began to plague her – including insomnia, melancholy, dizziness and heart palpitations – but numerous visits to medical specialists failed to shed any light on her ailment. It was common for women's symptoms to be dismissed by the male-dominated medical profession, which conflated their conditions with mental weakness or 'hysteria'. Without a formal diagnosis, Dorothea resolved, not always successfully, to be stoic and uncomplaining. She was devoid of self-pity and yet her collection of vague symptoms left her with a sense of humiliation. Though she found it embarrassing to admit to this apparent weakness and wanted to push through it, some days she was overwhelmed and felt too unwell to get out of bed. It was at night she felt it most intensely. When sleep eluded her, she would spend hours lying in the darkness trying to stay ahead of her anxieties: 'the ghostly pack / Wolfishly is baying / At my back', she wrote of the feeling in her poem 'The Wolves Pursuing'.[14]

What was described at the time as 'nerves' might today be categorised as anxiety or depression. Yet there may also have been an underlying condition at play: at least one of Dorothea's relatives was later diagnosed with sarcoidosis, an autoimmune disease which could also account for many of Dorothea's symptoms including fatigue, chest pain, shortness of breath and fainting. Whatever the cause, her illness was a terrible burden to carry at a time when women's symptoms were so often discounted.

Dorothea's anxiety was not without foundation. She had experienced the trauma of losing her brother and her future held many uncertainties. Her life was predicated on her family wealth and eventually, it was assumed, on the fortunes of a husband. Her poetry, plays and fiction were an outlet for her creativity, but she wanted something more. An unpublished and untitled poem from early 1907 speaks directly to Dorothea's frustration at the notion that marriage was the only respectable path for a young woman:

> They say that women's lives are only Love,
> That naught else really counts, that we must wait
> For that fulfilment. It is well, but yet –
> Would I might go and bathe me at the Spring
> Of all romance – I'd act instead of dream . . .
> Heavens! The things I'd do, were I a man.[15]

It was during this period of frustration that Dorothea was to meet a woman who would become central to her life and art.

∽

Born in 1882 at Petersham in Sydney, Ruth Bedford was the second daughter of Alfred Bedford and Agnes Stephen, whose father, Sir Alfred Stephen, was a chief justice and member of the New South Wales Upper House. Ruth's family moved in the same circles as the Mackellars, thanks to her grandfather's connections.[16] A few years older than Dorothea, Ruth was striking, although not exactly pretty. Her face was angular but her dark, deep-set eyes reflected her thoughtful and compassionate nature. She was eager to please but never pushy, allowing others to take the lead but happy to use her warmth and intelligence when called upon.

Dorothea's friendship with Ruth Bedford was to be a lifelong one, and would spark an extraordinary literary collaboration. Yet pinpointing the exact timing of their fateful meeting has proven difficult. In *My Heart, My Country*, Adrienne Howley insists the pair met at school, when Ruth – a cousin of the Knox sisters – joined Dorothea in the classroom at Rona. But in the introduction to Dorothea's edited diaries, Jyoti

Brunsdon claims that Dorothea first encountered Ruth on her trip to London in 1904. However, a newspaper article in the *Daily Telegraph* quotes Ruth revealing that she had made her first trip to London in 1912.[17] Later, in a 1961 radio interview with Hazel De Berg, Ruth stated that she didn't meet Dorothea until they were 'grown up', although she doesn't specify what age that might be. Perhaps the poetry holds the key: Ruth's 1903 poem, 'Dear Land of Mine', shares striking similarities in theme and structure to Dorothea's 'My Country', suggesting the pair may have initiated their literary discussions as early as that year, when the two women were eighteen and twenty-one years old respectively, and must have thought themselves quite 'grown up'.

Whenever they met, it was clear that the attraction was mutual and immediate, on both an emotional and a creative level. Dorothea learned that Ruth was an avid reader, loved children and animals, and had an affinity with the bush, enjoying any opportunity to escape to the countryside. Dorothea quickly recognised a kindred spirit. Ruth would later describe herself and Dorothea as the oldest and dearest of friends, recalling: 'We only had to meet once to know that we wanted to meet very often, and a few days after we had met she rang up and said, "Can you swim?" I said "Yes", and after that we went swimming together almost every morning in the summer and enjoyed it immensely.' They also began writing to each other whenever they were apart, and even when they were in the same city. They described in detail the settings, the streetscapes and landscapes they found outside their doors. Most of all, they wrote about poetry and plays, sharing their verses, critiquing each other's work and urging each other on. This writing life was to become integral to their friendship – their correspondence allowed them to discuss literature and poetry, life and romance, and the Australian landscape, which became almost a third wheel in their relationship. Their creative collaboration soon became as necessary to Dorothea as breathing.

Dorothea continued her preoccupation with her imaginary characters into adulthood, and Ruth followed her lead. Dorothea wrote about her characters in her verse books and fleshed out ideas for scenes and plays. She moved back and forth between storylines for up to half a dozen different plays at any one time, adding more characters and narrative arcs to plays that seemed to be developing well, and dropping others that were not working. The letters between Dorothea and Ruth quickly became part of the writing process, and they began to correspond with each other in character, taking on the roles of the 'play' people they were developing. They gave their characters names, ages, backgrounds and intense, layered relationships which were teased out in their letters, fuelling their imaginations as they practised dialogue and developed plots. Ruth later explained the process:

> Another of our playtimes, I may call them I suppose, was the acting of people. We would just give some idea to each other of who the people were and why and what their sex was and so forth, and then we'd turn into those people. It's a most amusing way to spend your time, and though people who had never done it would just simply think it silly, it really teaches you a great deal about people, because bits of yourself come up that you didn't know were there. As I suppose most people realise now, that was how the Brontës wrote their books.

There they were seeing no one whatever but a curate or two, and the only man their brother Branwell, and they used to act among themselves all the time, and those people were the people in their books. I remember reading a paragraph in a diary of Emily's, I think; 'We went for a walk on the moors. We were the Bondells.' That meant they turned into their family of Bondells. When I went up to where they have a collection of Brontë letters, I saw quantities of tiny, tiny letters in microscopic writing, and these were the letters their play people exchanged, but I don't think anyone who had not done plays like that themselves would have realised what they were.[18]

Several of the characters Dorothea and Ruth wrote and acted in their plays would become the protagonists in novels the two young women would go on to write together over the next decade. Antoine 'Tony' St Croix was the first of their young adventurers and would become the hero of their 1919 novel, *The Little Blue Devil*. Abandoned by his father after his mother's untimely death, Tony sets out on his own at the age of ten, gaining a job on a trading boat from the port of Marseilles in his home country of France. Ruth and Dorothea would eventually act out many scenes involving Tony on his adventures around the world and, as he grew to adulthood, his various love interests. The acting sessions were later documented in Dorothea's diaries. Letters written as play characters still exist among Dorothea's papers, and one from Ruth, playing the character of Jenny Lawless from a collaborative play they dubbed *The Mad Marriage*, addresses Dorothea as Quentin, Jenny's husband. It shows how thoroughly they remained in character:

My dearest Quentin,
It is quite a long time since I wrote you any letters . . . father and Mildred will stay to dinner tomorrow night. It is quite extraordinary to consider what a very different sort of father my children have to mine, and when you most disapprove of him you must consider how well I've turned out. I miss you most awfully, especially at night but most parts of the day too and I hope you do the same by me. Nobody's kissed me since you left, except of course the children.
Your loving wife,
Jenny Lawless

Dorothea would write later of Ruth that she had met 'a fellow dreamer who understands'. In the beginning, the letters were simply confidences between friends, but they later grew into something more complex and thrilling. Although the intricate and intimate nature of the correspondence was likely never suspected by their families, it's easy to imagine the excitement with which the two young women rushed to collect their mail, in the hope of discovering the instantly recognisable cursive writing on that one special letter nestling within a bundle of crisp white envelopes.

Chapter 5

Core of My Heart

Lying on the grass by the Namoi river under the veil of a weeping willow one summer's day early in 1908, a twenty-two-year-old Dorothea was far removed from the social pressures she had left behind in the city. Kurrumbede station, a property northwest of Gunnedah on the Liverpool Plains of New South Wales, was a refuge for her, and she visited often. Having overcome the 'wobbles' of her illness, a sense of calm came over her as she settled in for a long stay in the countryside.

Charles had bought the sheep and cattle farm in 1905, hoping it would be a new start for his family. He had sold Torryburn in the Hunter Valley in 1901 – the memories of happy days the family spent there with Keith were too much of a burden. Charles engaged architect and family friend John Reid to build a homestead, and given Reid was best known for his commercial buildings, it was unsurprising that the result was less than romantic; a slightly austere Edwardian stone and slate house. Over time, the many outbuildings grew to include cottages, labourers' quarters, stables, a stallion yard, a hay silo, a buggy shed, dog kennels and an underground meat locker – the trappings of a bustling successful farm. Charles installed Eric as manager of Kurrumbede. His middle son was like a fish out of water in Sydney, but when mustering, drafting or playing polo he was in his element. The family bought the neighbouring farm, Rampadells, soon after purchasing Kurrumbede, to consolidate their land holdings – now amounting to almost 6,400 acres – and to allow Mac to eventually co-manage it with Eric. Located on the beautiful Namoi River about 280 miles north of Sydney, the farm was diversified, combining wheat cropping with raising sheep and cattle.

Ever fond of the water, Dorothea could never resist the opportunity to remove her shoes, roll off her stockings, and ease her feet into the water of the river that ran through the property. It was cool and clear but shallow and deathly still as there had been no rain to fill the river and send the water surging and bubbling downstream. Refreshed, she pulled an exercise book and a pen from her bag and set to work. She was trying to refine a poem she'd been working at, off and on, for several years.

She had begun writing the lines that were to form the first stanza before leaving for England in 1904, while the family was staying at Buckland Chambers. According to a *Women's Weekly* article, Dorothea had been 'lounging around after a game of tennis with two teenage friends, all speaking of their trips to England. One friend especially lauded the English countryside as "so green, tidy, and civilised"' compared to the sprawling Australian landscape.

'You shouldn't try to compare the two,' retorted the budding poet. 'They're so different. I do admire England, but don't feel at one with it.' Walking home mulling over the conversation, Dorothea began that famous poem with her friend's 'love of field and coppice'.[1]

She had also taken umbrage, in the lead-up to her trip to London, at some of her fellow Australians' references to England as 'home'. As Howley reported it, Dorothea was quick to put them right:

'You are so lucky to be going home,' some told her.

'I'm not *going* home, I'm *leaving* home,' said Dorothea.

'Oh Dorothea . . . don't you feel when you come back the Heads are closing behind you like prison gates?'

This attitude annoyed Dorothea. 'The Heads are the gates to my home,' she insisted. 'And I return through them with joy.'[2]

Ruth's 1903 poem, 'Dear Land of Mine' – eventually published in 1912 – had played with similar themes:

Dear land of mine, I will not send
One envious thought beyond the foam,
Though travellers to the world's dim end
have told of treasures, rare and fine,
They speak of England still as 'home'
It is not mine.[3]

Dorothea carried a deep affection for England, writing in her diary as she sailed into Plymouth, 'England came nearer and nearer and it was so lovely, so lovable, so utterly unlike any other country in the world that I found myself crying'. But she wanted to draw attention to the stark differences between the landscapes of England and Australia. At a time when many of her class struggled with the duality of being Anglo-Australian, or saw themselves as British expats, Dorothea was proud to call herself Australian. The English countryside seemed to her too far away and fantastical, almost like an Impressionist painting, a little out of focus. She hoped the poem would be less a mournful longing for the familiar and more a powerful love letter to a land which ignited such great passion in her. She was happy with the opening verse, which captured England's austere beauty, even as it softly disowned it:

> The love of field and coppice,
> Of green and shaded lanes.
> Of ordered woods and gardens
> Is running in your veins,
> Strong love of grey-blue distance
> Brown streams and soft, dim skies.
> I know but cannot share it,
> My love is otherwise.

The opening stanza, while designed to evoke the ordered, subdued English countryside, was also laying the groundwork for what was to come. The images are soft and subtle, 'brown streams' and skies that are 'dim' and 'blue-grey'. The formal English gardens are stark in comparison with the wild nature of the Australian bush, and this would provide the perfect background for the bold brushstrokes that were to follow. The rough edges of the Australian countryside suited Dorothea's restless spirit and desire for freedom, and she was ready to declare her love for her country.

The line 'My love is otherwise' is playful and coquettish, as if her head had been turned by a new and more exciting lover. It also hints, perhaps, at the ambiguity surrounding her own sexuality and her lifelong sense of 'otherness', of not quite fitting in. This first stanza positions the poet as an outsider, looking towards the object of her love and longing.

But Dorothea wanted to push the ideas further. She wanted to come up with something original that captured *her* perspective, but that would also be instantly recognisable to her fellow Australians. She wanted to write a poem that would capture the ancient and mysterious country of Australia; its ambiguities, its dangers, its grandeur. Her country was like no other continent on earth, yet capturing its essence always seemed slightly out of reach. Every time she thought she had found the right words, the right rhythm, it slipped away. It was like trying to hold the river's water in her cupped hands.

Throughout the first half of 1908, as the devastating drought wore on, Dorothea continued to tinker with the poem. In truth, she had been writing, revising and editing it since she was a teenager, and early versions of some of the lines appeared in poems she had composed following the breaking of the drought at Torryburn, when she had danced in the rain. She wanted to clarify her vision of the landscape and her physical and emotional response to the dramatic contrasts of Australia's climate.

Dorothea had herself been born during a time of drought, as reported in the *Evening News* of 1 January 1886: 'According to some authorities, the year just closed has been the most disastrous one for the colony.'⁴ Questionable farming practices adopted by the settlers were already beginning to impact the land. An intractable dry spell devastated large swathes of the country from 1895 to 1903 in a phenomenon known as the Federation Drought. As a young girl from a wealthy background, Dorothea was, for the most part, protected from the struggles of a country finding its way to nationhood. But the long-term effects of drought during her formative years crept into her being and into her poetry.

The juxtaposition of drought and flood; the concept of a wilful yet lavish land with beauty and cruelty in equal measure consumed her, and at last the words came:

> I love a sunburnt country,
> A land of sweeping plains,
> Of ragged mountain ranges,
> Of droughts and flooding rains.
> I love her far horizons,
> I love her jewel-sea,
> Her beauty and her terror—
> The wide brown land for me!

Dorothea casts Australia as a femme fatale, a seductress who has the potential to ruin those caught in the thrall of 'her beauty and her terror'. The land's thirst for rain over the next few decades would eventually become a metaphor for her own longing for love.

The young poet wanted to capture something of the landscape's specificity: she hoped to describe that moment in the middle of a hot summer's day when the air seemed to be sucked out of your lungs and it appeared, for a whisper in time, that everything stood still; the exotic native plants that shocked with their audacity were alive in her mind. She had been amusing herself with painting a watercolour of a dragonfly – she often saw them whizzing backwards past her window at Kurrumbede, and marvelled at their dexterity and bejewelled beauty. The oldest of insects, folklore suggested the dragonfly was a messenger that could deliver secrets between this world and others. And it was as though she had received such a message: it was the many colours of Australia – as multifaceted as the wings of the dragonfly – that she wanted to render into words:

> A stark white ring-barked forest
> All tragic to the moon,
> The sapphire-misted mountains,
> The hot gold hush of noon.
> Green tangle of the brushes,
> Where lithe lianas coil,
> And orchids deck the tree-tops
> And ferns the crimson soil.

There is something romantic about the 'sapphire-misted mountains', and there are hints, perhaps, of sexual discovery in the 'green tangle of the brushes' and the coiling of the 'lithe lianas'. The poem was becoming a seduction in full colour.

But Dorothea wanted to say something, too, about the inhospitable nature of this land, and how much its inhabitants had suffered in return for its beauty and bounty. That year, the newspapers had been punctuated with stories about drought and drought-busting rains. Columns recorded the woes besetting the bush and the men and women trying to eke out a living there. The Bong Bong Picnic Races near Moss Vale in the Southern

Highlands attracted only thirteen horses that year. Beneath its dust, the track was 'too dangerously hard for many to risk their steeds', according to the *Town and Country Journal*. On 15 January, the same journal reported that conditions were dire: 'Nothing short of water famine is feared unless rain soon falls.'[5] Crops were described as 'withering up', with farmers resorting to measures they had not tried for forty years, such as sinking casks in swamp beds to try to find water for stock. Dorothea had seen the devastation first-hand as crops perished, animals died of starvation or dehydration or both, and hard men of the bush were brought to their knees. But how to render their pain, and how it affected her, in a poem?

> Core of my heart, my country!
> Her pitiless blue sky,
> When sick at heart, around us,
> We see the cattle die—

The poem was taking shape, and in late January, as Dorothea continued to whittle away at it, the rains finally came. The *Sydney Mail* reported a great flood in the Hunter River because of the 'recent phenomenal rains'.[6] On 4 March, the same newspaper described the impact of similar drought-breaking downpours[7]:

> The outlook across the plains, instead of being bathed in heat haze, is clear and clean to the horizon. In place of dry crackle and snap, the bush murmurs softly and sweetly. The wallaby leaps over rocks from whose crevices mosses and new ferns peep out . . . soil, leaf, flower, creeper, are all better for the rain and so also are the humans.

Having experienced drought and the sweet relief of breaking rains throughout her life and once again this year, Dorothea knew the direction her poem must take. To her, Australia was a country of incredible resilience. She was always surprised at how quickly the rain transformed the landscape. Crops were replanted, herds were replenished and spirits soared.

> But then the grey clouds gather,
> And we can bless again
> The drumming of an army,
> The steady, soaking rain.

Sitting at her desk in her bedroom, Dorothea could gaze out the window at the gardens and orchards that surrounded Kurrumbede homestead. Her mother loved the garden and, as she had done before at Torryburn and Dunara, worked hard to curate a beautiful mix of trees and flowers. While others might have done the planting, it was Marion who designed the gardens down to the last leaf – and her hard work had been repaid. Roses in beds alongside stands of apple, pear and plum trees; a quintessential English garden in the middle of the Liverpool Plains. The bees, happy at their work among the blooms, mirrored Dorothea's sense of purpose as she attempted to finish the poem that she had been working on for so long.

> Core of my heart, my country!
> Land of the Rainbow Gold,
> For flood and fire and famine,
> She pays us back threefold—
> Over the thirsty paddocks,

> Watch, after many days,
> The filmy veil of greenness
> That thickens as we gaze.

Still, there was something missing. The heart of the matter. Now, she had visions swirling in her head of precious stones deep beneath the earth, cut through with every imaginable colour like buried treasure.

> An opal-hearted country,
> A wilful, lavish land—
> All you who have not loved her,
> You will not understand—
> Though earth holds many splendours,
> Wherever I may die,
> I know to what brown country
> My homing thoughts will fly.

That was how she truly felt. We were indistinguishable from the land and it from us. Its rivers, streams and mountains were our lifeblood and if we listened closely, we could hear the country's beating heart.

Finally, Dorothea laid down her pen and closed her verse book. She was pleased with the imagery – there was a certain sensuality about it – but she would shoot it off to Ruth for a once-over before committing it to the whims of a newspaper editor. She believed she had captured something in her 'scribbling' but she couldn't know of its trajectory once released into the world; that it would change her life and become both a blessing and a curse.

Although the poem consumed Dorothea's thoughts for much of her stay at Kurrumbede, there were other pressing matters to attend to. She was there with her brother Eric and her friend Dorothy Owen, who was visiting from Sydney. Dorothea had made herself scarce to allow her brother and her friend some time alone. It was clear they had a romantic attachment and she thought Dorothy would make an excellent sister-in-law – indeed, she already felt like a sister. To some extent, Eric's newfound happiness with her friend was a relief. Always sensitive and reserved, after Keith's death Eric had seemed even quieter and more withdrawn, and Dorothea had been worried about him. So it was a delight whenever she found the two of them lounging on the verandah, smiling at each other, or in the sitting room, listening to the gramophone. Eric was attentive in his own quiet way, and Dorothy loved to watch him play polo, his swashbuckling style at odds with his innate shyness. Dorothea's friend was pretty and good-natured, and they all spent many happy hours rehearsing scenes from her plays. A courtship between two of her favourite people gave her great pleasure.

When she saw Dorothy and Eric ride up to the fence and dismount one morning, Dorothea was quick to notice a vibrancy about them, perhaps even a flush on Dorothy's cheek. When Eric came striding towards his sister to announce their engagement, Dorothea was thrilled.

That afternoon, Eric wrote to Charles and Marion to tell them the news while his new fiancée also wrote to her parents advising that Eric Mackellar wanted to speak to them on their return to Sydney. The couple did not anticipate the reaction of Dorothy's mother, Jessie Owen, who was incensed that Eric had proposed without first seeking her approval. Dorothea was aware that Mrs Owen was a formidable woman who liked to throw her considerable weight around. But surely she would only want her daughter's happiness?

It soon became apparent that Dorothy's mother was also enraged by what she considered the unchaperoned nature of her daughter's visit to Kurrumbede. She felt that the young couple had not been properly supervised, and immediately dispatched her husband to make her anger known to the Mackellars. Dorothea recorded her own confrontation with Dorothy's mother in her diary. She and Eric had returned to Sydney just after the brouhaha over the engagement broke out, and early one morning Dorothea decided to take matters into her own hands.

Ringing the Owens' doorbell, Dorothea could already hear the overwrought tones of the lady of the house haranguing her daughter. A furious Mrs Owen called Dorothea into the drawing room with all the indignation she could muster. Dorothy was seated on a sofa, cowering and unable to meet her gaze.

After an awkward exchange of greetings, Dorothea sat down uninvited. She tried to be diplomatic, suggesting that Dorothy's happiness should be uppermost in everyone's mind. This seemed only to infuriate Mrs Owen further.

'You must remember that I am a married woman and you are a little girl. How dare you say that I am biased in this matter by anything but Dorothy's eventual happiness?' Mrs Owen raged, according to the extensive notes on the interview preserved in Dorothea's papers. 'I have always fought your battles. Many people have warned me against you, but I did not believe them. I know now that they spoke the truth and that you are dangerous.'[8]

Dorothea undoubtedly felt it a bit rich that *her* character was being assassinated when it was her brother who had caused offence, although being called dangerous would have appealed to her imagination. She opened her mouth to speak but was cut off by the older woman.

'Once a person has deceived me and acted in an underhand and dishonourable way, I never believe in them again,' fumed Mrs Owen.

'I can assure you that I feel the same way. At least on this we agree,' Dorothea replied, keeping her voice low and controlled. She was determined not to let her emotions get the better of her.

'Whatever else you are,' Mrs Owen continued, 'you are not a fool, and you must have seen what was going on under your nose.' It was true that Dorothea had noticed and suspected the attachment, but she could hardly have imagined that it would be unwelcome to her friend's mother. But she could see that there was no reasoning with the woman, and she knew that Dorothy would not go against her mother. She rose, looking at her friend sadly, and let herself out.

In the following months, Mrs Owen wrote a series of letters to Marion, expressing outrage that seemed disproportionate to the alleged crime. Their correspondence reveals Marion's thinly disguised contempt for the flighty and dramatic Mrs Owen. On 15 September, Mrs Owen complained bitterly that Eric's approach to the engagement was much too casual and his 'curt' letter belatedly seeking permission to marry her daughter was an insult:

> When I thought of Dorothy at Kurrumbede (and knowing her almost too affectionate nature) with Eric in love with her and Dorothea arguing for it, you must not be surprised that I wondered if, being part of that atmosphere, Dorothy would be of sane mind?[9]

Mrs Mackellar responded with a letter that only just managed to retain a respectful tone while communicating her bewilderment at Mrs Owen's fury. Dorothea, for her part, insisted she had not influenced her friend, and that Mrs Owen had misconstrued the nature of their relationship. In another letter, on 26 September, Mrs Owen feared her daughter had been compromised:

> I think a very great wrong was done by your son making love to Dorothy unchaperoned. It seems to me if at any time, a girl ought to be sacred, it is when she is in an unprotected position.[10]

It seemed Mrs Owen was intent on breaking the engagement with Eric and, as a consequence, the friendship between Dorothea and her daughter. It may well have been that she wanted someone more powerful for her son-in-law, but it's hard to believe that the reliable, respectable and wealthy Eric – with his impeccable family connections – was not worthy of Miss Dorothy Owen. Ultimately, Eric was not to be lucky in love and Dorothea was to lose one of her best friends. And it seems likely that Dorothy Owen, too, was wounded by the failed engagement – Miss Dorothy Owen continues to make the odd appearance in Sydney's social pages throughout the next decade, and it is not until 1919 that there is record of a Dorothy Owen marrying a James Fletcher. If this was indeed Eric's Dorothy, she would have been in her thirties by then.

The poem that Dorothea worked so hard on, for so long, first appeared in *The Spectator* in September 1908 under the title

'Core of My Heart'. It also featured in a number of Australian publications as 'Core of My Heart – My Country' and eventually as 'My Country', in a nod to economy of space in a headline as well as a sign of growing nationalism in a still-young nation. The poem would officially be renamed 'My Country' in Dorothea's first collection of poetry published three years later; she clearly saw the merit in the simpler, more emotive title. And although the title perhaps carried a sense of belonging and possession that was blind to the existence and the suffering of Indigenous peoples who had been dispossessed of *their* country, few white Australians who read it in the newspaper would have seen it that way at the time.

Whatever title it was given, the poem was met with immediate acclaim. An article in the *Sydney Stock and Station Journal* reported:

> Hurrah for Australia! One of the best poems ever written reaches us from the London *Spectator*. It was written by Miss Dorothea Mackellar, daughter of Dr Mackellar . . . We have much pleasure in reprinting the poem and can only suggest that if any man (or woman) can set it to a ringing tune, it would make a grand National Anthem for Australia.[11]

The overwhelming response to her poem took Dorothea by surprise. But her family were a little more critical, she later recalled, insisting that one couldn't immediately see the paddocks greening after the breaking of a drought and questioning the use of 'lianas' rather than simply 'vines'. There was a suggestion that soil could not be described as 'crimson', and this line would later become 'warm dark soil' in deference to the critique.[12] However, not everyone agreed with the change. Several years later, then Victorian Governor Sir Thomas Gibson-Carmichael queried the decision in a letter to Henry Hyde Champion, the editor of the journal *Book Lover* and later Dorothea's publisher:

> She must have a very true eye (from my point of view) for colour. Surely . . . in the poem as I read it in the *Spectator*, the words were, 'and ferns the crimson soil?' I remember it struck me at the time as perhaps exaggerated, but when I went for the first (and only) time into the Queensland bush, 200 miles north of Brisbane, I thought it so true.[13]

The poem was to become all things to Dorothea, both a triumph and a burden, the reason for her literary longevity but also a roadblock to her ambition. The poem followed her throughout her life – sometimes as an affectionate companion and sometimes threatening to overshadow any further literary strides. Everything she did was compared to it, and nothing ever seemed to measure up. The poem was to bring her fame on three continents and the kind of national acclamation reserved for celebrities. Her every utterance, social engagement or travel plan was detailed in newspapers across the country. And yet she could never seem to move on from the poem that had won her fame.

Several years after the publication of 'My Country', the *Australasian* published a new poem by Dorothea called 'Australia'. The final verse again celebrated Dorothea's image of her country as woman and lifeblood:

> Let others praise the rose and white,
> For rose and white is fair to see;
> her smooth brown skin and scarlet mouth,
> and tawny hair is life to me.[14]

This echoed the comparison between England and Australia in the earlier poem. It spoke to Dorothea's desire to write something which might again grab the imagination of the nation, but 'My Country' cast a long shadow, and this new contender never made it into any of her collections.

Much of Dorothea's early poetry had been characterised by Georgian symbolism, with frequent references to nature, the moon and mostly benign supernatural creatures such as fairies and nymphs and dryads. There was a striving to elevate the everyday, to give the reader an idealised view of the world, or perhaps what the world could be. But 'My Country' was a departure for Dorothea from all that came before. It was grounded in a realism that was closer to Modernist poetry – although she would struggle to make the leap to that aesthetic in later years. Dorothea had left the romanticism of the bush balladeers behind and painted in bold, confident brush strokes that were Post-Impressionist in their use of colour. Yet the dark undertones were never far away, always menacing, threatening. It was these chords that struck the reader, reverberating with some secret and compelling knowledge.

The poem's dark and foreboding or 'gothic' elements could perhaps be tied to the turbulence in Dorothea's own life: her restlessness, and the sense she was always waiting for the horror to come, perhaps recalling the tragedy of Keith's death. There had long been a deep-seated fear of the Australian outback on the part of white settlers who could not quite come to terms with the extremes of its climates and its geographies. And the poem captures this odd sense of something sinister lurking – that otherworldly or supernatural element that was evoked when people disappeared in the Australian bush without a trace. As author and academic Stephanie Trigg wrote, the silence around

Indigenous culture and denial of prior occupation created a gothic consciousness of 'something deeply unknowable and terrifying in the Australian landscape'.[15]

∽

In October, soon after 'My Country' was first published in Australia, there was an article in the *Sydney Mail* which foresaw a growing sense of nationalism that would become synonymous with the poem:

> It sounds the right note – the clear, ringing, triumphant note of love and trust in our country – our Australia. It would seem that the world is slowly coming to a realisation of the possibilities of the Commonwealth. That a wrong impression long prevailed was largely the fault of Australians . . . Certain it is that while Canadians and, nearer home, New Zealanders have always trumpeted the greatness of their homelands, Australians, with a far better country, have said little or nothing of its richness, beauty, and splendour, and have allowed the nations to believe that drought and isolation were permanent conditions. It was false to say so – foolish to allow it to go unchallenged . . . The truth is that Australians do not appreciate their privileges. We want no war, nor threat of war; but should ever the time come when we are in danger of losing the grandest, sunniest, happiest country in the wide world, the people of Australia will at last realise the truth. Australia! – the name itself will one day arouse a passion of patriotic love. A little more thought today of the blessings that are ours would not be amiss. [16]

Though clearly patriotic, 'My Country' was not intentionally jingoistic, but it was nevertheless occasionally co-opted for political and nationalistic causes. What Dorothea could not have predicted was that the looming Great War would take the poem to new heights of success.

It was during the war that 'My Country' began to achieve the canonical status it would hold for the next century.[17] Prior to this, it had been associated with a strong sense of nationalism, but it was not until the war that Australians truly adopted it is an anthem. Suddenly, homesick diggers were quoting the poem, longing to see 'a sunburnt country' and 'the wide brown land' once more. Stories emerged of Australian soldiers in the trenches of Europe clinging to the lyrics of the poem tucked inside their uniforms as a reminder of home, or sending the verses to their loved ones to let them know they were thinking of them. A decade later, writer and poet Zora Cross – a contemporary of Dorothea's – described how moved she was when, on discovering an old schoolbook belonging to her brother who died in the war, she found that beside the final lines of 'My Country' – 'I know to what brown country / my homing thoughts will fly' – he had written the words 'same here'. The poem was also referenced in a Brisbane *Daily Mail* article about a young digger and budding playwright killed in the war, whose diaries mirrored this longing for home:

> 'Surely anyone who has read the last four lines of "My Country" will think of them often out here,' wrote Adrian Consett Stephen, author of *An Australian in the R.F.A*. 'Out here in the trenches amid a sodden country, soaking beneath its sodden skies. Is it possible that somewhere the sun is blazing on surf and yellow sands?' It is another example of the

grim irony of war that this young Australian, whose letters and diary are now given to the public, should have met his death in action some two years after the above words were written.[18]

Australians had finally found their anthem and it cemented the reputation of the young poet who had created it.

Chapter 6

A Rising Star

The rise and rise of 'My Country' over the next decade was extraordinary, and the national and international recognition for Dorothea was to be both instant and enduring. She could not have imagined how popular her poem was to become, or that it would take on a life of its own and that she would be swept along on its tide. It continued to appear in newspapers and journals around the country, from big city mastheads to tiny local papers like the *Wollondilly Press* in regional New South Wales. 'My Country' had caught the mood of the people, and it would be reprinted across several continents over the next decade, appearing in wide-ranging publications in Australia over the next century.

Meanwhile, Dorothea was becoming more active in the literary and social scene in Sydney, and by 1909 she was excited to become one of the founders of the Bush Book Club alongside its patron, Lady Poore, who was the wife of Admiral Richard Poore – then the Commander-in-Chief of the Australian Navy. The book club raised money and purchased books for people living remotely who could not afford or could not access reading material. Dorothea was passionate about the scheme, believing that books could lift people out of ordinary or difficult circumstances and transport them to new worlds. A report in the *Sydney Morning Herald* showed qualified support for the book scheme while revealing a patronising attitude towards people living in the bush:

> It is quite true that reading is often a quite illiterate occupation, and that most often in the case of the bush dweller it is not likely to reach the rank of the higher moral virtues . . . the main object of a Bush Book Club should be to afford a sane and humanising recreation.[1]

In her autobiography, *Recollections of an Admiral's Wife,* Lady Poore admitted she had caused controversy with her perceptions of country people despite her good intentions:

> In recommending its establishment, I was lucky enough to bring down a heavy shower, if not a storm, of criticism upon my head by saying that if Australians in the bush had more opportunity for reading, they would cultivate the imagination in which they appeared, to me, deficient.[2]

Over the next two years, more of Dorothea's poems began appearing in a range of publications in Australia, England and America. Her short stories, too, were finding a market. In 1909, the *Sunday Times* published 'Recollections of an Ancient Mariner':

> The Ancient Mariner was seated on a rock at the harbor's edge, smoking and likewise taking an active interest in a yacht

race which, in fact, he seemed to be personally conducting: for he was calling out directions to all of the crews in turn, addressing individual members by name.³

Early the next year, Dorothea discovered her 'Boggabri story going the rounds of the American magazines and they had illustrated it with a black bushman attired in leaves'. Another short story, *The Lie* – written that year under the penname C.L. Prevost, after her play character, Kid Prevost – was later published in the *Southern Sphere* and *The Australasian*.⁴

It was during this period that journalist Charles 'Charlie' Bean, Dorothea's friend and a vocal advocate for her work, convinced her a collection of verses would be well received. Henry Hyde Champion – or H.H.C., as he was known – had opened the Australasian Authors Agency in 1906 and had begun negotiating to publish Dorothea's first volume of poetry, with Bean acting as a go-between. H.H.C. and his wife Elsie had been running the Book Lovers Library in Melbourne, and he also edited a monthly publication known as the *Book Lover*. A larger-than-life character with a booming voice, a moustache and a monocle, Champion left a military career in the United Kingdom to become an anti-war activist. After emigrating to Australia, he suffered a stroke in 1901 and was left partially paralysed with a limp and slight speech impediment, which made his physical presence even more memorable. An imposing figure, Champion's indefatigable efforts contributed much to the literary life of Australia at the time. Although Bean was due to leave for London to work as a correspondent for the *Sydney Morning Herald* – where he would make his name as a renowned war correspondent, documenting the Australian experience in Gallipoli – he would continue to play a role in Dorothea's career from a distance, helping her to forge literary connections at home and abroad.

∽

The year 1910 found Dorothea and her parents again staying at Buckland Chambers in Sydney with Dunara leased. Dorothea never tired of the view from the apartment above Charles's surgery, especially at night when people strolled arm in arm among the trees in Hyde Park below. Governor Arthur Phillip had great foresight when he reserved paddocks in the centre of the fledgling town for parklands in 1792. At first, it was used as a common for gathering firewood and grazing animals until its proclamation by Governor Macquarie in 1810, when he named it Hyde Park after the London landmark. Architect Francis Greenway had imagined it as a 'grand quadrangle of a Neoclassical town plan', but originally it was used for horseracing and later for cricket matches.[5] Now, depending on the time of day, it was a bustling thoroughfare for agents of commerce or a quiet concourse for courting lovers.

Dorothea never walked there without a chaperone as she knew some of its dark secrets. Only the year before, after a lovers' tiff that had started on a park bench, one Robert Macey shot new love Mary Agnes Brooksbank before turning the gun on himself. The quarrel had apparently been about Mary joining the Salvation Army – which may have worked in her favour, since she survived the shooting.

By 1910, the city of Sydney was home to more than a million people and its streets were abuzz with commuters, horse-drawn wagons, trams and the new motor cars. Suited men and women in long skirts and broad-brimmed hats darted across the tram tracks while cyclists rolled through town alongside trams and wagons in the shadow of magnificent sandstone buildings. It was an exciting time. Australia was known internationally as a 'social laboratory' for its radical welfare legislation.[6] Largely due to the lobbying of women activists, Australia had seen a decline in infant mortality, the raising of the age of consent, and the introduction of technical education for girls, which had all greatly improved the lives of women and girls.[7] Charles Mackellar had also had a hand in many reforms – particularly in relation to improving the plight of single mothers – that were viewed as quite radical in other parts of the world.

Dorothea moved easily between the society of Sydney's intellectual and administrative elite, and life on her family's country property at Kurrumbede. She was the 'ideal' Australian girl – beautiful, sophisticated and fashionable, with a growing literary reputation. While she was cultivated and spirited, she was also a romantic with a deeply sensitive side. Sometimes she felt everything around her seemed heightened, so that colours were too bright, sounds too loud and tastes too strong or bitter. This sensory overload was exhausting and more than a little unnerving. But Dorothea knew that it was a double-edged sword, because it allowed her to extract great joy from life; intense emotion and passion and desire that was thrilling at times and always fed into her creative spirit. Whenever it became overwhelming, Dorothea knew she had to retreat somewhere quiet to recuperate, or flee to the tonic of country life.

With this in mind she joined her godmother, Florence Binnie, at her holiday home on the edge of the Royal National Park in mid-January to enjoy the peace and quiet. The wealthy indulged the practice of moving between city and country properties on a regular basis and, with staff on hand to meet their every need, there was little more to do than relax.

Dorothea wrote in her diary that she and her godmother 'Breakfasted in our wrappers on the veranda, lazed nearly all the morning'. Another day, Dorothea and Florence 'hired a boat and rowed far up the river. It was delicious. Everything is looking beautiful and the black swans chased us and begged for bits of apple.' They arrived home just before a rainstorm, which they watched in comfort from the verandah. 'This place never looks the same for two hours together,' Dorothea commented.

That night, they took a moonlight walk up the hills with Florence's dog Koti doing an excited dance every time he came across a native creature lurking in the bushes. Rock wallabies came to greet them, quite used to the many tourists, hikers and holidaymakers who swarmed the national park every summer. It was magical there, and Dorothea again felt the restorative benefits of being in nature. 'The moon was beyond reproach. We do feel so much better,' she wrote. The sights and sounds of the bush, and the languid pace of life, both restored and inspired her.

∾

Back in Sydney several weeks later, Dorothea went for her regular swim in the ocean pool at Rose Bay. The family had moved back to Dunara at Point Piper, so Dorothea was again close to all her favourite haunts. It was Valentine's Day, and the water was clear and inviting. She had been taking swimming and diving lessons and was quietly pleased with her proficiency. Strong and athletic, she liked to push herself physically. There was a freedom in swimming, of being in the water, of feeling the salt water on her skin. Skimming across the surface, diving deep to the bottom and re-emerging into the crisp morning air was a thrill she craved. But another thrill beckoned, too.

Ruth was coming over later in the day. She and Ruth had discussed acting their plays together with a view to, one day, producing them in the theatre. This was an exciting prospect, but one Dorothea had never seriously entertained before, because the general feeling among the upper classes was that theatrical types were a bit 'unsavoury'. But under Ruth's influence, the plan seemed like a real possibility, and Dorothea relished it, writing in her diary: 'It's fun being different people!'

When Ruth arrived at Dunara, the friends went up to the rooftop terrace where an enclosed stone wall allowed them to safely sit at the top of the world, with a view of the city and the ocean, until darkness fell. They were working on a play about their old friend, Kid Prevost. Dorothea had been developing the character since her teenage years but Kid was taking on a greater depth with Ruth's input. Kid was born in a rectory in the north of Ireland, but his adventurous spirit led him to live in South America. There, he fell under the sway of the masterful villain Urquiza, and became a horse thief until his rescue by the beautiful Katherine Hammond. A few years later, Kid's escapades would would continue when he was cast as the protagonist in Dorothea's 1913 novel, *Outlaw's Luck*.

At twenty-four, Dorothea knew that there was much speculation about her marriage prospects. She had no shortage of suitors, but none had captured her heart or made her pulse race as it did when she and Ruth played their characters, creating ideal heroes and heroines and imbuing them with all the passion 'nice' girls were required to keep hidden in polite society. She wondered how her parents might react if she were to suddenly announce she planned to become an actress. It was impossible, of course, but she could fantasise about it. And some women became actresses without losing their place in society, she knew: that very week she had been to the Palace Theatre to see *The Fencing Master*, starring her friend, the glamorous and fashionable Grace Palotta.

Grace, who was born in Vienna and was five years older than Dorothea, first visited Australia in 1895 with a touring company from London's Gaiety Theatre. With a reputation for style and elegance, women followed her stage career and her fashion advice in journals such as *The Lone Hand*. Grace had even published a novella, *A Viennese Romance: The Life and Adventures of an Actress*, several years earlier.[8]

Both Dorothea and Ruth were taken with Grace's beauty and her vitality, although her writing had been panned in the *Tasmanian News* for lacking 'literary style and polish'.[9] Whatever her private view of Grace's literary style, Dorothea saw Grace as an enigma, impossible to know because she was entirely self-sufficient:

> It isn't wholly satisfactory when a person gives nothing in return for what you bring but when she doesn't evince any need of you at all – when there isn't one treasure of yours that will help her, nor even one shining trifle in your gift that will please her for a moment – then indeed friendship becomes impossible.

Inspired, nevertheless, by the mysterious actress, Dorothea and Ruth continued in their attempts at theatre, even on trips to Bondi beach: 'the surf was so glorious', Dorothea wrote in her diary. 'So we paddled and Ruth was nearly swept away and drenched from top to toe. We dried ourselves on a hot flat rock and we acted the Prevost Play. I think it was so courageous in cold blood on a salt morning.' And later during a picnic at Diamond Bay:

> It was a heavenly day and there were heaps of mauve and white violets . . . we acted the Kid Prevost saga for hours. The landscape did fit in. It was too good for words. The feeling is on me still, I can't think myself free of the play. It went awfully well. She loved it too.

∽

The following Thursday night, the Mackellars dined with the 'Charlie Fairfaxes'. Charles, a lawyer and the grandson of the prominent newspaper scion John Fairfax, who founded the *Sydney Morning Herald*, and his wife, Florence, were regular dinner guests. Dorothea was pleased to be seated next to their son, James, or 'Mr Jim' as she called him. Mr Jim had talked excitedly to her about poetry and publishers. After dinner, Dorothea and Mr Jim retired to the billiard room where he showed her his published collections of verse including *The Gates of Sleep and Other Poems*.

Mr Jim had left Sydney for London in 1904 and established himself as a poet, moving in literary circles with American poet Ezra Pound and Australian poet and novelist Frederic Manning. It was partly through her friendship with Mr Jim that Dorothea was accepted into London's literary circles and formed many important friendships.

In the days that followed, she was busy either accompanying her father on his official engagements, including a reception for Japanese officers at Parliament House, or enjoying shopping expeditions which led her to buy a much-admired three-cornered black hat with a gold quill. But always in the back of her mind, she was longing to escape to meet up with Ruth and continue from where they left off in the adventures of Kid Prevost. Kid was having trouble with his latest romantic interest, Carol – the pair had fallen in love but they were terribly unsuited.

While Dorothea had crushes on both men and women, and Ruth often commented that she liked children, people and books in that order, Dorothea did not quite have the language to describe her relationship with Ruth. All she knew for sure was that she couldn't wait to be with her, and she missed her desperately when they were apart. Friendships between women were expected to bridge the periods in life that came before or after marriage: childhood and widowhood. However, friendships that interfered with relationships with men by assuming too much importance were viewed as abnormal.[10] Dorothea and Ruth were romantic with each other in the context of the characters they were playing. If the characters were in love and kisses and touching were required as an expression of that love, it was only the deep creative spirit at work. Their relationship did not attract undue attention from family members despite long sessions of acting in their bedrooms, on the roof or in the bush, away from prying eyes. There was an intimacy between them, there was no doubt about that. Their play-acting exuded a sexual aestheticism that included desire and a certain physicality. Women at that time were often at risk of being considered either too sexual or devoid of sexuality, with both sides of the spectrum viewed with suspicion.

Love scenes were never far from the young women's imagination. Together, they acted scenes from the play they called *The Little Blue Devil,* with Dorothea playing the hero, Tony, and Ruth playing his latest love interest – an Italian aristocrat. Dorothea described the scene as 'serious love at 11.30 am at a bathing house!' Dorothea confided in her diary that she had 'never been fuller of electricity' than she was that day with Ruth. And that autumn, Ruth had also written some verses for Dorothea about their time spent play-acting. Entitled 'Babies on the Roof', it was dedicated 'To the Other Baby (damned bad lines in return for a beautiful evening)' and was recorded in Dorothea's diary:

> Yet the land of Let's Pretend
> Opens for them wide
> Here is life that has no end
> Here is love untried.

As the weather cooled and March gave way to April, a watershed moment in Australian politics occurred when a federal election was held on 13 April 1910. Andrew Fisher led the Labor Party to a commanding victory over Alfred Deakin's newly formed Liberal Party made up of former anti-socialists, protectionists and independents. A huge swing to Labor allowed the party to claim a majority in both the House of Representatives and the Senate for the first time. Dorothea managed to cast her vote despite some 'muddle' at the polling booth, and later that evening she and Ruth joined the people gathering to hear the election result.

The crowd that crammed the city centre to celebrate was 'huge and good tempered', she wrote.

On 30 April, Dorothea attended Commemoration Day at the University of Sydney, which coincided with the twenty-fifth anniversary of the granting of full academic rights to women. 'Commem Day', as it was known, was often characterised by wild celebrations, with students taking the opportunity to let down their hair in an otherwise strict and sober environment. Walking through the grounds towards the Great Hall – surrounded by dignified sandstone buildings on this auspicious occasion – must have made Dorothea wistful. When she had observed classes, she had thrilled at the lecturers with their serious faces and their passionate voices, and the students with their hopeful expressions and dubious questions. Undoubtedly, Dorothea would have been visited by the feeling of opportunity lost. What might her life have been like if she had been allowed to gain a degree, as many of the young women present were now doing? After she was seated, she watched as the chancellor of the university, Sir Henry Normand MacLaurin, tried to address the noisy crowd. The *Sydney Morning Herald* reported that his speech 'was so completely interrupted that after a strong appeal to the undergraduates he left more than half his address unread'.[11]

By 7 May, the city was once again bustling, this time covered with flags at half-mast as the people of the Commonwealth heard the news that King Edward VII was dead. It was unexpected and shocking news, and the Mackellars went into mourning alongside their countrymen. The weather, cool and overcast, suited the sad occasion.

But Dorothea had much to look forward to: in June, she was to visit Queensland as the guest of Charles's old friend

Sir William MacGregor, former governor of Newfoundland and now the governor of Queensland. She was to tour North Queensland with the MacGregor family for what was to be the governor's first official visit to the north of the state, and he was taking his second wife, Mary, and his youngest daughter, also named Mary but known to all as 'Babs'. Dorothea was enlisted as a travelling companion for Babs, and she was looking forward to spending time with her lively friend – she intended to record every detail of her trip in her diary.

Chapter 7
Mr Dods

Dorothea set off for Brisbane by train on 3 June with high expectations, and was delighted to find Captain Hugh Scarlett – the Governor's aide-de-camp – waiting for her when the train pulled into the railway station. She could not help but notice his handsome face and warm smile as she was ushered into a luxurious Mercedes with red leather interior, and her bags were retrieved from the train. She smiled back at him, holding his gaze a little longer than necessary, and thought this might be an even more enjoyable trip than she had anticipated. At Government House, she was warmly welcomed by Sir William and Lady Mary MacGregor.

Three days later, the MacGregor party was on a train to Rockhampton, with bananas and palms seeming to multiply before their eyes as they rattled past, and tawny grass and green eucalypts could be seen from the windows. On arrival they were met by the mayor and schoolchildren proffering bouquets of purple orchids. They attended the annual Carnival of Rockhampton which revealed all manner of bizarre attractions and freak shows including so-called 'man-eating' snakes, although Dorothea pointed out they didn't *actually* observe a snake eating a man, and were therefore unable to verify the claim. From there, the group joined the SS *Lucinda* and continued their journey via the Fitzroy River and out to sea.

Captain Scarlett seemed quite taken with Dorothea and took every opportunity to talk to her – until Lady MacGregor came upon them and shooed him away. Dorothea laughed at this unnecessary policing; Captain Scarlett always acted with propriety. She enjoyed his company and she sought him out for moments alone, sometimes mischievously, in order to trigger a flustered Lady MacGregor into calling from the other side of the boat: 'What are you two up to now? Come and join the rest of us so I can keep an eye on you!'

The next day they travelled through a beautiful strait between two islands, Keswick and St Bees, where they paddled ashore, gathering shells and eating oysters. It was idyllic. Dorothea was dressed in a light lace frock which ended well above her ankles and allowed her to slip her feet into the cool rockpools, the dress only getting a little wet as she held it aloft. Dorothea was surprised when Captain Scarlett, his trousers rolled to just below his knees, walked on oysters in the rock pools without knowing what they were and hopped about in pain. Apparently, he had never seen them growing in their natural habitat.

After reboarding the *Lucinda,* they sailed through the Whitsunday Passage with its stunning scenery and on to the Hinchinbrook Passage, which she found even more beautiful, 'like a smooth blue and silver opal. The big mountains had bright silver clouds on them like Jupiter's'. The wind freshened and they raced up to Cooktown, where the governor was to open the agricultural show. Arriving in the rain, the party stayed overnight before being taken by carriage and grey horses to a wine party, and then to visit hospitals and schools.

'I never saw such a lot of blackfellows before,' Dorothea wrote, using the language of the times. It seems likely she would have encountered Aboriginal people in her travels in regional Australia and around the family property at Gunnedah. However, her social status and the nature of the circles in which she moved meant that Dorothea would have had few, if any, meaningful opportunities to interact with First Nations Australians, who were rarely mentioned in her diaries.

On 15 June the party went to see a beautiful garden renowned in Cooktown for its homegrown produce. Dorothea was enamoured of the tropical landscape and the languid way in which the locals went about town or worked on the plantations. It was a way of surviving the intense heat by preserving their energy, but she felt there was something so poetic about the way they moved and spoke in a quiet, slow, easy manner, as if they had all the time in the world. They could not and would not be rushed.

At the garden, they ate granadillas and drank milk under a jackfruit tree. She didn't want the afternoon to end, she later recalled. The next day, they travelled from Cooktown to Port Douglas and Cairns, and then west to Chillagoe by a railway that passed the Barron Falls. Here, the climate was different from the coast: dry and clear. The group stayed with a mine manager and his tall, blue-eyed wife in their tropical house and then drove to the popular Chillagoe caves under a bright moon. A 'scrumptious' supper was spread out in a huge cave which served as a makeshift dining room, with lamps creating flickering shadows on the stone walls. Dorothea and Babs were taken on an exclusive tour by 'a nice thin man called Campbell' to a cave no white women had previously entered. The pair admired the beauty of the cave, undoubtedly unaware that it might be a sacred place for Aboriginal people, and not for their eyes to see.

Moving on to Townsville and Charters Towers, Dorothea, adventurous as ever, was excited to descend into a goldmine:

> 3000 feet vertically, very dirty but awfully interesting: the cage you go down in, the queer trolley rattling down at an angle of 38 degrees. The naked men (well, half-naked) and the stifling passages where it isn't ventilated and the gold brick at the top and the quicksilver squeezed through a cloth. I loved it all.

Back in Brisbane by July of 1910, Dorothea attended the opening of the Queensland Parliament with the MacGregors. Newspaper reports described the women's gowns as steadfastly black because of the ongoing period of mourning for King Edward. Furs and ostrich feather boas were donned in many cases, the prevailing style of gown being the popular tailored Russian-style coat and skirt: 'Miss Mackellar, Sydney, who accompanied them, came in a coat and skirt of black serge with tricorn hat of black chip, finished with wings; she also wore white fox furs.'[1]

On 21 July, Dorothea left Government House to stay with another friend of her father's, architect Robert 'Robin' Dods and his American-born wife, Mary. Charles had met Robin when he travelled to Sydney to do design work for the Bank of New South Wales during Charles's presidency of the bank. Dods, who quickly became 'R' in Dorothea's diaries, was described by his biographer as a man who possessed 'immense charm, wit, and natural ability with discriminating and impeccable taste. He was passionate about his work and derived great pleasure from it.'[2] He was also interested in politics, literature and the arts, and became a champion of Dorothea's writing almost immediately after meeting her and reading her poetry.

Dorothea loved staying with the Dodses, finding their home in Abbott Street – New Farm, which Dods had designed – wonderfully peaceful. It was a similar sensibility that Mr Dods brought to her: a calmness; a sense of security that she could not really explain. In the evenings, Mrs Dods would retire to bed and Robin and Dorothea would spend hours talking. She loved their literary discussions and the single-minded attention he lavished on her. 'He is such a dear. It makes things really hard,' she confided to her diary. And it was soon after meeting Mr Dods that Dorothea developed a secret code to use in her diary to protect her privacy. The code consisted of a series of characters in place of letters: there were circles and squares, crosses, stars and diamonds, all representing either a letter or a punctuation mark.

Dorothea's diaries of 1910 throw into doubt a claim she made later in life that, in 1908, she had become engaged to an unnamed fiancé. In an interview with Adrienne Cowley, author of *My Heart, My Country*, Dorothea reportedly claimed she had broken off the relationship after her unnamed fiancé had told her he didn't want her to visit Brisbane at the invitation of Sir William MacGregor. According to Dorothea, an American fleet – the Great White Fleet, as it was called – was visiting the city, and her fiancé was worried about her taking the trip unchaperoned. 'If you have so little trust in me that you expect I will fall into the arms of the first sailor who makes advances, you little know me, and I no longer wish to know you, much less marry you,' Dorothea claimed to have told him.³ However, while the American fleet did visit Australia in August 1908, the only ports of call reported were Sydney, Melbourne and Albany. Further, Sir William was not appointed governor of Queensland until December 1909 and did not live in Australia until then. It's possible there was a short engagement around this time, and that later in life Dorothea mistook the date and circumstances, but it remains largely a mystery, as there are only fragments of diaries from 1908 and there is no mention of the broken engagement in any of her future diaries.

Her relationship with the very married Robin Dods, on the other hand, was blooming. Dorothea took every opportunity she could to spend time alone with him, whether they were attending social functions or at the Dodses' home, New Farm. She had just turned twenty-five and her 'R' was a man in his forties, married, a father of two and a friend of her father, so the stakes were high. A sensitive and cultured man, his mother's death in 1908 had devastated him. His grief and the loss of some architectural commissions led Dods to take a year off work to travel in North America and Europe with his friend Robert Lorimer. It's not clear how much time, if any, Mary spent accompanying him on this trip but his long absence suggests their marriage was under pressure. With Lorimer, he travelled in Italy before catching influenza. Deciding the northern winters were not good for his health, he reluctantly returned to Australia.⁴

On 9 August 1910, Dorothea and 'R' attended a ball for the new Mater Misericordiae Hospital, for which Robin had been the architect, with Mrs Dods missing the event due to ill health. The ball was described as an unqualified success by the *Brisbane Courier*.⁵

Between 300 and 400 dancers occupied the floor. The hall was elaborately decorated ... pillars around the ballroom were completely hidden from view by greenery, in which was mingled pink roses and wattle blossom.

On the drive back to the Dodses' house that evening, something happened between Robin and Dorothea. What exactly is not clear from her diary, but Dorothea seemed to think that their relationship had been resolved in some way: 'He does like me but he was very good driving home and I tried to help him and we succeeded. It will be alright now I think.' About a week later, however, Dorothea reported suffering a 'collapse' during which her teeth were chattering, and wrote how much she hated her 'weakness'.

On 23 August, a lunch date with Robin at the Brisbane Botanic Gardens was 'intimate' and Dorothea felt coquettish and flirty as they spent a leisurely two hours together. Mr Dods was 'just a boy', Dorothea wrote in her diary. Then she picked up Babs MacGregor and Elisabeth Dods, Robin's daughter, and they motored to Government House for tea. When Dorothea arrived back at the Dodses' house that evening, Mary Dods retired early due to a headache, leaving her husband and the young Miss Mackellar alone in the drawing room. They talked for hours, arguing on all sorts of matters, mostly political, and Dorothea felt she could hold her own despite her host's experience. Whenever the conversation became too personal, though, Dorothea changed the subject and regaled Robin with stories from her overseas trips. Robin was easy to divert. But nothing would ever stop her being 'a little fool' when it came to 'R', she wrote later.

After almost six weeks with the Dodses, the atmosphere in the house was growing increasingly uncomfortable. On 25 August, Mrs Dods appeared tired and nervous and Dorothea began to think she had outstayed her welcome. 'I think it is just as well that I'm going away, dear as they are.'

She spent a week visiting friends to try to sort out her feelings for 'R', but by 10 September, she was back at New Farm. She simply couldn't stay away. Dorothea reported having 'nerves' and feeling ill, and that 'Mrs Dods has nerves but I of all people, and to her of all people, ought to be patient'. She later explained that Robin had tried to give her a lovely old Italian pendant, but she refused it. '*Ahime*!' she wrote in her diary. 'Woe is me. I wish oneself would *let* oneself do these things – no, perhaps I don't really.'

When Dorothea received a letter from Ruth, the timing could not have been better. Her friend was the antidote to her confusion and despair over Robin and, realising how much she missed her, Dorothea decided she must return to Sydney soon to tell her everything. Things were so much less complicated with her other 'R'. Ruth had sent Dorothea a poem she had written for her called 'Something Wrong':

Something whispers, 'She is not here';
Something sighs, 'She is still away';
And I am missing my dearest dear,
Night and day!

A few days later, Dorothea left Abbott Street, arriving home by train on 19 September to be met by her mother and father.

A week later, a letter arrived from Robin telling Dorothea he was coming to Sydney and asking if they could meet.

The clandestine nature of their relationship was thrilling for Dorothea, although she was careful to write about it in her diaries in very pragmatic terms. Dorothea's secret code was often employed during this period as she sought to keep the nature of their relationship under wraps. Dorothea was still experiencing the bouts of 'nerves' or 'wobbles', and when they met, Robin tried to convince her to seek out a specialist to check the condition of her heart, but she was reluctant. She sometimes felt as if she was going mad, because the 'attacks' or 'turns' could come out of nowhere and the symptoms were vague – appearing in different combinations from heart palpitations and dizziness, to sweating and fatigue. She hoped no-one thought her a fraud or attention-seeker, but she also wondered if the condition might be psychosomatic, perhaps brought on by stress. Though 'hysteria' was a medical diagnosis still applied to women in the early twentieth century, Charles had assured her she was far too sensible and practical to be predisposed to the fanciful dramatics he had witnessed in various asylums. She wished with all her heart that she could rid herself of the debilitating episodes – adventure was everything in life and she did not want to be held back from any of it.

On 30 September, Ruth visited Dorothea, bringing with her some sketches for what would become *The Little Blue Devil*, the novel on which they had agreed to collaborate. The novel's hero was based on Dorothea's play-character, Antoine St Croix or 'Tony', the orphan who travelled the world and lived on his wits, at the whim of merciless seas and devilish villains. The eventual title of the novel, which came later, was taken from a Rudyard Kipling poem called 'The Egg-shell', the story of a witch who takes to the sea in an eggshell and wreaks havoc on sailors:

The wind took off with the sunset—
The fog came up with the tide,
When the Witch of the North took an Egg-shell
With a little Blue Devil inside.[6]

In the poem, the eggshell is a small, fragile torpedo boat and the blue devil is the boat's captain, a naval officer in a blue suit. Kipling had based the poem on old Irish folklore, and Dorothea loved the idea of the witch sailing the seas to hunt her hapless victims. The title of their novel was just one indicator of the rich imaginary world that Dorothea and Ruth shared, a collaboration that was to span many years and result in two published novels.

But although Dorothea could escape into a fantasy world with Ruth, it was not long before she was confronted by her feelings for 'R' once again. The Mackellars and Robin Dods attended the annual Australian Club Ball on 4 October at the Sydney Town Hall. A gossip columnist breathlessly described the 'no expense spared' approach to the decorations:

> The colour of Tuesday's ball was pink and blue, hundreds of dozens of pelargoniums and azaleas being woven into the lovely scenic picture . . . art and nature rivalled each other in effect like a fairy picture! The only things missing, the goblins and the fairies.[7]

At the ball, Dorothea complained that she was unwell. That evening, her symptoms included feeling 'nervous and shaky' and as if she might 'scream at people', but she managed to put on a brave face, although, in her own words, she could hardly stand or speak. She left the ball early with Robin and despite the fact that she felt awful, they drove to a park. After an awkward conversation in which both admitted to having feelings for one another, they agreed that they needed to be sensible. For days afterwards, Dorothea felt terrible and confused. To make things worse, it had been a couple of days since she had seen Ruth and she was missing their acting sessions. In some strange way, too, she missed the characters, whose own troubles could always be worked out by story's end.

Throughout the week, Dorothea continued to feel unwell – she was experiencing pains in her chest 'like knives' – and Robin again urged her to have her heart checked. Finally, family friend and surgeon Dr Robert Skirving made a house call and declared that while Dorothea was run-down there was nothing 'organically' wrong with her. Dorothea found it 'frustrating and humiliating'. If only someone could decide what was wrong with her she might be able to find a remedy! She wanted nothing more than to be strong and robust.

Robin was visiting Dorothea almost every day despite their promise to be 'sensible'. He even visited her bedroom and demanded her bed be moved to allow better light for reading, and he and Mac took care of this. In her diaries, Dorothea did not speculate about what Charles and Marion thought of this married man showering their daughter with such attention and visiting her in her bedroom. Perhaps they thought his age and marital status precluded him from having anything but honourable intentions. Dorothea admitted in her diary that she and Robin were intimate on some level, but there is little detail. She wrote they 'were very weak and gave in without saying anything – but he knows I like him now and I'm glad in a queer way. It is only a "little", but I never did it before and it shakes me dreadfully'.

Soon after, Robin returned to Queensland. A cryptic line in one of her journals, not dated, says gloomily, 'I am a wrecker of happy homes'. And yet, despite her misgivings, her romance with the married Mr Dods continued.

As a way of distracting herself from affairs of the heart (she missed 'R' furiously whenever he went home to Brisbane) and her various ailments, Dorothea had thrown herself back into her writing. She hoped she might surpass the success of 'My Country' and that her best poetry was still to come. She had also begun compiling the 'booklet', as she called it, which she would submit to H.H.C. as her first collection of poetry. Dorothea chose some unpublished verses as well as others that had appeared in a range of publications including *The Spectator*, *Harper's*, *The Bulletin*, *The Sunday Times*, *The Bush Brother*, *Southern Sphere* and *Appleton's Magazine*.

On 22 October, her poem 'Colour' was published in *The Spectator* in London, echoing her love of the Australian landscape. In a progressive move which went against the Eurocentric fashion of the day, it placed Australia squarely in Asia with its 'Asian marble' and 'cool green jade'. In its bold artistry, it rivalled 'My Country', with more frenetic brushstrokes and an even more colourful palette:

> Great saffron sunset clouds, and larkspur mountains,
> And fenceless miles of plain,
> And hillsides golden-green in that unearthly
> Clear shining after rain

It would forever remain one of her favourite poems.

Despite enjoying a busy round of social events in November – and spending every spare moment with Ruth – Dorothea managed to put the final touches to her manuscript. On 23 November 1910, it was duly despatched to H.H.C. Her first collection, *The Closed Door and Other Verses*, included 'My Country' and 'Colour', and would be published the following year.

Chapter 8

The Closed Door

On the romance front, 1911 brought Dorothea no shortage of suitors, although their chances of capturing her heart must have been low, given her feelings for Mr Dods. One Mr Newmarch – a friend of 'Mr Jim' Fairfax – proved to be dedicated and determined in his pursuit, but Dorothea refused to take him seriously. Without ever using his first name, she described him as having a very young voice when he phoned to ask if he could visit her. She referred to him as 'it' in some of her diary entries, which was the playful fashion of the time. 'It writes plays and very good verse, a bit of a genius, I think. Father talked to "it" nearly all the time. 25 years old.'

Newmarch visited Dorothea at Dunara on 3 January of that year, and her impression of him did not improve entirely, but there was a reluctant affection. They sat together under a Moreton Bay fig and looked out over the harbour as they spent several hours deep in conversation:

> The genius came and I took him in hand and oh my soul and body. He wants to marry me. He has promised not to speak of it again. He told me all his affairs, which are tangled, and his woes, which are tragically boyish and he's very young and egotistical and sensitive and he will be hard to keep in hand. Jealous and frightfully high-strung. Poor child.

She began to refer to Newmarch in her diaries as 'The Child', perhaps because his relative youth – he was the same age as Dorothea – was in stark contrast to the maturity of Mr Dods. A little over a month later, when 'The Child' came to visit, she confided: 'He is easier to manage when we are face to face than at a distance. But I see the breakers ahead.'

Meanwhile, Dorothea had several writing projects keeping her busy. She was working feverishly on *The Little Blue Devil* alongside Ruth, each of them working on different chapters then coming together to discuss and rewrite. Dorothea was also translating *coplas*, a traditional verse form, from Spanish to English. A Madrid newspaper had run a competition the previous year which resulted in more than 600 poems being published as the *coplas modernas* (modern verses). She loved the passion in the language, the spirit and the romance. It was a joy to bring the poems to life in English for others to read.

In early March, Dorothea and Ruth met at Diamond Bay,

> on a perfect day, all blue and gold. We acted ever so much and I was almost too happy to breathe. Ruth was a dear and there were charming lizards and goats about (one who played at being petrified) and we were wicked and stayed very late. I'm afraid I tired her, poor darling, but she did like it too, and

it was all most satisfactory. We began two new plays and did lots of pleasing things.

Two days later, Dorothea and her mother set off in the Rolls-Royce, driven by their chauffeur, Boyle, for Kurrumbede. Out of the city, the car stalled as the chauffeur tried to negotiate deep water at a crossing. Other motorists who saw their predicament managed to push the car out of the water and tow it to nearby Maitland, but the outcome was a broken cylinder and a car that was going nowhere. While Boyle stayed with the car, Dorothea and Marion read 'sixpenny novels' as they waited for the evening train to take them on to Gunnedah.

When they arrived at Kurrumbede, the women noticed that recent rain had thickened the paddocks with lush green grass and the garden was plump and flourishing with natives and succulents alongside English roses. Dorothea rushed down to the river that ran through the property to see a team of bullocks, twenty-eight in all, taking timber across the waterway. It was impressive, she wrote later, to see the magnificent animals heaving with effort, their sinewy muscles working overtime to take the weight of the logs, and all the while a flattened sun flooded the sky with orange.

She loved being in the country: the stillness, the changing hues, the sounds of creatures scurrying and wriggling in the undergrowth – and something else, a wistfulness that was at once familiar and unsettling. Dorothea recognised the contradiction of the great peace and uneasiness that came with being in the Australian bush, and she was compelled to try to capture it in her writing. In 1875, English journalist and author Marcus Clarke had written of a phenomenon he called the 'weird melancholy' of the Australian bush[1]:

What is the dominant note of Australian scenery? That which is the dominant note of Edgar Allan Poe's poetry. Weird Melancholy . . . the Australian mountain forests are funereal, secret, stern. Their solitude is desolation. They seemed to stifle, in their black gorges, a story of sullen despair. No tender sentiment is nourished in their shade. In other lands the dying year is mourned, the falling leaves drop lightly on his bier. In Australian forests no leaves fall. The savage wind shouts among the rock clefts.

It was something like this that Dorothea seemed to grasp at in much of her poetry. She recognised the vastness, the loneliness, the ever-present menace infused in the landscape that was both terrifying and enthralling at the same time.

Charles, who had arrived at the property some days earlier, was heading back to Sydney but managed to anger Dorothea by telling her that she was not to ride one of the bigger horses: 'Dad went away and before he went he suddenly said I must not ride Silver,' she wrote furiously. 'No time to argue, but it made me angry and depressed me so much I really can't write any more about Monday.' It was frustrating; she was a formidable horsewoman, even when riding side-saddle.

There were times when Dorothea felt she was still treated like a child despite proving over and over that she was capable of holding her own on the farm. Yes, some days she was nervous and exhausted but that didn't mean she should be wrapped in cottonwool! Eric and Mac could do whatever they wanted, and she had seen what a tonic the farm had been for them. Eric had a particular affinity for the bush and the animals. His love of polo continued unabated through the local polo club. Perhaps he felt closer to their brother Keith on a polo pony, as it had always been a shared passion. Dorothea longed for some of that same freedom, and when no-one was looking she would sit astride a horse like her brothers and gallop across the paddocks.

Dorothea continued to work on *The Little Blue Devil* while luxuriating in the carefree lifestyle the countryside gave her. She wandered alone across the property without the constraints of her mother fussing or the layers of clothing she might be wearing at some charity luncheon in the city. She enjoyed the privileges that came with her family's wealth and standing – particularly the access to travel and to many wonderful social events and all that entailed – but there was another part of her that longed to be free in what she wore, how she styled her hair, and what she said and did.

In mid-March, Dorothea found herself, as she often did, down by the river. Slowly she rolled down her stockings, carefully removing the grass seeds one by one before taking them off. Dipping her toes in the cool, clear water she watched a lizard sunning itself on a rock and wondered what might come of the book Champion was publishing for her. She imagined what it might mean if her reputation, and therefore her literary credibility, were to grow. She dared not think of herself on the same level as some of her literary heroes, but if her work was taken more seriously, her parents might consider allowing her to pursue a proper literary career. Consequently, her need to marry might become less pressing. She walked home barefoot with her head full of daydreams.

The next day Dorothea rose early and gathered armfuls of roses for the house – the rain overnight had brought them into full bloom. After church, she went riding with Eric, and together they rounded up some 'stubborn' sheep and moved them across the paddocks, following the line of the river, only stopping for a moment to watch the swans and a single black duck. The following day she again saddled up and left with Eric to go mustering, not coming home until after sunset.

She recorded in her diary that she was spending time writing most days: 'Wrote some *Little Blue Devil*, wrote verses about the sunset rainbow. Looked at the splendid moon with the telescope.' While Kurrumbede gave her the peace and quiet she needed to write, a certain married man was never far from her thoughts and she was hatching a plan to travel to Brisbane in the next couple of months to visit Babs MacGregor and, of course, her 'R'. Dorothea's suitors back in Sydney – including 'The Child' and a man by the name of Norman Pilcher – were still enthusiastically pursuing her whenever she was in her home city, but they were little more than distractions for Dorothea. Her heart was with Robin Dods. During those long stretched-out days on the farm, there were times when she felt physically exhausted, her very bones aching, but she slept better at Kurrumbede than anywhere else.

Dorothea arrived back in Sydney on 23 March and Ruth visited several days later. They were acting characters who would later come to life in their 1914 novel, *Two's Company*: Remington, the stoic mining manager, and his 'adopted' son, 'Rags'. 'The former very angry and troubled, the latter in a passion of fear and shame', she wrote of the odd pair.

Meanwhile, her poem 'Burning Off' had been accepted for publication by *The Spectator* in London and appeared on 1 April:

They're burning off at the Rampadells
The tawny flames uprise
With greedy licking round the trees
The fierce breath sears our eyes.[2]

Dorothea was not sure it was one of her best efforts, but *The Spectator*'s literary editor was clearly taken with it. She had been a little worried when earlier the editor had written to her friend Lady Poore, patron of the Bush Book Club, urging Dorothea to take more care with her technique:

> I had to send back some of her things today, simply because they were so rough in the execution, with extra or limping feet. One of them called 'Burning Off' was really a splendid picture of burning trees at the Rampadells, I think the name was. If you should come across her, beg her to take more trouble with the form and finish, but encourage her to any extent, as she has real vision and a passionate love of nature.[3]

On 8 April, two weeks after returning to Dunara, a finished copy of *The Closed Door* arrived in the mail. Dorothea was thrilled to finally hold the book in her hands, writing: 'I never dreamed it would be so soon. Mother and I awfully excited and so was Ruth when she came.'

May brought further news about *The Closed Door*, with H.H.C. writing to tell Dorothea her collection of poems was the fifth-bestselling book in the country. She was delighted with her success, although she kept it to herself; it was unbecoming for a woman to talk too much of her own achievements.

A review of *The Closed Door and Other Verses* in the *Sydney Morning Herald* on 13 May observed that few would have known of Dorothea when her poem 'My Country' appeared in *The Spectator* in 1908. The publication of her first poetry collection was to bring her into the light. It was deemed to her credit that, while her point of view was essentially Australian, she did not strive for 'Australianness'. Compared with the 'ghastly burden of bush rhymes and back block ballads, and all their hopeless impediments of scenario', the reviewer wrote, 'Miss Dorothea Mackellar's little book offers one of the too rare examples of verse that is quite Australian but is also intent upon the light that never was on land or sea, Australian or otherwise.'[4]

Many of the reviews written by men used patronising language like 'little' or 'slight' to describe Dorothea's work. However, a review in the *Daily Telegraph* on 20 May gave an early verdict that her lyrics had a surprising depth:

> Miss Mackellar makes her thoughts and feelings 'carry' ... the capacity to think and feel is innate. These poems touch Australian scenes not only descriptively, but in a way that reveals their sympathetic effect on the author, and so, by transference, on the reader.[5]

The review recognised that her poetry had an important impact on readers, including aspiring writers, and particularly women. In her diary, young journalist and fledgling poet Marjorie Quinn described coming across Dorothea's first collection some years later in a small red paper-covered book in Dymock's Bookshop in Sydney:

> We ambitious scribblers especially reveled in such natural, and captivating verses written by a young Australian, when far away, about her own country that she so much loved. I read and re-read it, bought it (at the price that was easily managed) and treasured it and have it packed among my books to this day.[6]

She believed the poet had a rare natural talent: 'Poetry was evidently innate, *poeta nascitur not fit*, or "poets are born, not made".'⁷

❦

By the end of May, Dorothea found herself back in New Farm at last. She described Mary Dods as being nervous while she, Dorothea, was 'all shivers'. On the very first evening, Robin and Dorothea fell back into their routine of having an after-dinner drink and a chat in the salon after Mary had gone to bed. That night, Robin looked formal in his suit but relaxed and handsome. Dorothea felt flushed – or perhaps she was simply glowing, having carefully chosen a topaz lace dress to complement her hazel eyes. During their talk, Robin tried to convince Dorothea to break with Henry Hyde Champion as he was sure she could find a more suitable and influential publisher. However, Dorothea felt a sense of loyalty to H.H.C. and always wanted to avoid rows or unpleasantness whenever possible.

Most mornings, Robin brought tea to Dorothea. Some days she met him in the city for lunch or shopping. A snatched half-hour was thrilling. They were enjoying a friendship and an intimacy that they knew was illicit, but for Dorothea that was part of the pleasure. She knew nothing could come of it, and yet she hoped. She felt so relaxed in his presence and capable of saying almost anything. And 'dear' Mrs Dods seemed happy to have her around, she reasoned. It was almost, she wrote, as if her hostess was relieved that Dorothea could spend time in the evenings indulging her husband's interests with long conversations when she, his wife, was exhausted and had retired to bed.

Was this the truth of the matter, or was it Dorothea's way of justifying the rather unorthodox triangle that was developing at New Farm?

Dorothea was still with the Dodses when a review of *The Closed Door* by critic Archibald T. Strong was published in the Melbourne *Herald*. It was generous in its praise: 'Miss Mackellar sees all things with the receptive eye of the true poet, and clothes her fine intuitions and perceptions in language which is always musical and graceful, and not infrequently of high and sustained beauty . . . Miss Mackellar is that rare being, a true poet, possessing genuine inspiration and power of song.' But Strong did question Dorothea's experience, suggesting that 'as the authoress acquires fuller knowledge of life and a richer variety of emotional experience, her poetry is certain to gain in range and depth'.[8] It must have been galling for the young poet, who had not only travelled far and wide, but also felt that she'd had her fair share of 'emotional experience'.

Life was becoming more difficult in New Farm as Robin pressed his affections and Dorothea resisted. She decided to put some distance between them to give herself time to think. In July, she left to visit friends in the country, travelling north-west to Ipswich and Nanango, where she was 'ankle deep in red dust', before moving on to Cressbrook. After several weeks revelling in the landscape and farm life, including the freedom of again riding a horse astride rather than side-saddle – quite unusual for a woman of her station – she received another invitation from the Dodses to return to Brisbane and stay with them for the following three weeks. She could enjoy the Royal Brisbane Show and there would be a number of dances and balls to attend, the letter assured her. She must say yes, it urged. When she arrived back in Brisbane, she found her mother Marion had already telegraphed to say she could stay on with the Dodses. Dorothea had intended just to stay overnight then continue on to Sydney, but now she felt she had no choice but to stay longer, describing herself as 'angry and trapped'.

Yet when she returned to New Farm on 24 July she found it hard to stay angry with Robin. Two nights later, she was back to teasing him over dinner in the presence of Mary Dods who, in Dorothea's mind at least, was the one insisting she stay. During this period, Dorothea again met Robin most days in the city. At Finney's department store, Robin insisted on buying Dorothea stockings. She described the encounter as 'childish and funny because we saw ever so many of our friends'. The fact that they were openly flouting convention by being seen in public together was sure to have tongues wagging in polite circles, and it seemed some of Dorothea's friends were less than impressed, including Babs: 'I fear I'm rather on her nerves.'

On 4 August, Mrs Dods retired to bed early again and Dorothea was more confused than ever. 'It's not easy. She's so nervous and I am growing to like him better. I can't help that,' she wrote. Four days later, Robin and Dorothea attended the Assembly Ball, where Dorothea enjoyed herself immensely, taking part in at least eight dances as she and Robin tried to ensure they were not too long in each other's company. But on the drive home, despite the presence of a discreet chauffeur, Robin pulled her into his arms and kissed her. 'It will be some time before I forget the drive home . . . he was touching me and I said I was rather a bad little girl and it hurt him. We were both upset and it got much more serious.'

The next night she felt anxious but compelled to take things in hand and tell Robin how she was feeling. She was emboldened by their encounter and felt things must be resolved one way or another. Attending another ball, she was waiting for a moment when she might have Robin to herself while putting on a great show of playing the very eligible young woman. After her twelfth dance, quite flushed and with her heart racing, she managed to steal him away from the crowd and into an empty vestibule. His closeness made her breathless, but she found the courage to speak.

'I've never felt this way before,' she blurted out.

She confessed to her diary that she felt 'desperate – and yet not miserable', after telling Robin that she loved him. She moved her lips towards his, her whole body trembling, but they pulled away at the last minute. Confused and heartbroken, she turned on her heel and left. They spoke no more about it that night.

It seemed Robin, for his part, was not happy with his young paramour's newfound forthrightness and reacted badly, sulking – as if he, and he alone, could take the lead on such matters and therefore remain firmly in control. Dorothea sensed a change in him and drew back. It was complicated, and she began to resent his ambivalence and his willingness to play with her emotions. Had he been leading her on? Was it only in her chasteness that he found pleasure? Dorothea was unsure what she should do. The next day, she left the Dodses' house and lay on the banks of the Brisbane River, smoking, watching the steamers go by and trying to understand her feelings about Robin.

Dorothea's period came that night, and she was in terrible pain. Heavy and increasingly lengthy menstruations were causing problems for her, and she often signalled her period's arrival in her diary with a swastika – long before the ancient symbol was appropriated by the Nazi party. She remained in her room with hot water bottles and Robin came to visit her when he arrived home in the evening, suddenly tender once again. Her pain and vulnerability and his presence in her room made her feel shy and awkward. He stayed in her room for dinner at the suggestion of his wife, who had retired to bed, too ill to eat. They talked and read poetry, but Dorothea didn't find any clarity around their relationship. Of course, she knew it would ruin her to be involved in the destruction of a marriage and a very public scandal. It seemed inconceivable that Robin would leave Mary, but then, what was the long game? Why was he torturing her, and could she be seduced as long as it remained their secret?

The next day she was preparing to take the train back to Sydney when Robin came to her room early in the morning to say his goodbyes. She didn't want to leave him and she felt ill both physically and mentally – heartsick might describe it better. Loaded with hampers to provide sustenance on the way home, she boarded the crowded train, where she had her own compartment, allowing her to fret and worry and cry. Eventually, she managed to sleep fitfully for the final part of the journey home.

She was met at the station by her mother and they returned to their temporary home in Buckland Chambers. Dorothea's low spirits were evident to Marion, who was worried about her daughter. Dorothea managed to convince her mother that it was her difficult monthly periods that were the cause of her misery. It was decided that she would see the eminent gynaecologist, Dr Edward Thring, as soon as possible.

While her health was causing others some concern, it was Robin who was never far from her mind. In a later poem called 'The Other Woman's Word', she described her confusion and genuine distress over loving another woman's husband:

Most sweet, most proud, most lovely thing—
'Dearest' you never said.
Most wonderful and darlingest
You've called me: those are not the same,
Would you believe I love you best
For holding back that name?[9]

She longed to confide in someone but felt it was impossible. Her parents could never know. Her father would be furious to think his friend, an older married man, might have taken advantage of his daughter, or compromised her in any way. Ruth, for her part, might not understand, but it was with her dear friend that Dorothea longed to discuss every small detail.

On Saturday 19 August 1911, Ruth came to visit, delivering the finished manuscript of *The Little Blue Devil*. She stayed for lunch and, in the afternoon, she and Dorothea acted a little scene from *Two's Company*. Afterwards, they took the car and drove to Dunara – although it was currently leased, Dorothea could still gain access to the garden. She and Ruth gathered snowdrops from the banks that sloped down towards the harbour. The next day they posted the manuscript to London with great hopes that it would be well received.

Both her swains, Norman Pilcher and 'The Child' Newmarch, continued to pursue Dorothea, calling her often and inviting her out, but she put them off, telling them she would be leaving shortly for Kurrumbede with her mother. They duly set off on 30 August and broke the trip at Muswellbrook where, despite the presence of a chauffeur, Dorothea took the wheel, driving from Scone to the Liverpool Ranges. It tested Marion's nerves; she kept imagining her daughter was going to drive into herds of cattle that were grazing by the side of the road, but they made it safely to Gunnedah and then to the homestead.

Eric was shearing, so mother and daughter unpacked and settled in for a relaxing afternoon that would entail the 'slow and luxurious reading of letters'. A letter from Robin took Dorothea a long time to read, and she was not finished by dinner when Eric arrived home. She desperately wanted to tell him about Robin, and her wonderful, upsetting, thrilling, impossible secret – but she could not. Instead, Eric cranked up the gramophone and they listened to 'What Do You Think of Hoolihan?' by the American vaudeville comic Ed Favor. Marion didn't care much for the music, but she was patient and indulgent with her children, as always.

Eric was grateful to have his mother and sister at the farm, where he led a rather lonely existence most of the time, with only the farmhands for company. His polo-playing provided some respite and Saturday games were the highlight of his social life. A *Daily Telegraph* article that year headlined 'Eric Mackellar's Hard Riding' celebrated his exploits on the polo field: 'Eric Mackellar was prominent because of his exceptionally hard riding. He rode as if something had bitten him and bumped fearlessly into everything.'[10]

Mac was working on the nearby family property, Rampadells. He visited often and Dorothea was happy to be in the company of her brothers. These were men who had her best interests at heart and did not seek to make her confused or miserable. Dorothea spent her days writing to Ruth and Robin – her two 'Rs', as she called them – strolling to the river, visiting the shearing sheds, reading *Life* magazine and Arnold Bennett's *The Old Wives' Tale*, gathering flowers and watching the cattle muster. Her diary describes a young woman who was enchanted by the landscape, in which she found such inspiration for her writing. On a deeper level, Kurrumbede was a source of great nourishment for matters of the heart and soul, which she recorded faithfully:

> Watched the shearing and made rhymes about swallows. Walked to the river and wrote to Ruth. Clover and cattle and she-oaks and brown water. Rode out with Eric and Mr Dewhurst, moved sheep from Racecourse to Emu. Hot thundery day, pinky iridescence in the clouds, blue haze and mirages everywhere, lagoons with trees. Looked at all the dams. Seven solid hours of riding. Very sleepy and contented.

The next day's mail brought many books and letters and a request for permission to print 'My Country' in an anthology in England. It was addressed to 'Miss Dorothea Mackellar, Poetess, Sydney, Australia', causing her some amusement as she was not used to the title.

Soon after her return to Sydney on 16 September, Dorothea described in her diary a conversation with Ruth that was 'a comfort to her'. They walked in Hyde Park together when the 'sky was peacock blue and all the stars were out'. But whether she finally confided her feelings for Robin to her friend, or she and Ruth discussed their own complex relationship, the diaries do not reveal. In either case, it is certain that Dorothea was much in need of comfort of all kinds, as both her worries about Robin and her terrible menstrual pain had been increasing.

In October, Dorothea entered The Terraces, a private hospital in Paddington later known as the Scottish Hospital. It is not clear what surgery was being undertaken but it was likely linked to the frequency of her periods and prolonged bleeding. It may have been a curettage designed to ease excessive bleeding. The surgery was carried out the next day and was considered successful. Dorothea, who had a private room, was to spend the next month recuperating, with many visitors and much attention from family and friends.

The room filled with flowers – roses and lily of the valley, stocks and peonies, sweet peas and carnations covered every available surface. As well as her parents, Eric and Mac, there was a steady stream of visitors including her friend Meg McPhillamy from Bathurst, her godmother Florence Binnie, Jim Fairfax and, of course, the luckless but loyal Norman Pilcher and his love rival 'The Child'. Ruth also visited with a new suitor, Reginald 'Rex' Sessions Barrett, whom Dorothea thought was very nice, although she wasn't sure he was right for her sophisticated friend.

In Sydney for work, Robin visited Dorothea before leaving on a business trip to Melbourne. Dorothea hated saying goodbye, but he returned four days later and came directly from the train to see her. Norman Pilcher visited the following day, but Dorothea felt the strain of trying to be amusing. 'I wish men didn't get upset when one is tired – and oh dear I was tired.'

On Thursday 26 October, Norman, 'The Child' and Robin all came to the hospital, but Dorothea refused to see anyone but Robin. She knew she was being unfair to the others, stringing them along perhaps, but having all three of them visit her was a ruse of sorts to legitimise Robin. If it had only been him visiting all along, then eyebrows may have been raised. But today she only wanted her 'R'. She was aware of something passing between them that was more than before, a sexual awakening, exquisite longing, agonising desire; everything beautiful and terrifying at the same time, and she clung to him as if she were drowning. She later wrote in her diary: 'I can't stop him making love to me now – and I don't wonder. It must be hard for a man when a girl is so quiet and yet – just waking up – and I can't change myself in that way.'

Robin remained discreet and cheerful until the end of the visit, when Dorothea lay limp 'and scarcely realised how close things were'. Later, she left her room to sit on the balcony and take in some much-needed fresh air. Although she had seen Robin only hours before, she wrote a letter to him. She realised that whatever the nature of her relationship with 'R', it was impossible, and they must find a way to unravel it – permanently.

In November 1911, an article signed with the initials E.E.D., possibly authored by fellow poet and critic Enid Derham, appeared in the journal *Commonweal*, which claimed for Dorothea a new accolade, the 'first real manifestation of a national self-consciousness'.[11] The review suggested that finding art or literature that amplified a distinctly Australian voice was proving difficult. The reviewer claimed poets such as Henry Kendall, Marcus Clarke and Adam Lindsay Gordon chose Australian subjects but handled their subject matter in an English way. For E.E.D., later poets such as 'Banjo' Paterson and Henry Lawson did not have an outlook that was 'lofty enough or wide enough' to strike a truly Australian note, and charged these poets with explaining too much 'which is not necessary when you are speaking to members of the same family'. Dorothea, E.E.D. asserted, was the first genuine Australian singer who was singing *of* her own *to* her own:

> She yet shows a rarer and diviner touch, a loftier and more dignified personality than any of our previous singers. She is an idealist and a mystic; and this it is, perhaps, that gives her verse that air of serene distinction wanting in her predecessors.

Only three years after the publication of 'My Country,' critics were understanding that Dorothea was bringing something fresh to poetry – an Australian voice that stood apart from the English and American poets. The bush balladeers before her had used the familiar trope of the frontiersman or outdoorsman, highlighting the masculine pursuits of shearing, droving and shooting. Dorothea feminised the images of the land but not in a way that was passive, flowery, or reminiscent of the English rose. Her images were searing and burned their way into the reader's consciousness. Her language was clear and free of the old poetic language that borrowed from Victorian verse. It also spoke to Australians in a way they recognised, piquing in them an emotion that was at once comforting and challenging.

After leaving hospital, Dorothea travelled with Charles and Ruth by train to Parramatta, where they were met by Marion with the family car to take them to the Blue Mountains. They would stay with Dorothea's godmother, Florence Binnie, in Kurrajong Heights, where she could recuperate. It was mid-November and the day was scorching hot. A sulky – a light, one-horse carriage – was waiting at the bottom of the hill, which was too steep for the car to negotiate. The following day was milder, and Dorothea managed a short stroll to the garden gate before retiring to the cool green of the garden with Ruth. A hammock was strung between a pine and a pittosporum on the slope overlooking the glorious orange orchard that climbed the hill.

After several days of languid stupor punctuated by gentle conversation and reading, the two young women decided to try their hand at a new play. They began developing their characters and acting out scenes before walking down to the orchard by the sarsaparilla vines and under the apple trees. Then back to the hammock, where they 'lay end to end eating little pinky-yellow apricots underneath whole scores of different kinds of birds who sang in the trees'. Dorothea was, she said, 'too happy to write much'. The lazy days brought her a contentment she had not felt in many months: 'A walk in the wild wet woods. Brown ferns and pinky-red leaves and coppery-gold – and waratahs and many sorts of loveliness and great grey veils of blowing rain and a splendid dark purple storm down in the plain.'

Dorothea and Ruth ate wild cherries and slept out in the hammock all night. 'The dawn was clear, red and honey-coloured and the mist, a calm sea over the plain. And the moon set late.' Dorothea had arranged to leave the next day, but Ruth was staying on for a couple of weeks. She hated the idea of leaving her friend, and they sat on the grass in the moonlight, talking and feeling melancholy, before falling asleep together in the hammock one last time.

In December the family was preparing for a grand tour of the Middle East and Europe before landing in the United Kingdom, where Charles would again be researching the treatment of delinquent and neglected children. He was also planning to attend the first International Eugenics Conference being held in London in July the next year. Eugenics was a controversial social program which proposed sterilisation and other methods for weeding out the 'weak or feeble-minded' based on a range of spurious criteria.[12] At that time, the horrors that would be committed in the name of this new 'science' were still largely unrealised. For Dorothea, the trip would mean leaving Ruth behind and she was beginning to dread it. It was only Ruth who could take her mind off her other 'R'. Robin and Dorothea were no longer seeing or writing to each other by this point, and she was certain it was for the best, although she felt heartsick when she thought of him. There's no record of them ever meeting again, even though the Dodses moved to Sydney just a few years later. Dorothea's beloved 'R' died in 1920.

Ruth was the distraction Dorothea needed, and she admitted in her diary that she was 'growing to live' for her time with Ruth, which was 'folly but sweet', and she vowed to spend as much time as she could with her before she left for the Middle East. Ruth's mother was seriously ill at this time, so the friends could not meet as often as they wanted, but they did have some 'blue-gold days' bathing at Bronte, swimming at high tide through the clear waves that pummelled them and fizzed and crackled over their heads even as they were bursting through the surface to gasp at the air.

Ruth's mother died the day after Christmas that year, and Dorothea went to Ruth, who was 'brave and self-possessed although white as a ghost'. She promised to see her friend again soon, and on New Year's Eve they went to the Royal Botanic Garden, where they walked and talked and promised faithfully to write often until they would be reunited in London the following year.

Chapter 9

The Grand Tour

New Year's Day 1912 dawned hot and grey. The Mackellars were due to leave in a few days on the RMS *Orama* but the excitement filling the house that day was not about their impending journey but rather the knighthood bestowed on Charles in the New Year honours. The telephone rang repeatedly, but Dorothea was trying to keep the news from her mother, as Charles wanted it to be a surprise when it was announced in the newspapers the next morning. Dorothea gave an interview to the *Sydney Morning Herald* and the *Daily Telegraph*. She suspected her mother might not want all the fuss that would go along with a knighthood, but her father thought it would make Marion happy and proud. It seemed that they were all trying to be happy for each other. Mac had called from the country to congratulate his father, having read the news in the evening paper, but he had been warned not to tell his mother.

The next morning, Dorothea ran to celebrate with her mother, who had at last heard the news and was in a state of happy shock and was pleased for her husband. Charles returned from an early-morning visit to his office in a light-hearted mood, bringing with him piles of letters which had come in the first post. Dorothea could see her work replying to so much correspondence would be onerous, but she would have a chance to tackle the task on the ship. *Sir* Charles Mackellar! She was pleased for her father and the well-deserved recognition of his hard work and public service. Dorothea left her parents in the drawing room and, having had the car brought to the front of the house, she slid behind the wheel and drove to the city to pick up Ruth.

They motored to Diamond Bay in Vaucluse: 'We climbed right down to the sea and sat on the rocks with our feet dabbling in the adorable little rainbow-coloured pools.' They talked and tried to act, but found that all their play people had 'not exactly died but gone far away'. They managed to call some of them back and, after acting, they lay by the water.

Dorothea and her parents were to set off on 6 January, blissfully unaware that the greatest tragedy in the history of transatlantic crossings would take place later that year, turning the world of travel on its head. The *Titanic* had not yet hit the iceberg and the wealthy upper classes had taken to the world of cruising with gusto, embracing the greater luxury and reduced travel times the modern cruise liners offered. Dorothea was busy packing and writing thankyou letters for her father, up to forty a day, as congratulations for his knighthood poured in. Worn out, she lay on the floor when Ruth arrived to soothe her nerves. They talked of Ruth's plans to meet Dorothea in London in May, but it seemed there was some tension with Ruth's beau, Rex Barrett, about her trip. He was concerned about her being so far away for an extended period of time.

Ruth followed them aboard the ship for lunch, a tradition allowing wealthy passengers to host their friends and say their goodbyes onboard. A great storm came in, which did not fill the Mackellars with comfort before the long journey ahead; a journey that would take them to Melbourne and Perth before heading to North Africa and on to Europe.

The *Orama* was built for the Orient Steam Navigation company in 1911. A new M-class ship, it boasted bigger and better passenger accommodation with 'handsome and lofty dining saloons and a music room sumptuously furnished as to carpets and upholstery, quiet and restful as to its scheme of decoration'.[1] The solo traveller could enjoy a spacious two-berth cabin and five thousand miles of travel by sea for just a guinea a day. If you could afford it, the lure of the company's advertising brochures and the pull of exotic ports must have been hard to resist: 'Lisbon and the islands! The Canaries, Madeira and the Azores with Gibraltar and Tangiers thrown in.'[2]

At lunch on their first day at sea, the Mackellars sat at a table hosted by the Anglican Bishop of North Queensland, George Horsfall Frodsham. Dorothea rather liked the bishop, who was quite the storyteller, regaling the guests with tales of his schooldays with playwright and bon vivant Oscar Wilde. In the evening, Dorothea walked with the bishop on the boat deck after dinner while he sent a newfangled marconigram, a message sent by radio telegraphy. That evening, Dorothea wandered up on deck. 'It was thrilling up there in the dark and the wind and there was such an enormous dazzling blue spark,' she wrote after spotting a meteor.

They docked in Melbourne on a freezing cold morning, but Dorothea was cheered by the arrival of Henry Hyde Champion. She had only ever corresponded with H.H.C., who she knew to be a colourful character by reputation. Nonetheless, he was an imposing presence in the luncheon group that day with his monocle and moustache. He created a memorable impression on Dorothea, who noted his limp from an earlier stroke, but did not pity him, as he had so little pity for himself. H.H.C. was accompanied by his wife, Elsie, sister of renowned suffragette Vida Goldstein. Dorothea was a little nervous because H.H.C. had truly been *her* champion when it came to her poetry, and she wanted him to feel that his efforts were not wasted.

A week later, they left Fremantle for North Africa. There was a great camaraderie on the ship and lively music and dancing after dinner, but Dorothea was less than impressed with some of the male company. 'They were dancing on deck and the music drove my brain wild but I don't like any of these more or less puffy youths well enough to stand and hope they will ask me, it is always suggestive of a slave market, so I stayed away altogether.' Fancy dress balls were de rigueur, and costumes from Bizet's popular opera *Carmen* were kept in the hold of the ship and brought up for one of these occasions. Dorothea wore a crown of red-gold and tobacco leaves (the first act of *Carmen* takes place outside a tobacco factory in Seville). 'I didn't mean to dance but succumbed,' Dorothea wrote.

Dorothea had an insatiable curiosity and could not bear the narrowness of the topics women in society were expected to find interesting. Early in the journey, she asked if someone could give her a tour of the ship and the chief engineer took her all over the vessel. Later she described the view from the decks:

> The sea is a marvellous lapis lazuli blue. There are great beams of pale blue light, rayed like the wriggles in watered silk,

going deep down below the surface, and the surface itself is fretted with delicate, cross-cut ripples, all sorts of marvellous patterns you can scarcely distinguish, how exquisitely soft the breeze must be. The sunsets are wonderful now . . . thin sharp greens and oranges with a very brilliant little silver boat of a moon sailing through it all. I love bathing in the phosphorus at night, in the dark, blazing stars and trickles of flame over my body.

Arriving in Colombo in what was then colonial Ceylon (now Sri Lanka) on 25 January 1912, the passengers disembarked for a day trip described by Dorothea:

Nice brown babies! Nice white little humped hillocks and yellow stucco walls and red roads and lolling palms and burning blue sky. Dinner at the Galle Face Hotel in the cool, with the sound of the sea all around us.

Back on board the *Orama*, she was excited to receive a letter from Charlie Bean announcing that her novel written with Ruth, *The Little Blue Devil*, had been picked up 'on good terms' by the English publisher Alston Rivers. 'It's awfully good of Charlie, he is taking a lot of bother about it,' Dorothea wrote to Ruth as soon as she could.

Out at sea, Dorothea passed some of her free time reading, while also finding herself the object of much attention by an Italian passenger she nicknamed 'Mr Rome'. They played deck quoits together and spoke of Egypt and marriage, in general terms. Her companion danced eagerly and talked to her for hours in the moonlight on the upper deck, causing Dorothea to muse in her diary, 'he's making a dead set at me'. He told her she had an innocent face and she confided she had never been treated as an 'ingenue' before.

On 5 February, the Mackellars left the ship in Port Said, Egypt, and headed for Cairo. Dorothea felt unwell and was not helped by all the rushing about as the family played tourist. It was the return of one of her mysterious bouts of ill health. To her credit, she rarely complained and continued to travel to many exotic destinations and undertook many arduous journeys which were not for the faint-hearted. In this, as in many areas of her life, she was a contradiction: countrywoman and socialite, tomboy and fashionista, dutiful daughter and champion of women's rights, nervous and courageous all at once.

The family took a train through a desert with white sand and plants that looked to Dorothea like Australian saltbush. All the while, she recorded the landscape:

> There were slim blue-gowned men and black-gowned women and camels loaded with incense and donkeys loaded with half the world and children just like all other children. And creamy flat-roofed towns with swirling writing stuccoed on the walls.

They arrived in Cairo and settled into the Continental Savoy Hotel, which would be their base to explore the antiquities Dorothea had read so much about. The next day, Dorothea and Marion explored parts of the city:

> In the bazaars we saw beautiful Egyptian women with white-rose skins and chestnut hair under their white veils, buying

things and giggling even more than other girls. I got red slippers there and was drunk with the colour and the bustle and the scent – yes the smell. Carpets and brasses and sweetmeat sellers and jewel merchants and slipper sellers and beggars.

They headed for the pyramids and the Sphinx on the outskirts of the city, following a well-worn tourist trail and riding camels across the sands with a deep and burning blue sky above them. Visiting the Museum of Cairo, they saw the 'ghastly' mummies and the statues of sacred rams standing guard. Later that night, Dorothea wrote of her repulsion at the extraordinary wealth of the Pharoahs: 'They lived in luxury that they didn't appreciate while the peasants sweated and bled and starved and died in their millions – and I think we are still rather like that . . . it's rather sickening.'

The next day the family travelled by train to Asyut, where they boarded the paddle-steamer *Ramses* which was to take them up the Nile to Aswan. They saw great limestone cliffs, dazzling white with tombs featuring carvings of wolves and crocodiles. Arriving in Dendera, they took a ferry across the river to Thebes, where they came upon a funeral procession of a woman they believed to be Coptic Christian. The body, wrapped in a red shroud, was carried high on a bier, followed by a crowd of black-robed mourners who were wailing and beating their breasts, tears streaming down their faces.

Even far from the social scene of Sydney, Dorothea, who was now twenty-six, found many admirers. She wrote about a passenger on the boat, known only as Mr Mason, who had taken a romantic interest in her, and had pulled her aside so he could speak to her confidentially:

> It really was one of the queerest conversations I have ever had ... he said he could read me like a book and so on. I can size him up so far, but I don't know quite how much is humbug yet. It appears he has been on board all the time but I never saw him before yesterday. It amuses me to be treated in such a fatherly way ... he's about 37 or 38 I suppose.

On 21 February, after another trip ashore, Dorothea wrote about Mr Mason in more complimentary terms as 'the blue-eyed man of understanding', admitting that he was impressive and warm. 'He meant no harm but I explained that one of the privileges of age such as mine was to accept endearments only when inclined for them.'

The morning after arriving back in Cairo, Dorothea quickly replied to a letter from Ruth that had been waiting for her at the hotel. She and her parents spent the day at the agricultural show and shopping, and in the evening there was a dance, 'all red coats and paint and feathers and glitter'. At dinner that evening, Mr Mason declared his feelings:

> It was a most beautiful night and there was a moon. There was also Mr Mason who did his level best to get some conversation and only succeeded in getting about one minute. But he made the most of his time, observing rapidly that he loved me to distraction and I scared every man away and he would cancel his passage if we were going to stay on there. He did his best to persuade father but of course it wouldn't be convenient. He is quite mad but kind.

Meanwhile, Ruth was having her own romantic interlude. She had become engaged to Rex Barrett, the man she had been seeing for some months. Ruth was almost thirty and seemed genuinely excited at the prospect of becoming a bride. In a letter to her fiancé on 4 March, Ruth wrote wryly of the revisions she was working on as 'typing nearly all day at that ridiculous novel'.[3] She mentioned a letter from Dorothea which was posted from Port Said, passing on Charlie Bean's news that *The Little Blue Devil* had been accepted by London publisher Alston Rivers, who wanted the manuscript finalised as soon as possible. 'Isn't it fun? I don't know if they are putting our own names or nom de plumes. Aren't you proud?' Ruth asked him. 'But, of course, bear in mind that it's a "mere-smear" yarn really,' she added modestly.

It appeared Rex was still unhappy about Ruth's plans to travel to England to spend most of the year with Dorothea. Ruth tried to reassure him:

> Dear heart, dear husband-to-be (how strange) you mustn't say that on March 20 you will feel I am going right out of your life. You know nine months won't change either of us, and you know as well as I do that separation truly doesn't – cannot, when two people love each other. It hurts but it cannot touch the things that matter.
> Goodbye darling,
> Your Ruth.[4]

By the end of the month, however, they were no longer engaged. And with Dorothea away, poor Ruth did not even have her dearest friend close by to confide in.

The Mackellars were now travelling aboard the ocean liner SS *Omrah* to Algeciras in Andalusia, Spain, passing the Rock of Gibraltar: 'Beautiful beyond words as we steamed across the bay in a clear green twilight that changed to blue. The broad band of lights round the base of Gibraltar were pinker and twinkled more than any I have ever seen, and the great harbour lights at the water's edge were yellow-white, like tropical stars.'

They stayed at the magnificent Hotel Reina Cristina with a fountain in the patio of chequered marble and a garden with orange trees covered in sweet-smelling blossom. The next day they explored a climbing, twisting little cobbled town coloured with yellows, browns, pinks and greys, all toned by the weather. They walked to the seashore and looked at Gibraltar, with the smell of salt in their nostrils and the wind rising ominously. Travelling on to Granada, the Mackellars relished their roles as tourists, riding on donkeys to the shrine of Our Lady of Lourdes. 'It's a fascinating grotto and the miraculous water is delicious to taste.'

After visits to Granada and Malaga, Dorothea and her parents arrived in Seville, where they attended a bullfight among 14,000 spectators. There were ladies in the boxes with their colourful shawls draped over the railings. A great black bull came running out and immediately killed a horse, shocking Dorothea: 'The only thing the descriptions hadn't made me realise is the horrible passivity of the horses. One of the picadors was injured and I lost count of the murdered horses. Once the horses were out of the ring, I didn't mind watching at all.' Dorothea stayed to the end, but she promised herself never to attend another bullfight as long as she lived.

∾

Finally arriving in London at the end of April, Dorothea succumbed to exhaustion after her many months of travelling.

When she closed her eyes, she could easily call to mind the Liverpool plains near Gunnedah, imagining them fanning out in front of her, the mauves and pinks and hints of gold shivering in the distance. When she opened them, she was staring at the stark white ceiling of her bedroom in the ornate Regency flat at 85 Jermyn Street London, which would be home to the Mackellars during their London stay.

Dorothea was looking forward to the whirlwind that was the height of the social season in one of the greatest cities in the world. As an attractive, intelligent, educated young woman from a wealthy and privileged family, her company was much in demand and she was intent on making the most of a frantic round of theatre dates, dinner parties and dances. Although it was not a title she gave herself, she was a poet with a growing reputation which only enhanced her allure, and many eligible young men sought her attention. It was undoubtedly flattering, but her astute young mind longed for an intellectual equal and she found some of her handsome and well-connected young suitors thoroughly banal. She took refuge in her writing, acting and rich fantasy life. Her age and single status were no doubt a topic of conversation in many of the city's drawing rooms, but Dorothea refused to be corralled into a marriage of convenience. It was an exciting time for a young Antipodean beauty to be in London – and soon she would be joined by her best friend.

On 1 May, Dorothea was making her way to Charing Cross Station to meet Ruth, who was coming up from Southampton after the long journey by ship. In the back seat of a town car, her excitement was building. She knew her friend would need to recover from the fallout of her broken engagement, but she felt sure Ruth's good spirits would be restored. After all, the engagement to Rex Barrett had turned out rather a shambles. Dorothea had yet to ascertain who, in the end, had called it off, but either way she felt it was for the best. She must have been keenly aware of the demands on her friend's time if she were to take on the responsibilities of a married woman. Though Dorothea wanted her friend to be happy, she also wanted them to be able to continue their writing and play acting together.

She couldn't wait to share the cultural life of London with Ruth, and was just as excited to explore the many quaint country villages they would visit across England. Still, Dorothea missed Australia, its open plains and expansive skies. Despite the lure of England, she was always afflicted with that peculiar longing known as homesickness after she had been away for a period of time. Ruth would be an antidote, a breath of fresh air. She and Ruth would tour England and Europe while developing their plays, and nothing would give her more pleasure. Dorothea's parents had finally agreed to leave her and Ruth alone in London when they returned to Australia later in the year. They would find a little flat together with their own 'scribble corners' where they would write. Dorothea could sense a new freedom and it made her giddy – it would be the first time she had truly lived independently.

Even with Ruth for company, Dorothea's parents were nervous about leaving her in London. They were also concerned about her making the return journey to Australia alone the following year, so they had hatched a plan. They wrote to Eric to suggest he make plans to be in England by April 1913. Eric soon wrote to Dorothea, agreeing to the plan, although he was not happy about having to make the long journey both ways on behalf of his sister. He preferred life on the farm.

Dorothea was also looking forward to retreating to the English countryside for a few weeks. Any time she and Ruth spent alone together was to be savoured, and she was anticipating a leisurely jaunt across the land of 'field and coppice / Of green and shaded lanes'.

Their novel *The Little Blue Devil* had just been published, to popular acclaim. Dorothea's mother Marion collect the reviews and pasted them into a scrapbook.[5] The London *Globe* reported that 'the authoresses have shown unusual force and power in their work and we shall look forward with interest for their future books', while the *Sunday Times* assured readers the book was 'the most attractive story of its kind we have read for many a long day', and the *Evening Standard* was equally effusive: 'It is fresh and original, with a farouche but delightful boy in it, who wins the reader's heart in spite (or because) of his lack of most of the graces of boy-heroes.' Their 'Tony' was a hero after all, and they could continue to flesh out more scenes. Perhaps there would be a sequel. This was a carefree time for the two women, who were enjoying their reputations as published authors and poets and the independence to travel unencumbered by chaperones.

On 20 June, the pair travelled by train to Cambridge, where they stayed at the Bull Inn, a beautiful Georgian building. In the afternoon, the women hired a boat and rowed down the toy river Cam, sliding under bridges and resting under willow trees. They spent several idyllic days enjoying the scenery and each other's company before returning to London.

That month Dorothea began work on the novel *Outlaw's Luck*, based on her play character Kid Prevost. Her novel written with Ruth, *The Little Blue Devil*, had now been released in Australia and the early reviews in their home country were as encouraging as the British ones. The *Daily Telegraph* reported the book was 'one of the best Australian novels written for quite a long while ... a thoroughly interesting and admirably written book, upon which the collaborators are to be congratulated'.[6] The *Sydney Morning Herald* review remarked that it was unusual for women to forge such a literary partnership:

> Collaboration is an unusual phenomenon in the annals of Australian literature; but when the collaborators are two young ladies who have already won name and fame in the poetry of our land, their joint efforts naturally arouse the liveliest interest.[7]

In something of a backhanded compliment, the reviewer reported that the story was 'remarkably' well told and was surprised that the adventurous parts seemed more convincing than those which concerned themselves with 'society' and 'love' – clearly the expected milieu of women writers.

For three weeks in July, Dorothea and Ruth took to the road, visiting no fewer than eleven cities and towns. First stop was Winchester, where they stayed at the fifteenth-century God Begot Inn with – Dorothea recorded with pleasure – delightful rooms named after famous royals such as King Alfred and Empress Matilda. But she was annoyed to find an Ella Wheeler Wilcox poem on the wall of their attic room. Wilcox was a writer of popular poetic homilies, including 'Laugh, and the world laughs with you, weep, and you weep alone', which were not to Dorothea's taste. She tore it down in disgust and concealed it under the dressing table.

They motored from Winchester to Salisbury and on to Exeter. The Devon lanes were so deep, Dorothea reported, that 'you can't see out of them at all and the banks are grown with tall nodding foxgloves and the hedges are hung with honeysuckle'. In the evening, they acted a little before a supper of raspberries and Devonshire cream.

∾

Back in London, on a glaring hot day in late July, Dorothea accompanied her father down to Greenhithe, Kent, for a prize-giving for the officer cadets on the HMS *Worcester*. The distinguished writer Joseph Conrad and his close friend Perceval Gibbon met them there. Dorothea had recently met the much older Conrad after a written introduction from her publisher, Henry Hyde Champion. Conrad had responded to H.H.C. in April of 1912 and, among other things, announced his intention to invite Dorothea to visit while the Mackellars were in London:

> Like all the sailors of the old wool fleet, I have the warmest regard for Australians generally, for New South Wales in particular and for charming Sydney especially. Directly, I have signed this I shall write to Miss Mackellar and tell her with perfect sincerity that we shall be delighted to see her here if her, no doubt, numerous social engagements permit her to spare us a day or two.[8]

Conrad was on his way to being regarded as one of the greatest novelists of all time with classics such as *Heart of Darkness*, *Lord Jim* and *Nostromo*, among others. His invitation was an insight into the regard with which Dorothea was held in the literary world. Conrad had begun his love affair with Australia more than three decades earlier, having first sailed there in 1879, then 1880, and again in 1887, when he arrived as commander of the *Otago*. Later he wrote: 'I have been all my life – all my two lives – the spoiled, adopted child of Britain and even of the Empire, for it was Australia that gave me my first command.'⁹

Dorothea found occasions like the prize-giving rather stuffy, so the company of Conrad and Gibbon was a delightful distraction. Gibbon, who was in a particularly impish mood, entertained Dorothea with talk of magic and snakes and Russian realists. He teased her about *The Little Blue Devil*. 'Please the pigs he'll forget to review it. He's very amusing and rather cruel,' Dorothea wrote.

Conrad and Dorothea subsequently bonded over writing and his fondness for Australia, and the pair became good friends. He was flattered by her appreciation of his books, which he confided he had not thought would be particularly liked by women. She became a regular at the Conrad country property – Capel House, a picturesque and roomy seventeenth-century farmhouse settled among orchards and surrounded by woods – located in Orlestone, a village in Kent.¹⁰ Dorothea especially liked his wife Jessie, with whom she could relax and be herself. Equally, Jessie felt Dorothea was an easy companion compared with some of the quixotic London literary types who swarmed to Conrad's country house.

Dorothea's father Sir Charles had come to London on business as well as to network. He continued to take a keen interest in adolescent and pediatric mental health and was now preparing to be an observer at the First International Eugenics Congress at the

Hotel Cecil before another official European tour. Leaving Ruth behind in London, Dorothea was accompanying her father in her role as translator, but being the only woman in the room – as she sometimes was – made her something of a curiosity among her father's colleagues.

The conference itself had her intrigued. Eugenics was still a relatively new concept at the time, but grand claims were being made about 'improving' the human race by preventing the inheritance of 'inferior' attributes and qualities. Those who might be considered to possess 'inferior' traits included people with disabilities, the mentally ill, criminals, members of the poor or working classes, and even those of non-Caucasian ethnicity. The term 'eugenics' (meaning 'well-born') was coined by Sir Francis Galton, a scientist and sociologist who built his theories on the back of his cousin Charles Darwin's book *On the Origin of Species*. Galton reasoned that if horticulture and animal husbandry could be used to build super-species in the plant and animal world, science could be applied to building better human beings.[11]

Dorothea was unsure what to make of it all, but she was curious to know more given that the theory had become popular in Britain, America and Australia in recent years and had supporters on both the left and the right of politics. The congress had attracted many luminaries from the world of politics and science, including First Lord of the Admiralty Winston Churchill, and was to be convened by Darwin's son, Major Leonard Darwin.[12]

Dorothea and Charles moved into the ballroom as a new speaker took the podium. He was German, and asked the attendees to consider how geniuses such as Bach and Mozart were made, and whether breeding programs could produce such geniuses in greater numbers. There were cautious discussions around the ethics of the sterilisation of criminals, 'drug fiends', the mentally 'sub-normal' and even epileptics. Some presenters aired their concerns that 'western civilisation was in danger of collapse, as society was preserving the weak and genetically undesirable and allowing them to breed at an alarming rate'.[13]

Undoubtedly, the sharp-eyed Dorothea would have been quick to notice that many among the attendees of the congress did not *themselves* meet the criteria of genius and athleticism that were being suggested as ideal for breeding. She would have enjoyed the cut and thrust of lively conversation with her father's peers – after all, she was articulate and forthright, and by her own reckoning possessed a sharp tongue. But the interactions also likely served to increase her frustration as a woman whose considerable intellect was often underestimated.

In August, Dorothea and Charles left Marion and Ruth in London and travelled to a 'Moral Education' congress at The Hague. From there, they moved on to Berlin to investigate how the Germans were dealing with 'mental deficiency' and delinquency in young people. Dividing their time between visiting institutions and social engagements, they attended a juvenile centre at Zehlendorf. Charles was impressed with what he saw in Germany, particularly in relation to the children's court, although he and Dorothea witnessed 'weeping mothers' in the courtroom. What astonished Charles was that advocates were appointed to look into the background of the youth offenders and give a thorough assessment of their home life and any circumstances which might mitigate their crimes. This seemed to both Charles and Dorothea a very progressive way of dealing with delinquency which would ultimately benefit both the individual and the common good. Charles was interviewed about his experience for the *Sydney Morning Herald,* and gave a report of what he had seen:

> On the judge's return it is usually a lecture which the boy receives; an impressive fatherly lecture, giving him, perhaps, for the first time, a clear idea of right and wrong . . . After the lecture, in the course of which the boy is probably weeping too, the young delinquent is told that he may go home.[14]

The article reported that the Mackellars were feted in Germany. The Secretary of State for Foreign Affairs gave a luncheon in the visiting Australian's honour, while Sir Charles was also the guest of the Kaiser at a gala performance of a military opera about Frederick the Great, *Der Grosse König*, at the Imperial Opera House. Kaiser Wilhelm II was known as a swaggering militant, and was later criticised for warmongering in the lead-up to the Great War, but Dorothea and Charles could not have known what lay ahead. She described the evening as an impressive affair, with the Mackellars sitting front and centre in the Royal Box with a perfect view of the Imperial Party:

> The Kaiser looks amazingly young and strong though they say he is ill. The Empress is much older. Prince Eitel, the Kaiser's second son, is a great big thing, the only big one of the family. The little princess, Victoria Louise, is rather sweet. It was a funny feeling to have such heaps of opera-glasses levelled at one, but I took kindly to it.

Dorothea and Sir Charles were back in London by the start of September, while Ruth was preparing to leave for Italy to meet her cousin Janet Stephen. *The Little Blue Devil* was selling well in Australia and the reviews continued to be favourable. Writing in the *Sydney Stock and Station Journal* under the pseudonym 'Gossip', journalist Robert McMillan revealed he did not know 'sweet Ruth' but he did know 'gentle Dorothea', and therefore had certain expectations of the book before reading it:

> there's going to be something sweet in this – an evening lullaby, a love story, a pathetic romance. You couldn't expect anything else from two girls with such musical names . . . sweetly innocent creatures who have no idea of the tragic relations of life. Rats! Girls are deep! My word they are . . . The story of *The Little Blue Devil* is a ripping yarn, full of queer things, and pathos and hard times and things you would never expect two girls to talk about, and 'damns' scattered all about the book as if it was written by an old bushman.[15]

Meanwhile, Dorothea had completed her Kid Prevost novel, *Outlaw's Luck*, while travelling in Europe. On 24 September, she visited A.P. Watt, founder of England's first literary agency, to see if there might be any interest in her manuscript. She left the bulky envelope at his offices and walked home.

After Watt eventually agreed to represent her, Dorothea received a reproachful letter from her publisher at Alston Rivers, who had heard through the literary grapevine that she was talking to an agent about her new book. But Watt informed Dorothea that the terms she'd been signed on at Alston Rivers were 'rot'. He would propose new terms which they would probably reject but which he hoped another publisher – the relatively new Mills & Boon – would accept. Mills & Boon was founded in 1908 by Gerald Mills and Charles Boon with an aim to promote fiction. The company had early success with British novelist Hugh Walpole and American writer Jack London, but it was not until the 1930s that the publisher became known for romance novels. Watt was right: Alston Rivers refused the new terms and Mills & Boon soon agreed to become Dorothea's new publisher.

Not long after, Dorothea was to enjoy yet another literary conquest. On 28 September, she was delighted to find that her poem 'September', which she had written only a week earlier, had been published in *The Spectator*. A few months later, the poem was reproduced in the *Sydney Stock and Station Journal* accompanied by an article, 'An Australian in London: Dorothea Mackellar', which praised the poem and Dorothea's contribution to raising Australia's literary stakes internationally:

> You can see the 'anxious faces, looking very strained and white' and you seem to realise London, somehow. Then you have the yearning contrast of Australia ('where my heart is') when the shearing is over, and the spring has begun. It is an exquisite poem and will help on the work for Australia that Dorothea Mackellar has done and is doing.[16]

After a search lasting several months, Charles accompanied Dorothea to a flat in Douglas Mansions at 31 Cromwell Road, South Kensington and agreed to lease it for his daughter and her friend Ruth. They were to move in towards the end of the year, when he and Marion planned to return to Australia. Hurrah! Dorothea was thrilled. She was now aged twenty-seven and hardly an innocent, but it was still a leap of faith for the protective Mackellars to leave their unmarried daughter in London without a chaperone, and Dorothea revelled in this newfound freedom.

Most days, she walked along the Embankment and through Billingsgate, enjoying the quaint names of the byways: Huggins Lane, Three Cranes Lane, Beer Street, Allhallows Lane. She wandered in the Tower Gardens, where 'the grey towers shimmering in the sunshine through a screen of autumn leaves and the sad loafers on the benches blended into the picture'. She also haunted the art galleries and museums. In October she saw the renowned Second Post-Impressionist Exhibition at the Grafton Galleries, which included works by Matisse, Cézanne and Bonnard as well as Cubists such as Picasso and Braque. Dorothea particularly liked Matisse but felt the Cubists were less successful. 'Why are all one's sensations supposed to be blackish grey? Mine aren't,' she wrote, acknowledging her own highly developed sense of colour.

One morning, she found a pile of letters waiting for her, and among them an autographed copy of Joseph Conrad's latest book, *Under Western Eyes*. She was keen to read the book and renew the acquaintance with Conrad and his wife as soon as she could.

Dorothea and her parents enjoyed two weeks in Paris before Charles and Marion were to continue on to Sydney via Rome. Dorothea travelled with them as far as Rome, where she met up with her cousin Pearl and, in late November, Ruth and her own cousin, Janet Stephen. On their last day in Rome on 28 November, Dorothea and her parents undertook some last-minute sightseeing on a cold, bright morning. They threw pennies in the Trevi fountain, saw the Capitoline Hill and the Temple of Vesta. They visited the Santa Maria in Cosmedin, which Dorothea described as 'one of the nicest churches in Rome, not Renaissance at all, and so well restored, queer and Byzantine'. She later met up with Ruth and said goodbye to her parents. 'We all hated it but were sensible. I think Father felt it most of all. It got very cold. They drove away in the dark and I hurried off and talked hard. Ruth is a dear.'

The young women were heady with the freedom of choosing their outings and their social engagements. There was an exhilarating feeling in the air. They went shopping and visiting galleries and had tea in the Piazza di Spagna. In December, the group visited Milan and then journeyed back to Paris across the Swiss Alps, where the snow thrilled Dorothea:

> Deep and dazzling, there was even snow by Lake Maggiore, and all the waterfalls were frozen, shining icicles. The forests came straight out of Russian fairy tales, loaded with cotton wool and it was a foot deep everywhere and sometimes drifted ever so high.

After the group had settled themselves in Paris, Ruth came into Dorothea's room with a bunch of violets, and they passed the time acting Rags and Remington, which was beginning to obsess Dorothea in a 'delightful but very uncomfortable manner'. The characters were from a play that would ultimately become the novel *Two's Company*, another collaboration between the two women. The plot involved Remington, an English mining engineer living in the Australian outback, who rescues a boy named Rags (short for Raglan) from a 'wicked' Chinese man. The theme of an abandoned and vulnerable boy making his way in the world appeared in all three of the novels Dorothea published, and clearly had a strong hold on her imagination. The casting of an 'oriental' as the villain bore all the hallmarks of the racism of the time – the first of Sax Rohmer's popular novels featuring the dastardly Dr Fu Manchu would appear in 1913 – even as Dorothea and Ruth pointed to the antagonist's exceptionalism, writing that the Chinese 'are a kindly race and very fond of children'.[17] Despite its unfortunate racial stereotyping, the book nevertheless had its happy ending: Remington and Rags settle into life together, and a woman called Viola ultimately becomes Remington's love interest and a mother figure to the boy.

With their Parisian interlude at its conclusion, Dorothea, Ruth and Janet travelled by train to Le Havre to meet a steamer which would take them on to England. They arrived in the blackest night, gliding up Southampton Harbour to meet yet another train that would take them on to London and the Rembrandt Hotel. There, they holed up to enjoy a quiet Christmas day before parting ways with Janet and making preparations to move to their flat at Douglas Mansions.

Chapter 10

Two's Company

On New Year's Eve 1913, after a joyous shopping trip to Harrods to buy household goods, including little flowering azaleas in pots, Dorothea arrived at the South Kensington flat which was to be her and Ruth's home for the next five months and set about unpacking. She was anticipating what the afternoon might bring. Finally, Ruth arrived and they talked, breathless with excitement, before an acting session energised by their newfound independence.

Most mornings, they ate breakfast together 'partly dressed or fully dressed' depending on their mood, enjoying the privacy not afforded them at home. Both had their 'scribble corners' where they could withdraw to write. Acting, writing, debating, storytelling, laughing and socialising together was a dream for them. While Dorothea was putting together another book of verses to be called *The Witch-Maid*, she and Ruth were also working on their play characters, including some of their old favourites. Sometimes they lay in bed and acted a scene with Tony and one of his love interests, Winifred. While Tony was a familiar and much-loved character in Dorothea's and Ruth's repertoire, becoming the protagonist in the novel *The Little Blue Devil*, Winifred did not make it into the book and may have morphed into Pamela, his hapless cousin and eventual bride. 'We do get our change out of these people,' Dorothea wrote in her diary.

Dorothea and Ruth were now aged twenty-seven and thirty respectively. They often attended the theatre while in London and on 1 March they went to see *Nell Gwynne: The King's Favourite* at the Lyceum – their excitement intensified by the fact that Ruth's friend, Minnie Tittell Brune, was starring in it. A review noted: 'Miss Tittell Brune made a most fascinating little minx of Nell and brought out all the good heartedness of the character.'[1]

Minnie was American but became a major star in Australian theatre between 1904 and 1908 after theatre impresario James Cassius (J.C.) Williamson met her in Europe and convinced her to tread the boards in the Antipodes. A household name in Australia and New Zealand, she appeared in plays such as *Peter Pan* and *Romeo and Juliet*. Both famously beautiful and a devout Catholic, Minnie sometimes found it hard to reconcile her faith and her career.[2] She often played opposite Roy Redgrave, who would go on to produce the great Redgrave acting dynasty.

Minnie visited Dorothea and Ruth's flat at Douglas Mansions and Dorothea was quite taken with her – especially when she agreed to join their acting sessions – and wrote of how easy it would be to flirt with the beguiling Minnie, employing the common parlance of the day:

> She is just as sweet and fascinating as R always said. She would be so easy to make love to, I nearly did, lots of times. And Ruth told her about our plays and she was very thrilled

and quite understood and she is going to play with us. It will be fun to have a real actress in them.

Dorothea and Ruth began collaborating in earnest on a book based on their play characters, Remington and Rags. Dorothea wrote in her diary that they had 'discussed the division of labour', and they gave the book a working title of *Remington's Boy*, later to become *Two's Company*. The descriptions of the Australian landscape were more successful than some of the dialogue the women produced, with Dorothea's rich and evocative imagery now a feature of her both her poetry and prose:

> An owl flew out across the path, so close they almost felt its wings. The crickets were chorusing loudly behind every stone, each one falling to sudden silence as the two passed and beginning again defiantly as soon as the steps had gone by. Great white stars shone in an indigo sky; through the trees they looked so near that it seemed as if an adventurous climber might pluck them.[3]

One foggy March day, the two made their way through the rain to the Thames to watch the famous boat race between Oxford and Cambridge from Minnie's flat overlooking the river at Hammersmith. Despite the poor weather, they could see thousands of Londoners and country visitors flocking to the nearby bridge to watch the boats pass under. As Dorothea reported, security was heightened owing to recent protests by suffragettes agitating for Englishwomen to be given the vote:

> the crews shot under the bridge with Cambridge leading by lengths – not a soul of those thousands allowed on the bridge

and it was strongly guarded by police because the suffragettes had threatened things. More by token when you go into a museum or gallery now, they make you give up even your small purse-bags. And by and by the Cambridge flag went down and the crowd began to melt . . .

Dorothea and Ruth walked home via Kensington High Street rather than get caught up in the traffic.

The popularity of Dorothea's poetry was growing, and her verses were often featured in London's *Spectator*. Her poem 'March Winds' was published at the end of that month, and soon after, the first copy of Dorothea's novel *Outlaw's Luck* arrived in the post to much excitement. Positive reviews appeared over the next few weeks in *The Times*, *The Spectator* and *The Scotsman*. *The Spectator* proclaimed the story was 'highly romantic and exciting, extremely sentimental, quite unconventional, and yet handled with perfect delicacy'.[4] It was not long before reviews began appearing in Australian publications, too, and Dorothea was no doubt surprised to hear that she was 'now settled in London in search of literary fame . . . and has been developing her talent for the writing of fiction to some purpose'.[5] The reviewer described her hero in detail:

> Kid Prevost, horse stealer and good fellow, is a curious combination of good and bad qualities, and gives one cause at least for sympathy in that he is certainly no humbug and doesn't whine when he gets himself hurt.

By May 1913, Eric was on his way to join his sister in London. Ruth's sister Freda was also travelling from Australia to England, and the lease on Dorothea and Ruth's little apartment was up. They packed their things and left Douglas Mansions with much sadness. Dorothea wondered if she might ever again have the freedom she had during her time there. She moved back to the Rembrandt Hotel, where Eric would also take a room, and Ruth moved to a flat with her sister.

It was during this time that Dorothea met Patrick Chalmers, a merchant banker and emerging poet. She described him in her diary as a 'small, very young, sandy Scotchman quite unaffected and inclining to be casual through nervousness. I like him'. Chalmers was, in fact, born in Ireland, but had grown up in Scotland.[6] He was a regular dinner companion and a favourite because of his easygoing charm, and he would allegedly go on to propose to Dorothea on the eve of the Great War. A version of their story was recorded by Adrienne Howley: 'They met, and Patrick and Dorothea soon fell in love. He was a banker, wealthy, discriminating and sensitive,' she wrote.[7] But the story goes that when Dorothea wrote to Patrick to inform him of her parents' approval of the marriage, the Great War waylaid the mail ship and her letter never arrived. By the time the war was over five years later, Patrick had married another woman.[8] The story, as told, was wildly romantic and tragic but appears to be a lively embellishment – whether on the part of the interviewer or the interviewee, it is hard to say – much like the alleged broken engagement of 1908. Dorothea clearly enjoyed Patrick's company when in London and felt a great affection for him and his poetry – the line 'What's lost upon the roundabouts / We pulls up on the swings' from his poem 'Roundabouts and Swings' is credited with bringing the saying into common usage.[9] However, her diaries fail to reveal any love affair. There is no mention of his proposal or any romance in their relationship, and no mention of her writing to him or telling her parents of his intentions. With a secret code to protect her privacy, it is hard to believe Dorothea would not have at least mentioned such heartbreak in her diaries, had it occurred.

Meanwhile, Dorothea and Ruth's social life continued at a frantic pace and they were enjoying many of the recreations available to women of their class. On a shopping expedition to Harrods they bought fencing clothes and took part in a fencing lesson at a studio, Salle d'armes, in London's Brompton Road. Dorothea described shopping at Liberty's emporium on Regent Street, where she bought 'glorious' opera cloaks in vibrant colours. And every outing was fodder for Dorothea's poetic endeavours.

About this time, Ruth introduced Dorothea to the poetry of Australian Enid Derham, who had published *The Mountain Road and Other Verses* the previous year. Although Derham's talent as a poet was not fully recognised until much later in life, there were similarities between the two women in style and content. Despite Derham being born only three years earlier than Dorothea and having a similar background, they led radically different lives. Derham pursued an academic career including a stint at Oxford, and became an English lecturer at Melbourne University, the first woman to hold such a position there.[10] A review of *The Mountain Road* was reminiscent of reviews of Dorothea's work: 'Mystical and illusive, her poems love to linger in a land of hidden glens, of peak and lawny hollow, where one may see visions and hear "the whimpering airs that cry by night, and never find their rest."'[11] Dorothea thought Derham's poems were wonderful, and she was at her self-deprecating best when she commented in her diary: 'They're miles beyond anything I could do. I'm glad for Australian poetry, of course, but I'm sorry for me.'

Not long after his arrival in London, Eric attended the English Derby and later regaled his sister and Ruth about an incident in which a suffragette, Emily Davison, ran onto the racecourse and seized the bridle of the King's horse, which took fright and rolled over, injuring Davison. While Dorothea wholeheartedly supported suffrage for women – which had been granted in Australia a decade earlier – she worried some of the public protests would result in tragedy. She questioned Davison's state of mind: 'An awful thing but the suffrage society repudiates her. I suppose if she dies, they'll make a martyr of her. Poor thing, mad of course.' Her prophecy proved true, and Davison later died from her injuries, becoming a symbol of feminist resistance.

On 1 July 1913, Dorothea acknowledged the onset of a terrible depression. Though it was not clinically diagnosed, she wrote in her diary of being 'abnormally depressed' and 'horribly depressed', and of never having had 'such nerves'. She was also feeling physically ill, which may have accounted for her low spirits. Her friends were concerned, and she eventually sought medical advice, attending the famed Harley Street rooms of Sir Watson Cheyne, who ordered her to bed under suspicion of appendicitis. Adding to her woes, her illness prevented her and Ruth from attending an event at the Poetry Bookshop, where they were to hear the great Irish poet William Butler Yeats reading his poetry. The bookshop had been opened by poet and publisher Harold Monro earlier that year and readings were held there twice a week. It was in a rebelliously sordid neighbourhood in the Bloomsbury district, with brothels across the street, and only a five-minute walk from the British Museum. Dorothea had been thrilled to discover the bookshop and attended readings regularly. While some poets who read there were deemed boring, Yeats's performance was later described as masterful, his poems coming to life, accentuating the melodic nature of his verse:

> A ripple of expectation ran through the packed audience, then a deep expectant hush as the poet stood silent for a moment framed in the candlelight against the dark curtain, a tall dark romantic figure with a dreamy inward look on his pale face. He began softly, almost chanting, 'The Hosting of the Sidhe', his silvery voice gradually swelling up to the solemn finale . . . [The poems were] all lyrics, some sad, some gay, some tragic, varying the pitch and tone of his voice to suit the mood, weaving a spell over his listeners.[12]

The Poetry Bookshop acted as a bridge between the Georgians and the Modernist poets. Monro had major success with the *Georgian Poetry* anthologies, which ran into five volumes between 1912 and 1922 and covered the early period of the reign of King George V. Their editor, Edward Marsh, effectively gave the name 'Georgian' to what he saw as a movement 'putting on a new strength and beauty.'[13] The description was designed to distance new poetry from the preceding Edwardian period as the Georgians were 'beginning to strike out on new and exciting paths'.[14] While Edwardian poetry had been a response to a changing world and new technologies, the Georgian poets focused on simple themes, exploring love and nature with a renewed romanticism. Later, Monro would be instrumental in the move towards Modernism, supporting the likes of James Joyce, Ford Madox

Ford, Ezra Pound and T.S. Eliot, although he twice declined to publish the latter's 'Love Song of Alfred J. Prufrock'. Dorothea's attendance at these gatherings gave her access to London's feted literary celebrities.

Poetic distractions aside, Dorothea's depression persisted and, with Eric and Ruth for company, she soon took refuge outside of London at Chipping Camden in the Cotswolds, where she complained that her heart 'hurt abominably' and 'wobbled'. Despite her ill health, she and Ruth explored the countryside, 'the fields yellow with harvest and the green orchards bright with apples and red plums'. They lay in the garden and watched 'the sky and the yellow-green fields and the elms that grew up the lane between the blackberry hedges'. Returning to London, Dorothea had surgery to remove her appendix, but she continued to experience heart palpitations and breathlessness. A visit to heart specialist Dr H.D. Rolleston did not provide any answers about the cause of her physical symptoms, although he recommended six weeks of further rest, which would be better taken away from London.

Dorothea dutifully followed her doctor's orders and travelled by train to Cornwall and the town of Penzance, hoping the sea air would restore her to health. Ruth remained in London. Staying at the Riviera Palace Hotel, Dorothea's room 'had magnolias and jasmine climbing around the windows . . . the pilchard boats set off from nearby Newlyn like a flock of grey gulls disappearing in the sea mist – quite a hundred of them grouping and scattering, smooth and silent as moonlight, and the most exciting thing was when Gustav Hamel, fresh from winning the Aerial Derby came flying past with a rattling rush and then away to sea like a heron with the sunlight on its wings'.

She limited her physical activities but managed to write some verse and to travel to nearby beaches. She motored to Lamorna through a storm of sleet on a day when 'the sea was rough jade-green and high-flung foam'. She lay on the shingly beach in the sun and watched the red-sailed fishing boats go out. The next day was wild and 'the foam dashed right over the front, the gutters were running white with it and the whole broad road was brown with kelp. Took a bath chair down to the beach and the sea was smooth and violet-blue one day and rough grey-green the next. Too breathless to watch it long.' The poem 'Wind and Rain' was written during this trip:

Half our burdens fell from us when we reached the shore
Where the shouting waves drove in with a steady roar –
Heaviness was blown away, hearts were born again
Driving to Lamorna in the lashing of the rain.[15]

On her return to London, Dorothea's doctor confirmed her health was improving but insisted she should not be exposed to city pollution while convalescing. This time she wrote to Joseph Conrad to ask if she could join him at Capel House, his home in Kent. When she arrived on 24 September 1913, his wife Jessie was there to meet her and the Conrads made her feel very welcome. Joseph and Dorothea talked long into the evening, and when Dorothea, exhausted, retired to bed, Jessie came to her room to make sure she was comfortable. Jessie was limping and she told Dorothea about several operations that had been carried out on her knee after tearing a cartilage, to no avail. She worried she might never regain full use of her leg. Dorothea felt deep compassion for her dear friend.

During her stay, Jessie confided that English poet Ford Madox Ford had asked to visit that same week. Conrad and Ford had been friends for years and Ford had recently left his wife for the volatile Violet Hunt – a fellow writer – following a scandalous affair. The unpredictability of their relationship, including furious screaming matches and what the Conrads described as 'mean scenes', was well known. Jessie had suggested Joseph should let Ford down gently by writing to say they had a full house. In *My Heart, My Country*, Howley records Joseph's explanation for not inviting the couple: 'It's the plates, don't you know. They spent most of their last visit throwing all our plates at each other. Most inconvenient.'[16]

When Dorothea left the Conrads to return to London, she began making arrangements for her voyage back to Australia. While she was looking forward to being reunited with her parents, the reality of the end of her year of independence was closing in. She and Ruth were putting the finishing touches to their novel *Two's Company*, and Dorothea knew they would not have the same freedom back in Sydney, where they each had the responsibilities of family to attend to, and the watchful eyes of their peers – curious about their insistent spinsterhood – to avoid.

On Friday 5 December, the eve of Dorothea's journey home – Ruth would follow later – she and Ruth completed the manuscript for *Two's Company* and sent it off to their agent. Dorothea hoped that by the time she sailed through the Heads and saw Sydney on the horizon, there might be good news awaiting her. Her hopes were well-founded – the book was accepted.

Part II

'COLOUR'

The lovely things that I have watched unthinking,
Unknowing, day by day,
That their soft dyes have steeped my soul in colour
That will not pass away—

Great saffron sunset clouds, and larkspur mountains,
And fenceless miles of plain,
And hillsides golden-green in that unearthly
Clear shining after rain;

And nights of blue and pearl, and long smooth beaches,
Yellow as sunburnt wheat,
Edged with a line of foam that creams and hisses,
Enticing weary feet.

And emeralds, and sunset-hearted opals,
And Asian marble, veined
With scarlet flame, and cool green jade, and moonstones
Misty and azure-stained;

And almond trees in bloom, and oleanders,
Or a wide purple sea,
Of plain-land gorgeous with a lovely poison,
The evil Darling pea.

If I am tired I call on these to help me
To dream—and dawn-lit skies,
Lemon and pink, or faintest, coolest lilac,
Float on my soothed eyes.

There is no night so black but you shine through it,
There is no morn so drear,
O Colour of the World, but I can find you,
Most tender, pure and clear.

Thanks be to God, Who gave this gift of colour,
Which who shall seek shall find;
Thanks be to God, Who gives me strength to hold it,
Though I were stricken blind.

Chapter 11

A Storm Brewing

Dorothea experienced the most intense creative period of her life in the four years leading up to and including 1914. She produced no fewer than five publications: two books of verse and three novels. By anyone's measure, it was an extraordinary period of inspiration and hard work. Dorothea had produced a book each year, starting with her poetry collection *The Closed Door* in 1911; then her novel with Ruth, *The Little Blue Devil*, in 1912; her own novel, *Outlaw's Luck*, in 1913; her second novel with Ruth, *Two's Company*, in 1914; and her second poetry collection, *The Witch-Maid*, in the same year. Writing was part of her daily practice. She loved trying words on, rolling them around in her mind and her mouth and testing them on the page. Dorothea read her verse out loud, always mindful of the musicality of her poems, the words as much a pleasure to her ears as to her eyes. Given the momentum of the past four years, she no doubt expected continued growth in the next chapter of her literary life, but she could not have foreseen the social and political upheaval that lay ahead.

The year 1914 had begun innocently enough, with no portents of the horror that was to come with the outbreak of war on a scale the world had never witnessed before. Dorothea and Ruth had returned to Sydney separately at the end of the previous year and the social whirl continued. At twenty-eight, Dorothea was acutely aware of her single status and the fact it was commented on in hushed tones across the city's drawing rooms. She knew that her parents were concerned for her future, although they never said it outright. They were grateful to her for helping them negotiate their heavy social demands as they grew older – a duty that often fell to unmarried daughters – but they would have preferred their daughter to be married and secure, with several children underfoot. As yet, there were no grandchildren to continue the Mackellar line and Charles and Marion were bemused that their offspring seemed so reluctant to marry and produce heirs. They were particularly puzzled by Dorothea, who they had raised to become the perfect wife: poised, well mannered, elegant, witty, well read. There was no doubt she had many suitors, and many were attractive and eligible, but none of them seemed to stick.

Dorothea divided her time between Sydney and her beloved Kurrumbede on the fertile Liverpool Plains. Only fragments of her diaries from this period remain, but it is clear that the dangerous geopolitics that would lead to war in Europe were not setting off alarm bells for Dorothea and her friends. At this time, she became acquainted with the writer Ethel Turner, author of several popular children's books including *Seven Little Australians,* published in 1894 to much acclaim. Ethel was fifteen years older than Dorothea and married to lawyer Herbert Curlewis, but the couple moved in the same social circles as the Mackellars. Ethel was preoccupied with balancing her responsibilities as a wife and mother and the demands of her literary career, while Dorothea was single, enjoying a busy social life and also working to expand her literary career. Despite the age difference, Ethel and Dorothea became firm friends and later Dorothea grew close to Ethel's beautiful daughter, the writer Jean Curlewis. Ethel wrote in her diary that the works of Dorothea and Ruth were the topic of discussion at a women's club in Sydney, an institution she seemed to disapprove of:

> To town in afternoon to Women's Club to listen to papers on Dorothea Mackellar and R. Bedford, a solemn and ridiculous waste of time that it is amazing such scores of women sit through every Tuesday afternoon. Why can't people read the books, hardly any had done that it seems, and have done with it. But to take your literature in public, in silly little doses at Women's Clubs. Heavens preserve me from such a repetition![1]

But the members of women's book clubs were not the only ones keeping tabs on Dorothea's career. On 26 May 1914, the influential critic, editor and publisher A.G. Stephens – creator of the literary 'Red Page' of *The Bulletin* – delivered the second in a series of lectures on Australian authors at King's Hall in Sydney. The lecture, entitled 'Some Women in Poetry', included Australian women writers such as Ada Cambridge and Mary Gilmore, and he noted their struggle for recognition with some melancholy. In a report on the lecture in the *Sydney Stock and Station Journal*, Stephens was quoted at length:

> 'The feeling I had when looking back was one of pity for the great mass of failure. They write for escape these women,'

he said, 'for escape from the sordid into the beautiful, from the reality they have known to the realm they conceive, from the petty aspects of life into the large vision of the universal mind.'[2]

He also singled out Dorothea's work for praise, calling her 'the only distinguished name in Australian literature' and describing her poems as 'little pictures in watercolour, washed in with skill and sympathy', reinforcing her standing in the literary community. 'Greater work has yet to be expected from Miss Mackellar', Stephens concluded.[3] She was more than ready to write it.

The assassination of Archduke Franz Ferdinand in Sarajevo on 28 June failed to spark apprehension in the drawing rooms of Sydney even after Austria-Hungary's declaration of war on Serbia. The looming war was not as much of an issue in the minds of Australians as the forthcoming federal election. Dorothea's novel in collaboration with Ruth, *Two's Company*, had been published by Alston Rivers in London and was selling well, and she was busy checking the proofs for her newest collection of verses, *The Witch-Maid*. Her diary entry on 2 August downplays the news of war, focusing chiefly on its negative economic impacts at home:

Went to Ruth for her birthday. At lunch, a man rang Mr Bedford to say that Germany had declared war on Russia. Hope it's not true – it was only on Thursday we had the news of Austria and Serbia and it's affected things so tremendously already – five firms in Sydney have failed in the last two days.

But just three days later, Britain declared war on Germany and Australia was dragged into the Great War, committing 20,000 troops in the first instance. The war was to dominate life for the next four years. Dorothea immediately volunteered for the Red Cross, recording that she passed a first aid test despite being nervous when learning to use bandages. Eric tried to enlist but was rejected because growing produce on his property at Gunnedah was considered more useful to the war effort. Mac was also rejected, due to trachoma – a bacterial infection that affects the eyes. While there is no mention of it in her diaries, there is no doubt Dorothea would have been relieved, despite her patriotism, to have her brothers safe at home for now. Later, Mac – along with his friend and future best man, Darcy Donkin – would sail for England to try their luck with the British forces. But for now, Dorothea was primarily distracted with her writing as well as the push and pull of Australian politics after Liberal Prime Minister Joseph Cook's failed attempt at a double dissolution backfired. The general election of 5 September resulted in a landslide victory for Labor.

Matters of the heart, too, were on Dorothea's mind. In October 1914, her diaries reveal a new suitor in her life – one George Le Maistre – and while there are no details about his appearance or his occupation, it is clear that they were quickly becoming very fond of each other. Charles and Marion must have approved, as he was a regular guest at Dunara. On 3 October, Dorothea agreed to attend an organ recital with Mr Le Maistre, but upon arrival at the Town Hall they soon discovered it had been cancelled. Rather than waste the evening, they took a stroll down to the Art Galley of New South Wales. Dorothea later used code in her diary to describe an intimate conversation which appeared to give her suitor false hope: 'Oh dear. It came out quite suddenly. It's my unfortunate frankness and his. I didn't know what to say. For though I don't love him, it is just possible that I may someday and yet I don't want him to stay here getting hurt. In the end, it seemed better to give him the chance he asked for. I never did that before. I am sorry.' It seemed George's feelings for Dorothea were more intense than hers but she felt reluctant to cut him loose. She enjoyed his company and having a suitor eased the burden of her unmarried status. But the conversation clearly troubled her, and she slept badly that night, for more than one reason:

> There were soldiers singing in the streets until 2 am. *'It's a long, long way to Tipperary—'*. I could hear it in the distance. Soldiers I think – and patrols collecting them. It was a beautiful moonlit night. And I had plenty to think about . . . there were a good many I liked better than this boy and yet I had always been quite sure of myself before. And my throat began to hurt and my head ached and I don't love him one bit. If only I *did*, I would not care a damn.

Soldiers singing in the street were not the only indication that a war was being waged. Dorothea and Ruth were helping with the war effort by preparing care packages for Australian soldiers overseas, and Dorothea had noted in her diary that it was 'hard to get into an Elizabet St. tram nowadays that isn't either loaded with khaki'd boys or with men going up to enlist'.

Perhaps weary with all the war talk in the city, Dorothea and Ruth took a holiday away from Sydney where they could indulge their play-acting to their heart's content. Picnics in the bush were a favourite pastime:

It was a most heavenly day, hot and still, and we went to the lost valley again and followed a great iguana who slid around a tree and showed us a rough path down to the house, near the struggling cannas and half-strangled sweet rose bushes. We went down to the creek and sat there all day and I paddled, and we did Ann [and] Tony at a picnic and Jenny in S[outh] America . . . We sat on a mossy rock higher up and loved the shining, beautiful bush and the waratah trees and the baby creek that went over the silver sand so clearly, to join the big one that was muddled with floodwater still . . . We walked home a quite different way, along a beautiful smooth path that appeared suddenly, right along the gullies by running streams and mossy rocks. It brought us out in the place where all the violets grow, quite near home, and the pink and purple mists through the tall gold-green trees and the sunset was glorious.

Back in Sydney after their break, George Le Maistre was spending more time with Dorothea and they were talking about a future together, at least on a playful basis. On 15 November, a diary entry recorded in code revealed that George had come in the afternoon and stayed to supper. They had a conversation that will still sound familiar in some circles, more than a century later: 'Discussed what university we'd send our sons to and what profession they'd be likely to choose – dear me!' The fact that Dorothea was imagining her future progeny with Le Maistre further contradicts her later assertion that she was engaged to Patrick Chalmers, with only the war waylaying their plans. In any case, the imagined sons never eventuated and the luckless

George Le Maistre disappears from her diaries, no doubt unwilling to pursue feelings that were not reciprocated.

If Dorothea was at all heartsore over this, she had much to distract her. She enjoyed the visual arts almost as much as literature and she was a regular at the galleries around Sydney, attending exhibitions and often purchasing works by her favourite artists. In November, she and Ruth attended a Society of Artists exhibition which included oil paintings by the well-known artist, cartoonist and novelist Norman Lindsay. Dorothea wrote that she wanted to buy one his paintings 'badly' but, in her opinion, the two best works had already been sold. Though she felt it was well drawn, Dorothea found Lindsay's *Bacchanal* 'far too tame and stodgy', remarking in her diary that the woman depicted in the painting 'had discarded all garments except a lovely blue scarf but was still a perfect lady'. Later, she would attend a Society of Artists Exhibition where some works by Lindsay were again on show. That occasion inspired an unpublished poem addressed directly to the artist, 'To Norman Lindsay on an Old Grievance':

The Grecian nymphs we read about
Were slim and shy and fleet,
And quite a lot depended on
the swiftness of their feet
So, Lindsay of the Master-Hand,
I take it rather hard
That you should make them solid *vrouws*
Who could not run a yard.[4]

Yet for all the cheerful posts in her diary, the war was never far from Dorothea's mind. Her last entry for 1914 recorded 'a successful raid on Cuxhaven . . . a good offset to the German baby-killing expedition to Scarborough'. This was a reference to an incident during which German battlecruisers shelled the port towns of Scarborough and Hartlepool in England, killing 137 civilians and injuring many hundreds more. The death of fourteen-month-old John Shields Ryalls after a shell landed on his home in Scarborough was a rallying point in the war. It prompted the then First Lord of the Admiralty, Winston Churchill, to declare the Germans were 'baby-killers'.[5]

Even with such dark goings-on in the world, on New Year's Day 1915, the *Sydney Morning Herald* was buoyant:

> With the rain falling over great areas of the Commonwealth, and with a promise of good seasons in the fact that it has come to follow up other rains, we may greet the New Year with lighter hearts, notwithstanding the war. While Australia's first duty undoubtedly is to fight – to the last shilling and the last man – her next duty is to produce everything that the Allies are most in need of; and the greatest wheat harvest on record as the mark of the coming months will be both a profitable and a patriotic enterprise.[6]

But Dorothea could not quite join in the optimism, and remained attuned to the desperation felt by Australians. Experiencing the tyranny of distance in a more poignant way than ever before, they were isolated from the action but not immune to the realities of war as telegrams delivered tragic news across the country with frightening regularity. Newspaper reports brought the horrors closer to home. On one particular Sunday in January, churches of all denominations invited people to join in a General Intercession to pray collectively for an end to the war. Dorothea's juxtaposition of the beautiful scenery with crowded churches brimming with devout or well-intentioned petitioners is sobering:

> It was a most beautiful blue and gold day, warm and fresh at the same time, and everything was looking its loveliest – and all the birds – the sort of day I thought, when I was very little, that they had in heaven. We walked to the funny little wooden [church] at Thornleigh. It was crammed to overflowing – lots of men sat outside. I'm sure it had never been so full before.

She wrote later that she felt heavy, more than usual, while her father looked worried and her mother seemed tired. 'I loved them much more than usual and was conscious it was not nearly enough!'

But there was balm for her worries in the form of a review of *The Witch-Maid and Other Verses* that appeared in the same week, which surprised Dorothea with its praise. The report in the *Daily Telegraph* described *The Witch-Maid* as a

> very welcome book of poems by Miss Dorothea Mackellar, whose lyric verse, dancing with movement and vivid with colour, is fresh and faun-like and deliciously alive. Hers is the gift of a keen visualising imagination reinforced by the ability to respond with full power to all impressions derived through the senses.[7]

The *Telegraph* suggested that Dorothea felt with 'supra-normal acuteness' both pleasure and pain, and that she was especially

Charles Mackellar c.1875.

Marion Buckland in 1877, shortly before her marriage to Charles.

Keith Mackellar.

Eric Mackellar.

Malcolm 'Mac' Mackellar in 1904.

Dorothea, age 4.

Little Dorothea.

The Mackellars at Dunara in the 1890s, from left to right: Dorothea, Mac, Marion, Eric, Keith, and Charles.

The Mackellars at the fountain in the grounds of Dunara. Marion and Charles (centre) are flanked by their elder sons Keith (left) and Eric (right). Mac and Dorothea are sitting at their parents' feet.

Left to right: Keith (standing), Mac, Marion, Eric (standing), Charles and Dorothea.

Torryburn, where the breaking of the drought inspired lines from 'My Country'.

Keith Mackellar in his mess dress uniform, 1898.

Keith in his Scottish Rifles uniform, 1898.

A stained glass window dedicated to the soldiers who died in the Boer War and donated to St James' Church in Sydney by the Mackellars. The face of St George is a likeness of Keith. (© Christopher Shain)

Postcards from Japan, found among Dorothea's papers.

Charles and Dorothea in Moorish costume on a trip to Granada, Spain, in 1905.

Marion Mackellar c. 1900.

Details from Dorothea's watercolour paintings.

Dorothea, c. 1910. (Courtesy of Jennifer Stiller)

The RMS *Orama* in Sydney in 1911, a year before Dorothea boarded the ship for her grand tour of Europe in 1912. (Australian National Maritime Museum)

The first class lounge (above) and smoking room (below) on the RMS *Orama*. (National Maritime Museum, Greenwich, London)

An oil painting of Dorothea c. 1905. (Supplied)

Mac in his First Lifeguards uniform, c. 1918.

Dorothea in costume for the Red Cross Day tableaux at the Palace Theatre, 1918.
(Photograph by Glen Broughton)

A photograph given to Dorothea by Jessie Conrad (left) in 1920. Joseph Conrad and their young son, John, are seated on the right.

Opposite left: Dorothea c. 1918.

Opposite right: Actors Snowy Baker and Pauline Frederick on location at Kurrumbede in 1919 for the filming of *The Man from Kangaroo*. Signed, 'To my old pal Eric.'

Dorothea c. 1925.   Dorothea c. 1930.

Farm life at Kurrumbede c. 1930s.

Dorothea photographed by May Moore in 1927.

Eric (centre) on horseback.

Dorothea became her mother's ears as
Marion's hearing worsened.

Sir Charles Mackellar, c. 1920.

Ruth Bedford in the 1930s.
(National Library of Australia)

Dorothea had many cocker spaniels throughout her life.

Frontispiece from *Fairies and Fancies* by Ruth Bedford, illustrated by Mela Koehler.
(National Library of Australia)

Dorothea in 1955. (Fairfax)

The view from Dorothea's home in Lovett Bay, Tarrangaua.

Interior of Tarrangaua during Dorothea's residency there.

Dorothea's personal book plate.

The original manuscript of 'My Country'.

Company Drill Made Easy and a children's picture book, both owned by Keith Mackellar and found among Dorothea's papers.

Some of Dorothea's verse books.

Dunara in 2017. (Wikimedia commons)

Plaque dedicated to Dorothea on the Sydney Writers Walk, Circular Quay. (Wikimedia Commons)

Kurrumbede during the 2018 drought. (Supplied)

A bronze statue erected to honour Dorothea in Gunnedah. (Supplied)

Tarrangaua. (Supplied)

Dorothea Mackellar's grave at Sydney's Waverley Cemetery. (Supplied)

sensitive to colour, creating a sense of shared recognition with the reader:

> Her poems, written either in Australia or about Australia are easily first in the quality of awaking a responsive thrill in the heart of the reader – which is the greatest by which real poetry may be recognised . . . and, of course, the author's famous poem, 'My Country', is included. Miss Dorothea Mackellar's pure and heart-touching lyrics are a joy to read.

However, the *Sydney Morning Herald*'s review of *The Witch-Maid* concluded that her second book of verses did not surpass her first, even as it praised her ability to paint vivid pictures:

> The later ones, as a rule, do not display quite the poignancy of feeling and the white-heat of passionate expression that we find in 'My Country', for example, or in 'Colour'. But this does not imply that the general quality of Miss Mackellar's poetry has deteriorated . . . she still possesses to a remarkable degree the faculty of conjuring up before our eyes an extraordinarily vivid picture in a single line or even a word or two.[8]

By March, Dorothea's poem 'Encounter' had been published by *Harper's Magazine*, and while she was always secretly thrilled with each publication, she wished the critics would not always compare her new poems to 'My Country', as she had begun to fear she would never write anything to rival it. 'Encounter' introduced a personified 'Death', a character who would come to feature in many of her verses as she tried to make sense of an 'unintelligible world' riven by war. Death, with his cruel curling lips, asks the poet:

> How has she failed, my sister Life, that you should call to me?[9]

∽

Dorothea and Ruth were trying to make the most of the warm autumn days despite the ever-present feeling that it was bad form to enjoy themselves when young men were dying on the other side of the world. Nevertheless, one 'blue and gold' morning they met at Circular Quay and took a ferry to Athol Bay, where they sat on the beach and looked at Sydney 'pale and clear and beautiful'. They went into the bush and sat on a rock to rehearse scenes from one of their plays, dangling their feet over the harbour where a fishing net was being drawn up:

> So we ran and looked at the silver jumping fish and by and by we went on and met the breeze around the corner and played in a mysterious massive old stone place ... oh, the path was lovely. It wound and climbed through beautiful bush but never quite lost sight of the sea and the water changed from ruffled turquoise to clear pale green, and deep red, and purple and dark green, and pale transparent blue and back to turquoise again ...

Afterwards, they swam and sunned themselves before catching a ferry back, with the sun 'an enormous red ball that sunk into pearl-grey shadow'.

By now, military parades had become a regular feature in Sydney. They were sometimes staged to welcome Allies, sometimes to send off troops and sometimes to celebrate troops who had returned – or at least those among them who were strong enough to march. It was both a solemn reminder of the devastating effects of war and a rallying cry to the next wave of brave young men the government hoped to recruit. Dorothea wrote about a parade she watched with her fellow citizens as they lined the streets of the parade route:

> In the place of honour came the French reservists from Noumea, very workmanlike in their blue with berets that had a red tassel on top. Then the Light Horse, a fine lot of men, so brown and lithe – and all the rest. They marched beautifully and the long brown caterpillar with blue-white glitter of steel over it seemed endless. It gave one to think – the crowd were quiet which is better than yelling. The time to shout hasn't come yet . . .

On 8 July 1915, Eric came to Dorothea in despair. He had travelled to Sydney from Gunnedah to talk to his sister, not wanting to have an intimate conversation over the telephone at a time when the patching of telephone lines at exchanges allowed telephonists to stay on the line and listen in. It seemed Mac had decided to leave Kurrumbede to follow his friend Snowy Baker to Hollywood. Eric felt the weight of responsibility for the country property suddenly on his shoulders, but he was also worried for his brother and the consequences of his friendship with the garrulous Snowy.

Reginald Leslie 'Snowy' Baker was a colourful character who was an athlete, sports promoter and actor. He had won several New South Wales swimming and boxing championships, was a representative rugby player and had parlayed his sportsmanship into an entrepreneurial career. Snowy was the quintessential raconteur, exuding charisma and a physicality that was attractive to both men and women. The lure of adventure clearly appealed to Mac, who had been refused entry into the army and longed for a life outside the farm. He also wanted to make his mark on the world; Keith's shadow was never far away. Snowy had hatched a plan to persuade Australian-born filmmaker Claude Flemming to return home from the United States to direct a film. Mac was eager to tag along. Eric was despondent. Kurrumbede was now in drought, and the war had seriously depleted the number of farmhands available to work the property. With Mac away, managing the property would fall solely to Eric, who felt keenly the pressure to prove himself to his father. Dorothea wrote about her brother's feelings of abandonment:

> As I was going to bed, Eric came in and I thought he wanted to talk and so he did and broke down worse than I had ever seen him. Talked for two and a half hours so there was time to say a good deal. Malcolm had hurt him badly – I am angry about it – and there were other things. Mac and a woman for instance. And marriage! Didn't sleep much.

She was referring to Mac's bombshell revelation to Eric that – on his eventual return from Hollywood – he intended to try again to enlist as a soldier. He also hoped to marry his love, Enid Woolf, a beautiful and well-connected girl from Perth. Enid's father, Louis Woolf, known as Arnold, was a well-known accountant in Perth, and counted former Prime Minister Edmund Barton and other leading federalists among his friends. Enid's sister Una married John Fraser, and their son John Malcolm would one day become the twenty-second Prime Minister of Australia. Enid was also the niece of Sir Samuel Hordern, of the prominent retail family Anthony Hordern and Sons, after which Sydney's Hordern Pavilion was named. While her pedigree was good, Mac's declaration of love for Enid appeared to blindside the Mackellars, and there was disapproval. Dorothea found Enid aloof and even prickly, and was greatly shocked and displeased by the fact that the young woman had, on occasion, been rude to Marion.

Whether related to her brothers' troubles or not, on 9 July 1915, Dorothea reported a 'general debility – a sort of suppressed nervous breakdown'. Before long, she was on her way to Kurrumbede, which usually proved a tonic for her. While some of her diary entries are missing over this period, it is clear that she had a relaxing time, enjoying the company of her brothers – Eric was in better spirits than he had been, and Mac had not yet left for America. That month, a booklet of war verses was being sold in aid of the Australian Wounded Soldiers Fund. It included well-loved bush poet Henry Lawson's 'Song of the Dardanelles', as well as Dorothea's 'Australia's Men'. Perhaps she had been thinking of her brother Keith when she had written the words,

> There are some that go for love of a fight,
> And some for love of a land,
> And some for a dream of the world set free
> Which they barely understand.[10]

Dorothea divided her time between Kurrumbede and Sydney for several months, and in September she wrote a poem at Kurrumbede called 'On Kelly's Ridge', which gives a troubling insight into how she was feeling about her life and her prospects. Imagining speaking to 'the queerest man you'd find', she laid out her troubles and her belief that she was a burden to her family:

> 'I'm thinking my youth goes by . . .
> And I've not the lives of a cat,
> And there's a weakness in all my bones—
> I'm thinking I'm young for that.
> I feel I'm a drag on the rest of them . . .
> I know I'm getting worse,
> For I haven't the strength to work at all,
> and that is a heavy curse.
> And there's whiles I think that I've wasted
> my life and made my choice like a fool—'
> So I talked on and he never spoke
> But watched me kind and cool.[11]

The strange man's response to the poet's woes is to say: 'You think too much of yourself . . . and that's the matter with you'. This idea of 'thinking too much of yourself' was deeply engrained in Dorothea, who was taught to be self-effacing; to embody a sense the humility expected of her as a woman. At thirty years of age, there was a distinct melancholy creeping into Dorothea's diary entries and her poetry. While this may reflect the war dragging on with all its implications, it also reflected her growing frustration over the lack of a clear direction in her life. Dorothea's life was busy, but she was unsure of what would become of her. Could a writing life sustain her? A poem called

'Flower of Youth' – also written at Kurrumbede during this period – hinted at the dark turn of her thoughts:

> Heavy with the dew of night, the almond blossoms lie,
> I've made my choice, my own free choice, the weight from me has lifted.
> I know it was for good I chose—and yet I want to cry.[12]

On 14 November 1915, Dorothea had returned to Sydney and there were bushfires raging through the nearby Blue Mountains. 'Everything was thickly veiled in creamy bushfire smoke . . . and all day the sun had been a flaming scarlet ball,' she wrote. The next day brought a dust storm, and

> There were odd feelings in the air – mother didn't feel well and Ruth came in the morning and I felt constrained to keep her all day but we were quietly sleepy and sick . . . Tuesday was a glorious day to feel and see and I got through a great deal but *what* does it matter, oh *what* does it matter?

Dorothea's feelings of futility persisted, and yet she saw fewer and fewer opportunities to change her circumstances. She was now thirty years old, and felt the call of duty in caring for her ageing parents. Dorothea had rejected many opportunities for marriage, and though she'd had agency in those decisions, it now seemed less and less likely that she would meet her match, and please her parents in doing so. Yet while her poetry occasionally reveals frustration at unrequited love and missed chances, there is nothing in her diary to suggest she truly regretted not marrying.

Meanwhile, Mac was sailing for America with Snowy Baker and Dorothea again travelled up to Kurrumbede. Eric was having trouble with the itinerant workers or 'wheat humpers', who were hired at two pounds a day to pile sacks of wheat in the storage shed. Dorothea complained about the workers in her diary, describing 'half of them' as 'lazing nags' who handled the wheat 'disgracefully'. The area was still in drought, and Dorothea reported hot, clear weather and starlit nights. There was no sign of rain. Since the livestock weren't hand-fed during times of drought – as would become the norm in later years – many animals died during this period. Dorothea bemoaned the 'rich harvest' that would be available for the itinerants who collected the bones of dead animals to sell to factories for fertiliser.

By mid-December Dorothea was back in the city, and though the war was still clearly on her mind, she was enjoying the summer weather, on a day she described as

> warm and cool, blue and gold – green with the coral trees flaming everywhere so splendidly that it was like a thousand trumpets. As I walked down Wolseley Road [in Point Piper] I had a strange swinging feeling – and then suddenly I realised what it was – that if there were no War (what an If!) I'd be happy. Not for years have I had that.

Chapter 12

Theatre of War

Hollywood arrived in the town of Gunnedah in 1916, much to the excitement of residents hoping to land a role in a new film that would star Snowy Baker. Mac had returned from America in July, along with Baker and director Claude Flemming. Flemming had agreed to make a film starring Baker, to be shot on location at Kurrumbede and the surrounding district. The locals were unfamiliar with the machinations of the revolutionary new entertainment known as the 'silent picture', but they were intrigued. There was some suspicion about the propriety of people who made acting their profession, but the imprimatur of the Mackellar family had given the project some respectability. There were certainly young men and women – and the occasional weathered old farmhand – who were prepared to audition for a role, even if just in the background as extras. Even Dorothea would eventually have a hand in the making of the film, after Baker asked her to put her literary skills to good use by helping with the all-important intertitles for the movie, which were critical to the success of any silent film.

The script, originally titled *The Call of the Bush*, was the winner of a competition run by *The Bulletin*. Snowy Baker would play Hugh Mostyn, who travels to England from his family farm in Australia to be suitably educated. Hugh returns to Australia years later as a gentleman, wearing a white suit and monocle, much to the amusement of the locals he encounters working the land. Employed as a jackeroo, he is teased mercilessly by the farm hands until his boxing prowess puts them in their place.

The script allowed Baker to demonstrate his athleticism. As Hugh Mostyn, he breaks in a wild brumby, takes part in a kangaroo hunt, and even defeats the local bully – played by real-life boxing champion Colin Bell – in a boxing match. Legend has it that their fist fight went on for a full five minutes and was captured on film in one take. Eventually, Baker's character falls in love with the farm manager's daughter after he rescues her from a rejected suitor.

The film proved a great success following its release in 1918 as *The Lure of the Bush*, reportedly taking 20,000 pounds at the box office and having a successful run in America after some scenes were re-shot in Hollywood. Alongside Baker's dynamic performance, the Australian bush stole the show, with the *Argus* reporting: 'A point which had a general appeal was the introduction in the course of the story of many features of bush life.'[1] Tragically, the fragile nitrate film – vulnerable to deterioration – was not preserved, and it is not known if Dorothea was credited for her intertitles, or what role Mac may have played in the production.

Still, whatever glory Dorothea had been denied for her intertitles, her poetic career was continuing in good stead. An article by literary critic T.F. Monk-Orran appeared in the *Sunday Times* in June 1916 under the headline 'Our Poets', and it claimed Dorothea as one of them. The article pleaded for greater recognition and rewards for Australian poets, and praised the efforts of women poets, including Dorothea:

> If Australia loved her poets as American poets are loved, we should be cheered by a constant high delight of song. But one can't have everything, can one? As it is, the poetical tribute to Australia that always seems to me to ring truest was written by a woman, . . . Miss Dorothea Mackellar . . . Every school kid should memorise it, and every Australian who wants to keep, in the best sense, young.[2]

During this period, many critics were pausing to consider the impact of the war on Australian literature. An article in the *Sydney Morning Herald* a month later addressed the progress of women poets, ruminating on how the dark times of war had influenced their writing:

> And since the tragedy and the sorrow of life have been written into everyone's heart, one might have expected that poetry would have receded still farther and farther into the dreamland of unremembered things. But, instead of that, poetry, and really good verse at that, is more largely read than ever and it has been quoted in a way that shows how very real the ideal side of us is. Women have not been found wanting in this field.[3]

At last, it must have seemed to Dorothea, women's contributions were beginning to be considered – not only in the arts, but in all aspects of life. On 6 October 1916, Dorothea attended a meeting of women at the Sydney Town Hall, at which Adela Pankhurst – daughter of the famous suffragist Emmeline Pankhurst – was in attendance. The women had packed in to hear Prime Minister Billy Hughes speak in favour of conscription. Some months earlier, Britain had asked Australia for additional troops, and while Hughes could have introduced conscription through legislation, he decided to put it to the Australian people through a referendum. The venue was packed with women lining the aisles from 'basement to gallery' with thousands more turned away. Dorothea managed to squeeze through the crowd and reported that she was hoisted out of the crush and onto the edge of a packed platform, which gave her a good view of the proceedings: 'On the whole, it was a wonderfully orderly meeting, considering what a high pitch everyone was at, and I was proud of my sex when there was a loud and smoky explosion in the Eastern Gallery, something apparently went wrong with the flashlight photography, and nobody turned a hair except for one male assistant who fainted . . . Hughes spoke very well.'

When an interjector could not be silenced, the organist was instructed to begin playing, and 'Rule, Britannia' was soon roaring in their ears. The *Herald* noted: 'That men interjected on occasion at public meetings was a well-known fact but that there should be interjections at a meeting of women which the Prime Minister was addressing was an un-heard of thing.'[4]

The Prime Minister's speech was published in the *Sydney Morning Herald* the next day: 'You must ask yourself the question, what will my vote do? Shall I, by my vote, plunge a dagger into the heart of my country? Shall I abandon my children at the

Front, my brother or my husband?'⁵ At the end of the meeting, almost every woman raised a handkerchief, a glove or an umbrella in support of conscription.

Dorothea had been drafted to write an article, on request from the Referendum Committee, which was published in the *Herald* on 25 October under the headline 'Faint Heart and Tender Heart':

> The anti-conscriptionists have tried to trouble us with that cowardly question, 'Would you vote to send away another woman's son?' It sounds terrible; but however tender-hearted we are, we hardly have the right to shrink from that. There is no hour of our lives where we are not dependent, unconsciously perhaps, and certainly without protest, on the suffering, the danger, the deaths of other women's sons and daughters.⁶

These were the words of someone who had already lost a loved one to war. But only three days later, a majority of Australians voted against conscription and Dorothea was philosophical about the result. Perhaps, for her, the notion that there might be a *choice* about whether to fight in support of the Empire was unthinkable, diminishing the ultimate sacrifice of her beloved brother Keith in the Boer War.

∽

The beginning of 1917 saw the Mackellars' country property Kurrumbede under attack. The Industrial Workers of the World, also known as the 'Wobblies', were a radical political organisation founded in Chicago in 1905, and had roots in anarchism and Marxism. The IWW advocated for a single united workers' federation instead of individual trade unions, and saw a general strike as a way of overthrowing the capitalist class and replacing it with workers' control of the means of production. Members of the Wobblies had burned the Mackellars' hayshed to the ground. Dorothea described the arson attack in her diary, writing that the fire 'caused tremendous loss. I hope they'll catch the brutes, oh poor Eric, it makes one furious.' Several months earlier, while the debate over conscription raged, a group known as the Sydney Twelve were arrested and charged with conspiracy to commit arson, perverting the course of justice and sedition. They were all convicted and sentenced to lengthy jail sentences of up to fifteen years. A judge's inquiry later exonerated six of the men, finding they were not justly or rightly convicted of sedition.[7]

In the years leading up to the war, wages had stagnated while the cost of living and unemployment climbed ever higher. This had led to disenchantment, and the growth of the workers' movement, which also cultivated an anti-war and anti-conscription platform. Shearers in New South Wales and Queensland wanted better wages, and many disobeyed their unions to support the Wobblies by taking direct action, which often included setting fire to farm buildings in protest. The Mackellars' hayshed was one among many burnt down in the fury.

Despite the attack on the hayshed, Kurrumbede remained Dorothea's sanctuary, and in May of 1917, she spent several happy weeks there with Eric. She wrote of long conversations in the evening, and farm chores during the day:

I planted all the grape and passion vines on Sunday and the rabbits ringbarked them that night. On Monday Eric and I drove over the wheat to see where the cattle had broken through. Lots of brolgas were stalking about, devouring. One had to be shot as a warning. Such a magnificent grey and scarlet creature, with jade green beak. It was horrible to see it struck out of life, though one didn't wish to sentimentalise . . . I love Eric so hard it hurts all the time, but it's warm too.

Ensconced in her country haven, Dorothea's poetry from this period reveals a tension between her public and private personas. In the poem 'Town and Country', she writes about trying to live in the moment in a context of war, about hiding her inner self and, perhaps, her confusion about her sexuality:

Yes, when I built my life again,
I left some pieces lying
That wouldn't fit into the plan
For all my earnest trying.
I won't pretend I have forgot,
Nor that they're here—for they are not—
But keep my memory sharp like knives
And thus enjoy two separate lives.[8]

She continued to battle ill health with familiar symptoms persisting – including fatigue, dizziness, heart palpitations and insomnia – but took comfort from the fact that Ruth remained a constant in her life. On 2 August, Dorothea drafted a poem for Ruth's birthday in her diary, which referenced the war, but also lauded the power of love to overcome it:

> Birthday wishes to my Ruth
> In an evil hour
> When the air is full of death
> And Desire's self perisheth
> Only Love endures, and Truth—
> Only they have power.

Dorothea was now thirty-two, and all mention of suitors and potential husbands fell away during this period – unsurprising, perhaps, when so many young eligible men were fighting overseas. Ruth was her steadfast companion at home, at dinner parties, the theatre, and in her charity and activist work. The newspaper articles which documented the Sydney social scene rarely mentioned Miss Mackellar without Miss Bedford. On one occasion, when a mutual friend invited Dorothea and Ruth to be joint godmothers to her new baby, Dorothea commented on her friend's unusual choice, saying, 'We all seem to be absurdly unorthodox'. If her relationship with Ruth was unorthodox, at least it was recognised in this oblique way.

Dorothea always wrote of her home city with great affection, and particularly after walks by the harbour's edge at Rose Bay. 'What a hilly, cliffy place Sydney is – steep steps and sudden turns, with silken blue water at the end of every lane and oleander and pomegranate over the garden wall.' But in late 1917, the city was beset by strikes: tram engineers, railway workers and bakers were all part of ongoing industrial action for better working conditions. Dorothea described in her diary a 'piercingly beautiful Spring day full of strikes and wars and pathos and irritation and one felt as if one had several skins too few'. Increasingly, she felt unsettled at home in Sydney, and on one occasion when Ruth came by for 'a little acting', Dorothea wrote about 'a violent fit of restless blues. Reds and purples rather . . . Dreadfully tired and restless and sick of being in one place.'

There were signs that Dorothea's sense of restlessness and futility were not hers alone – the people of Australia were ready to help with the war in any way they could. On 28 September, the city hosted War Chest Day, a huge fundraising effort with hundreds of stalls set up in Sydney's central business district. The day attracted large crowds, beginning with a procession of decorated motor cars, and it raised fifteen thousand pounds for the war effort. On 5 November, word filtered through that the new Bolshevik government had withdrawn Russia from the war: 'Pray God, it's not true,' Dorothea wrote. Almost as if to cushion the blow, the next day a request came through from Angus & Robertson to reproduce 'My Country' in a book celebrating the art of watercolourist Jesse Jewhurst Hilder. *The Art of J.J. Hilder* was published the following year, with the poem hand-lettered and illustrated by the artist.

But this fresh success could not soothe Dorothea's mixed feelings over the decision to hold another referendum on the issue of conscription. Only a year earlier, the move to introduce conscription had failed. The political fallout had led to an acrimonious split in the Australian Labor Party. Billy Hughes had again become prime minister, but as leader of the newly formed federal National Party. Both sides of the conscription debate were now appealing to women as mothers. A popular song at anti-conscription rallies included the lyrics: 'I didn't raise my boy to be a soldier . . . to kill some other mother's darling boy.'[9] As the war served to stoke nationalist fires, women voters were wooed as figures of 'suffering motherhood' in the rhetoric of both sides. Prime Minister Billy Hughes urged women to prove themselves mothers of a nation of heroes rather than be dishonoured as the mothers of a race of degenerates.[10] Those opposed called on women to vote 'No' to war, militarism and conscription, to vindicate the pains of childbirth by saving their sons. The referendum was held the following month, and in spite of the emotionally charged rhetoric, Australians again voted against conscription.

Other moral questions were also undoubtedly on Dorothea's mind. During the preceding few years, Charles Mackellar had been working on a paper entitled 'Mental Deficiency' with the help of an academic, Professor D.A. Welsh. The paper called for social reforms in relation to the 'feeble-minded'. This stemmed from Charles's investigation into the management of delinquent children during his visit to parts of Europe and the United Kingdom with Dorothea in 1912. He had long been convinced that environmental factors were the primary consideration in how the minds of children were formed. While working on his report on the *Treatment of Neglected and Delinquent Children in Great Britain, Europe, and America* (1913), Charles had begun to reconsider the question of nature verses nurture.

The eugenics congress he'd attended in 1912 had clearly influenced his thinking, and this new paper argued that the 'mentally feeble' should be separated from the general population and prevented from procreating, in line with the arguments of eugenicists. The rationalisation – popular on both the left and right of politics – was that if the 'mentally ill' were prevented from 'breeding', society as a whole would benefit. It was a controversial theory which seemed at odds with the many progressive policies Charles was responsible for introducing during his time as a politician. And though this particular paper makes for uncomfortable reading, many of the reforms for which he was now advocating *were* progressive for the time: he was in favour of the education of doctors in mental health as a specialty, more rigorous testing methods, and he saw the need to keep the 'mentally deficient' out of jails and industrial schools, favouring the development of more benevolent institutions. An article in the *Sydney Morning Herald* in November 1917 set out his arguments regarding what to do with the 'mentally defective': 'to leave them at liberty to propagate their kind without supervision commonly results in the commission of the worst sorts of crimes and adds a continually increasing burden to the charities of the State.'[11] What Dorothea might have thought of her father's work remains unclear, though it seems unlikely that she or Charles would have anticipated the terrible harm that eugenics would later wreak on the world.

More pleasant things were in mind as 1917 drew to a close, and Dorothea busied herself indulging in a Christmas tradition dating back to her time in London in 1912, when she and Ruth began exchanging handmade calendars, a ritual that would last more than two decades. The calendars were made using six sheets of beautiful, heavy paper linked with ribbons – two months to a page – which were carefully embellished with photographs, quotations, short poems and tiny reproductions of paintings to enhance a chosen theme.

Dorothea was also working on a new novel with a lead character called Deborah. It was based on a play called *The Unbroken*, although neither the playscript nor the novel would ever be published. By mid-December she was back at Kurrumbede, where once again nature would reveal its restorative powers. 'Drove out with Eric before breakfast, the garden a wilderness of sunflowers. Filled my apron with brand new ducklings like lightly poached eggs.' Hope was on the horizon.

Chapter 13

Armistice

In the landmark year of 1918, the world was at a tipping point and people everywhere were willing the war to be over. The Mackellars tried to maintain some sense of routine normality, but each day they wondered if the war would ever end. In May of the previous year, true to his word, Mac had enlisted as a lieutenant in the First Lifeguards in London, and they were beginning to wonder whether he would return to them alive. A month later, Sir Charles had received a letter from his youngest son with news that he had been recommended for a commission by a family connection, Lord Penrhyn. He'd made a special application to the War Office so Mac could bypass regulation training. Dorothea wrote she was 'very proud' but could not help but add: 'My heart sank when Mother told me – the training much shorter and the danger greater.'

A frequent visitor to Dunara during this time was Dorothea's friend Dorothy Macmillan – 'bless her clean human heart' – whose maiden name of Featherstonehaugh gave rise to the nickname

'Fethers'. Their respective fathers had introduced the two when they were little more than babies. Fethers's husband was away at war and she was grateful for the company and the hospitality of the Mackellars. During a hot and oppressive February, one of Fethers's twin sons died. Dorothea would later recall rushing off to be with her grieving friend, who she described as 'small and frail of body but strong in spirit'.[1] Towards the end of their lives, some four decades later, the two would become live-in companions.

But in April of 1918, there were excruciating rumours of peace being imminent, though an end to the war hovered just out of reach. Dorothea's depression was stalking her now, occurring more often and for longer periods of time. Even so, there were pleasures to be had. An interlude in July with Ruth at Kurrajong in the Blue Mountains, where they stayed for over a week, brought much-needed respite. It also signalled their enduring intimacy, and the fine line they walked between their friendship and the relationships of their play characters. Dorothea described acting scenes with Ruth involving Mr Savill from their play *Savill's Dream* 'in a slightly repentant mood. Such a relief after all those months'. She mentioned, too, performing 'Tony and Glynde letting off steam so that the fire shouldn't get too hot'. It seemed that even in their thirties, acting still performed an important role in Dorothea and Ruth's relationship, allowing them to express themselves to each other.

On her birthday, Eric surprised Dorothea with a black cocker spaniel which she promptly named Sheila. The puppy became her constant companion. At night, the 'new baby wept' until she took her to bed. Dorothea spent days carrying Sheila about in the pocket of her apron, like a 'mother-wallaby'. In a playful mood, she wrote affectionately about the dog in her poem 'The Youthful Sheila,' parodying Wordsworth's 'Daffodils':

> Awhile upon my feet she lies
> In vacant or in pensive mood
> 'Ere barking to the gate she flies
> To slay the wretch who dares intrude;
> And then her heart with pleasure fills
> She dances on the daffodils.[2]

Sheila was one in a long line of pet dogs in Dorothea's life, but she was a particular favourite who would be her shadow for many years to come. The arrival of the new puppy lifted Dorothea's spirits for a time, until an inexplicable, debilitating mood again set in. She wrote of feeling ill, and the 'humiliation of nerves'; stating that the 'depression was acute with very little to account for it, nervous and disinclined, as is usual these days'. At least, regular letters from Mac confirmed he was safe, for the moment.

But at last, there was real cause for joy. On 13 October the family heard news that Germany had accepted American President Woodrow Wilson's peace terms. There had been false hope before and the Mackellars decided they would wait for confirmation before celebrating. The peace rumours swirled around them, but they did not dare to imagine what a postwar world might be like. Dorothea wrote on 20 October, there was 'a creamy full moon in a windy green sky. And the news is good they have evacuated the Belgian Coast'. Ruth and Dorothea could not bring themselves to play-act. 'We think it's good news too – we haven't the same frantic need to escape from ourselves.' It was a poignant moment for Dorothea to acknowledge the escapism that motivated their acting: it had been a distraction from the war, but perhaps also a way to address a very different malaise in their lives.

The Mackellar family was at their beloved Kurrumbede – caught in the middle of another drought – when confirmation of the good news finally came through. Information that Austria had surrendered unconditionally was followed by word that an Armistice had been signed with Germany, but it was almost immediately contradicted. They tried to go about their day-to-day business and contemplate a future with optimism, but the way forward was still uncertain. Dorothea's depression was shadowing her, but she believed an end to the war would lift her spirits. Surely, that would put everything right, she had reasoned before. On 9 November, the news the papers brought was positive and there was a certain frisson in the air as they all dared to hope. News had filtered through that people in Sydney were beginning to cheer and dance in the streets, although still, it seemed, nothing was guaranteed.

The next day the Brouns – the family who lived on the property next door – visited Kurrumbede and the Mackellars to pass the time. There was nothing to do but wait. The war, much like the intransigent drought, had stretched out before them without an end in sight, and it was enough to drive the most optimistic of people to despair. But then:

> At the end of a hot afternoon, a storm broke on us after waltzing completely around the horizon. I got soaked to the skin, which was pleasant, while rescuing the chicks and ducklings from flood. I'll not forget the two dust-devils who strode across the plain just ahead of that black-purple storm.

When the announcement finally came on 11 November that the Armistice had been confirmed, there were celebrations across the nation, and the Mackellars drove into Gunnedah just in time to hear the tail-end of the Royal Proclamation. Dorothea wanted to share the excitement, but she felt nothing, writing: 'I can't take it in'. The family took the overnight train to Sydney, but Dorothea was unable to sleep. The noise was deafening at each station as locals flooded the platforms, making a racket with 'tooting and tin-cans'.

The next day, the *Sydney Morning Herald* spelled out the relief all Australians were feeling, describing the end of the war as an event greater in importance than anything in the experience of the modern world. It warned, however, of the looming gap in the skills, knowledge and creative genius of a generation of men:

> The flower of this generation has perished. The men who promised the greatest things in statesmanship, in science and the arts have gone, because their sense of duty was clearer than that of their contemporaries. Their loss is irreplaceable, but their sacrifice makes an unanswerable appeal for the democracy they have honoured and preserved.[3]

Mac, for his part, had served as a machine-gunner in France until he was injured and taken to hospital, just nine days before Armistice. His sister must have been deeply grateful to have her younger brother returning safely from war.

～

Back home in Sydney, Dorothea reported feeling tired and restless and useless. Ruth visited, but Dorothea insisted she felt 'decidedly ill' and must rest. She spent her time reading *The New Book of Martyrs* by Georges Duhamel which she found 'unbearable', likely because it described the experiences of a doctor in the French army. The nightmare the world had been plunged into for four long years was over, but its end was not proving to be the cure-all Dorothea had hoped for. Her depression had seeped into her bones like winter damp.

'Nerves' was a vague and insipid diagnosis reserved mostly for women's complaints, but in the years to come it would also be used to describe the post-traumatic stress disorder faced by returning soldiers. The broad array of symptoms associated with nervous conditions made them difficult to diagnose and treat, with people encouraged to rest, take restorative trips to the country, seek out healing waters or pray for miracles. Families with a social standing to protect were unlikely to have embraced a diagnosis hinting at mental illness, and so victims were expected to be stoic in their suffering. And it seems plausible that the idea of complaining of her dark thoughts and feelings was unthinkable to Dorothea, when war had taken the lives of so many men, and broken so many families.

The world was still reeling from war when a new enemy appeared: a pandemic was unleashed with the devastating spread of the Spanish Influenza, carried by soldiers returning home from the war. Its impact was underestimated in Australia in 1918, leading to a second wave the following year which brought a more sobering reality and a death toll of more than 12,000. It also tested a relatively young Commonwealth, as states sought to close borders and impose their own restrictions on their residents. An article in the *Sydney Morning Herald* in January 1919 illustrated the fractured approach to managing the pandemic:

> Now that the worst has happened the government of New South Wales is quite entitled to insist that Victorian infection shall be a home commodity. Meanwhile there are local precautions which require our attention. The wearing of masks has now been ordained, but there are other more general precautions which are still left to our personal sense of responsibility. The most important of these is the unnecessary crowding which can be seen every day in trains, trams, shops, and restaurants.[4]

Dorothea was thirty-three when the war ended. It had punctuated some of the best years of her adult life. Periods of depression continued to plague her, and her parents' deteriorating health had only increased their reliance on her. Her mother was profoundly deaf by this stage, and her father had begun the slow slide into dementia. The family decided to sell Dunara, deeming it too large and high maintenance for the ageing Mackellars and their daughter, and they moved to a property called Earlston at Wahroonga on Sydney's North Shore. The move was short-lived, however, as Sir Charles felt increasingly isolated from the city and his old friends. His apparent recklessness in leaping aboard the ferries that took him across the harbour to the city was also a concern for his family, who worried he would injure himself. By 1920, they would move back to the Eastern Suburbs, buying a property called Rosemont in Woollahra to give Charles more familiar surroundings.

As she had done all her life, Dorothea continued to write daily and was unwavering in her commitment to her creative pursuits. A review of her body of work in November 1919 by renowned literary critic Bertram Stevens praised her ability to find beauty in the ordinary. 'She sees the city trams as "jewelled beetles, flashing through the night". She pictures the lamps in Hyde Park as "those gold apples of the dark". And from her window, a crescent strip of the open sea in the distance enables her to conjure up all the charm and the wonder of remote lands.'[5] In the article in the *Herald*, Stevens asserted that Dorothea's extensive travels enabled her to see Australia in a new light:

> One has to travel away from the homeland to become sharply aware of the unconscious influences of accustomed surroundings and to appreciate beauty, that has been accepted as a matter of course. Miss Mackellar, recognising her debt, pays it handsomely, and in doing so helps many of us to realise the value of the gift of colour in Australia, which was so often considered sombre and melancholy, a haggard continent, in fact.[6]

And yet, amongst all of this praise, there were criticisms creeping into some reviews that Dorothea felt were unfair. Stevens suggested that Dorothea's comfortable world may have limited her ability to write on more personal matters and to make the leap to greatness: 'It is perhaps because of that lack of more poignant experience of life that her work, always charming and graceful in style, stops short of the major notes.' Even so, he recognised her particular contribution to the Australian songbook. 'Heartfelt joy in the beauty of outward life and particularly in the peculiar beauty of the Australian landscape, has been her chief inspiration, and in expressing it so well she has endeared herself to a large Australian audience.'[7]

Stevens's assumption that Dorothea's privileged life prevented her from reaching greater literary heights was a criticism that must have stung. And such critiques always seemed to emanate from a particularly male viewpoint. Would such a criticism be levelled at a male writer? She had borne the unutterable grief of losing her beloved Keith. She had suffered through unrequited love and frustrated desire. This was real life, as she had lived it.

For all of her achievements, the march towards modernism in literature – marked by a gritty realism and lack of sentimentality – was a leap Dorothea felt unable to make. Her poetry remained stubbornly Georgian in its romanticism and themes rooted in nature. By 1919, an anti-Georgian sentiment was evident, with modernists insisting that a new way of representing the world was necessary in a postwar environment. Modernists argued that upending tradition was the only way to deal with the social and spiritual incoherence of a postwar world. As Robert Ross wrote in his classic study of the Georgian movement, *The Georgian Revolt*,

> Emotions made taut by four years of horror had finally snapped; and being unable or unwilling to feel deeply, the postwar Georgian poets could scarcely have been expected to produce any but second-rate verse. Like the nation itself, many postwar poets were emotionally exhausted and they recoiled from the strains of war either to simple poetry which extolled the calm beauty of the English countryside or to the poetry of minutiae which required no sustained or strenuous emotional effort.[8]

It must have felt, to Dorothea, that the world – or the literary one at least – was moving on without her.

∽

The spring of 1919 brought with it another foray into the world of film, with Mac taking the role of foreman on another silent movie starring Snowy Baker, *The Man from Kangaroo*. Again, many of the scenes were shot at Kurrumbede, creating much excitement for the Mackellar family, the farmhands and the townspeople. A follow-up to *The Lure of the Bush*, it was the first of several films Baker made with Canadian-born director Wilfred Lucas and his American wife, actress and screenwriter Bess Meredyth. They were brought on board by the motion picture pioneer Edward John Carroll with the aim of spearheading an Australian film industry. A *Sydney Morning Herald* article reported high hopes for the fledgling endeavour:

> The scenic settings for the first production will be selected at Kurrumbede station, Gunnedah, by permission of Captain Mackellar and Mr Eric Mackellar ... Employment, it is stated, will be found for about 100 persons ... Mr Lucas said yesterday that the production of motion pictures was now one of the leading industries in the United States, and that there was no reason why it should not be one of the most flourishing industries in Australia.[9]

The Man from Kangaroo portrayed the travails of John Harland, a reformed boxer who becomes a preacher and is assigned to spread the good work in the Australian town of Kangaroo. As well as Kurrumbede, the film was shot on location in Kangaroo Valley, south of Sydney, with interior shots taken at the Theatre Royal in Sydney. The movie was a moderate success, but the production team made only two more films before disbanding, and Mac's film career was short-lived. Having been exposed to gas during the war, his health was precarious and he settled into the role of gentleman farmer at Kurrumbede. Although Dorothea loved to see Mac and Eric when she visited the farm, Mac's forthcoming marriage to Enid Woolf was a strain on the relationship.

Dorothea was especially protective of Eric when there were disputes between the brothers over the property, and she fervently hoped her older brother, too, might find a woman who would be the antidote to his loneliness and his natural shyness. At thirty-four years of age, her own single status was not lost on her, but she felt she was much better equipped than Eric to make her way in the world, even if she was destined to be alone.

Chapter 14

Wanderlust

Dorothea sailed for London – via Southeast Asia and Europe – in February 1920, accompanied by Eric, who was rapidly developing an alcohol problem. She hoped the change of scenery and the sea air would improve her brother's health. They had been forced to book the journey in stages, as the shipping routes were still disrupted in the aftermath of the war. They first travelled on a ship to the Dutch East Indies – later Indonesia – and Dorothea recorded the trip in her diaries. She described the Queensland coastline in her poem 'Whitsunday Passage':

Wet gold sky and clouds of violet
Low on the sea's jade-green
Tumbled islands of sheer chalcedony
The liner throbs between.[1]

On 19 February, the ship's passengers rose early and went ashore before taking a 'hot and dirty' train from Surabaya to Yogyakarta in Indonesia. Dorothea described travelling through flat country of timber plantations and fields of rice, sugar and tapioca, with volcanoes in the distance. Staying in Yogyakarta for several days, Dorothea and Eric walked the streets most afternoons, where they saw 'great ladies out shopping under tall gold umbrellas and great lords, very handsome, with jewelled knives in their belts and lots and lots of jugglers, dancers and strange puppets'.

They moved on to Tosari in East Java, where they rose one morning at 3.30 am and rode on horseback to Bromo volcano on a starry night. Dorothea wrote:

> I couldn't see the path at all. My pony was going first and Eric brought up the rear. The trumpet lilies gleamed softly through the dark on the banks on either side and smelled unbelievably sweet in the cool air. Over the high black shoulder ahead of me, the mountain of the Nymph's Bath. I saw the morning star, blinding silver and like a little moon. Never, even in the Indian Ocean, had I seen it so great.

They rode through the national park, emerged into open country and had breakfast at the top of a pass in an open work hut:

> Bitter cold ... all the strange green mountains with knife ridged sides, the sun just touching them were enough to take one's breath. Down the twisting pass we went and across the queer shady sand-sea dotted here and there with small bits of red lava to the livid sides of Bromo. It boils furiously and jets out choking sulphur. She's very deep and steep, the edge is pretty sharp. There is a great cloud at the bottom which sways aside every now and then to show gleaming

yellow sulphur and sometimes a hideously, bubbling sulphur pool. Nothing ever gave me such a sense of terrific force.

Next, they travelled to Singapore, and on arrival Dorothea was immediately taken to hospital, having fallen ill with dysentery on the ship. She recorded it as the worst illness she had ever experienced:

The next few days are vivid and yet smudgy like a dream. A lot of pain and no sleep, nice Sisters, awful scotch, drums, bells and gongs in the night-time from some temple nearby, Eric's visits, heat and cold, temperature 102 degrees, chirping lizards, the last of a waning moon – I never had the strength to turn and see her but I had her light. Once they began to allow me morphine it was much better because with sleep one can stand most things.

While in Singapore, Eric was playing polo twice a week and, according to Dorothea, creating a sensation. She found Singapore itself too active, commercial and controversial to be pleasant. 'The New Chinese are not as fascinating as the old and much more alarming,' she wrote. Yet she enjoyed being driven about at night with 'the Chinese all working hard or eating in the open-air restaurants by the light of oil flames and lamps and lovely traceried lanterns . . . the bustle is as stirring as shearing-time'. She and Eric drove to a big hotel at San Souci where there was a Filipino band playing. Sitting out under the cocos palms on the water's edge, she looked at the soft, bright colours of the dancing figures inside, and then at the moonlit sea.

On 11 April 1920, Mac married Enid Woolf with a ceremony and reception in Sydney reported in the *Sydney Morning Herald* under the heading 'Society Wedding':

> Keen interest was taken in the wedding of Miss Enid Woolf and Lieut. Malcolm Mackellar at St Mark's Church, Darling Point, on Thursday evening. The bride, who is a niece of Sir Samuel Hordern, has been staying in Sydney for some time. The bridal gown of white duchess satin had a train from the shoulders outlined with orange buds and pink tissue roses, the bodice being draped with lace.[2]

Dorothea and Eric were not present to see their new sister-in-law's satin train or lace bodice. The Mackellars were a close-knit family, but the relationship between Dorothea and Enid remained strained. With Dorothea's disapproval and Eric's escalating alcohol problem, it is also possible that the family had agreed it would be better if they did not attend Mac's wedding.

In her diary entries from April, Dorothea wrote that Eric had not been well for a week, suggesting that the culprit was his drinking. She loved him despite everything, and was immensely patient with her brother. But she also had her own perceived failures on her mind. During her time in Singapore, Dorothea wrote a poem called 'Vestal, 1920' which revisits the regret of not seizing opportunities for romance and love:

> The kisses that she did not take
> Pass unregarded to a common grave
> But through the black nights
> She is all one ache

For those she never gave.
Lover and husband, mother-lore
Renounced she, living as she chose to live,
And not for all these she mourns, but for
Her woman's right to give.[3]

Still, there were the many joys of travel ahead of her. Sailing on the *Dilwara*, Dorothea and Eric arrived in Colombo in Sri Lanka, then known as Ceylon, and were driven straight to the popular Galle Face Hotel. It was a familiar layover spot for rich tourists and Dorothea was delighted to discover some of her friends and acquaintances there. Eric, for his part, was nursing a vicious hangover and already considering where he might find his next drink. As luck would have it, Dorothea's actress friend Grace Palotta was entertaining guests in the hotel dining room and was 'vital and amusing as ever surrounded by rather attractive Russians'.

On Friday 7 May, Dorothea reported that Eric had a lunchtime injection and returned transfigured. On Saturday, she wrote that she and Eric were both having a course of injections – perhaps morphine, which was often prescribed for nervous conditions at that time – and they both felt a lot better. The siblings were forced to wait two months for a berth on another ship, but they made the most of their time, playing tourist. While visiting the city of Kandy and nearby Peradeniya, they encountered the sitting Chief Justice of Ceylon, Englishman Sir Anton Bertram, holding court in a temple. There was a pavilion at one end with a small and silent crowd, while several policemen strolled up and down. The siblings walked to the outskirts of the crowd and stood among the carved teak pillars. In contrast to the blazing white light outside, gloominess met them when they entered the temple. Someone was speaking earnestly in a clear-cut voice: 'We looked over the heads of the vividly swathed people and at the end of the hall, high above all those brown faces, there lolled a stately figure out of the 18th century, with flowing scarlet gown, white periwig and cape, disdainful, intent face, pale against the dark panels of the background. It was very dramatic.'

As they waited for the next portion of their pilgrimage, a temperature of 104 degrees brought a diagnosis of malaria that Dorothea greeted with 'indifference'. She was stoic in the face of severe physical illness – never paranoid or fearful – which was at odds with her reaction to the vague symptoms of her 'nerves'. By the time Dorothea had defeated the illness, it was mid-June and she and Eric were attempting to amuse themselves as their stay at the Galle Face Hotel was extended while they waited for their next ship. Dorothea wrote of leaving the hotel one afternoon before the 'wet, wild sunset' to watch a large group of Afghans at play: 'There were about 150 of them mostly young men, very smartly dressed in voluminous white cotton trousers, crimson or purple jackets stiffly embroidered in gold, broad sashes, turbans with gold embroidered conical caps of green, red, gold and purple velvet. They sat in a wide ring on the grass and two or three masters of ceremony walked up and down arranging wrestling matches.' Her special attentiveness for colour was always put to work when she travelled.

The next leg of the trip was aboard the *Naldera* for all ports to Southampton, which included Bombay, Aden, Port Said, Crete, Calabria and the Straits of Messina, via Etna and Stromboli and onto Marseilles. Eric continued drinking to excess, his behaviour increasingly erratic and unmanageable – he was becoming disruptive to the other passengers. In fact, at Aden, the shore-going party encouraged Dorothea and Eric to make their own arrangements. On 18 July, she wrote in her diary that her brother had become very unwell but the ship's doctor 'could not say positively what it was'. Dorothea loved Eric, but she found his behaviour embarrassing, and did not know how to help him.

A friend travelling on the same ship, Etta Close, was the only one to give Dorothea sympathy and an offer of help in the form of an intervention. 'Other people meant well but some were ghoulish. Then Miss Close offered to come ashore with us and because Eric's distress was making me frantic, I consented. She's a wonder!' At Marseilles, the three of them were put ashore and there followed a desperate search to find a hotel that would take them. A doctor was called – who discreetly diagnosed pleurisy, a condition of the lungs – and the women began around-the-clock supervision of Eric, who was in truth experiencing alcohol withdrawal. Etta and Dorothea took rotating shifts: 'Etta was beyond all praise for strength, patience, tact and human-ness.' Eventually, Eric was 'so thin you could spit through him but began to look less unearthly'. Having been forced to leave the ship to care for Eric, they scrambled to catch a train to Paris. They were provided with what Dorothea described as 'syringes and dope for me in case of the collapse which was predicted with gloomy joy'. They reached the train and settled in before bringing Eric his dinner through the 'rocking corridor', because he was too weak to walk safely to the dining saloon. Arriving in Paris, they found some rooms in a little hotel opposite the Gare du Nord. 'Etta and I went and had an orgy of shopping at the Galeries Lafayette (it was sale time) leaving Eric ensconced with some English papers.'

Crossing the English Channel on 6 August, Dorothea mused that the 'little channel waves were pointed and yellow-green, very sick they made me but the others, Eric and Etta, were well'. Disembarking, they made their way to London, where Eric and Dorothea established themselves at the Rubens Hotel. Dorothea could not contain her joy in returning to one of her favourite cities. 'It was good to be in London again and even the ordinary shop gave me a smile by its London-ness.' She resumed her round of engagements with the literary and theatre communities that had come to embrace her during previous visits. For Dorothea, London was the home of brilliant and interesting kindred spirits – artists and writers, young and ardent in the service of their arts. They welcomed her to the Tomorrow Club, a haunt of the enterprising literati of the age. The club was designed to allow literary types to come together, and it benefited from the efforts of one Thomas Stearns Eliot, who was to become one of the greatest poets of the twentieth century.

Dorothea had urgent shopping to conduct, rushing through the London streets on a grey day. She had no warm clothes, and while it was still summertime, the weather was decidedly wintry. She noted that many of the familiar parks and squares had emergency buildings in them – wartime relics that people wanted removed while the government dragged its heels. With her wardrobe fortified, it was off to Paddington train station with Eric and Etta for the journey to Etta's home in the village of Combe in Oxfordshire. 'A very quiet village of nice greystone houses and gay gardens,' she wrote. They stayed at Etta's house, Combe Cottage, and Dorothea must have been charmed by the place, for she described what she found there in detail:

Into a white walled porch ... to a low ceiled yew-beamed room with a magnificent fireplace and five Persian paintings on the walls. A little cottage room. Through its diamond paved windows, you get a glimpse of another garden and then you walk out to a great lawn, the square, the lily garden, the orchard and all. The sense of surprise is beautiful. I don't know which room I loved best. They all had the home feeling. We got up late and rested and had yams in the garden and cooled chops in the open to the little maid's disgust and astonishment.

On 16 August, Dorothea and Etta drove into Oxford and had tea with an acquaintance, Katherine Feilden. Miss Feilden had engaged architect Walter Cave to design a substantial estate and landscaped gardens that would become known as 'High Wall' in Headington. The garden had a series of formal terraces and enclosed gardens, with a glade, a rock garden and a stream. Dorothea was impressed with Miss Feilden's home, if not her living arrangements:

She has a beautiful house and garden even if the architect did swindle her. The garden is most cunningly arranged. It is not small, but it gives an impression of tremendous space. It was a hospital during the war. She's a nice little woman but as Etta said with affectionate pity 'a comfortable pussy.' And her echoing companion – a nice woman too but deliver me from that fate! The leisured spinster and her dependent, both in cotton wool.

This comment indicates that Dorothea did not consider herself a 'leisured spinster', although, as a woman of thirty-five years of age travelling the world, the label would have applied. She had long been accused by others of being wrapped in cotton-wool, but, in comparison to Miss Fielden, Dorothea seemed to consider herself an adventurous and modern woman who had seen and experienced much in the world.

∾

After returning to London following her Oxford jaunt, Dorothea went on to Overstrand in Norfolk, where she stayed at The Danish House with friends. The house was one of eight pavilions built for the 1900 Paris Exposition. Sir George Lewis bought the home for his wife, Lady Elizabeth, who had fallen in love with it – they picked it up and had the whole house shipped to Norfolk.[4] Dorothea found the place to be 'a picturesque and disconcerting abode. It stands right on the cliff and the North Sea gales shriek round its Norse gables and galleries – very black and white it is and futuristically furnished'.

Dorothea was visited there by her old melancholy, heightened by the windswept landscape, and yet her poetry revealed a sense of hope that she might yet find some kind of antidote to her restless spirit. In her poem 'I Will Not Think Her Foundered' she revealed a hard-won resilience: 'I will not think her foundered yet, / My ship that has never come in', she wrote, imagining a speculative future:

What is therein I may not tell,
But very certainly I know
It is in my heart's desire, and though
In this long wait my courage fail,

I shall believe that all goes well;
My tall ship has not struck a reef;
Those seas are deep beyond belief—
And she could weather any gale.
(*I will not think she has gone down—*
Hope is a swimmer hard to drown.)⁵

At the end of August, Dorothea travelled to Whitstable in Kent to stay with her childhood friend Meg McPhillamy, whose husband, Hugh Scarlett, had been aide-de-camp to Governor William MacGregor in Brisbane and later became Lord Abinger. Dorothea had held a warm affection for Hugh since their trip through North Queensland all those years ago. She wrote: 'Meg and her family are very nice, especially the three-year-old John with whom I fell instantly and violently in love. He is like a brownie. Hugh hasn't changed a bit. It was very nice playing with the babies and getting horse chestnuts for them. John can't help showing you where he has hidden the thimble and he's as friendly as he is impish.'

A week later, Hugh and Meg drove Dorothea part of the way to the village of Deal in Kent to see the Conrads, who were staying there to give Jessie Conrad a change of scenery. She had been cooped up for two years after another unsuccessful knee surgery. Dorothea took a train the rest of the way. Joseph met her at the station and he was 'more foreign than ever, and if possible kinder, the imposing car whirled us swiftly through Deal . . . it was heart-warming and I feel that they really were glad to see me and, of course, I was glad too'. She described a sumptuous lunch and an afternoon full of conversation that saw them 'mutually entertained'.

Later, she caught a train back to London, in a carriage that was 'a non-smoker but as all the men who got into the carriage after me smoked without asking if I minded, I swallowed my neo-Victorian prickliness and smoked too'. In London, Dorothea had agreed to visit her friend Patrick Chalmers and his new wife Winifred – Patrick was the subject of the story about the marriage proposal Dorothea had received and reportedly accepted, only to have her letter lost in the post during the war. She planned to go out of her way to befriend her old friend's wife so they could all spend time together, and she met Winifred alone at the station. 'Rather glad I was because of the opportunity of making friends (if she'd let me). She did. She is thin and fair and honest. I like her very much.' They travelled on by train to meet Patrick at the village of Goring on the River Thames in South Oxfordshire. She enjoyed Winifred's company, and her affectionate relationship with Pat was easily resumed.

> We walked to their house – on the whole a little less country than Wahroonga, and then he and I strolled down to the river while she did the flowers. They made me feel at home at once and I was very happy despite my bad stupefying cold. After dinner we yarned and said poetry in the old fashion and got on very well. Winifred is a dear. And she asked me to stay the next night so I said I would. It's so nice to be liked. Pat was pleased too. And their dogs are dears.

Next, Dorothea travelled to Oxford and the home of playwright and poet Catherine Dawson Scott, founder of the Tomorrow Club and later of the famed Poets, Essayists, Novelists (PEN) Club. 'It was a rather lovely day, golden leaves and blue mist as I came down after a highly satisfactory afternoon. She may perhaps be poor, but she is a kind hearty woman. I liked her.' The impressive gathering of writers that weekend was indicative of the literary circles Dorothea moved in. Alec Waugh, writer and older brother of celebrated novelist Evelyn Waugh, talked football with Dorothea, while she also enjoyed the company of John Davys (J.D.) Beresford, known for his early science fiction novels. She did not, however, find an affinity with poet Ford Madox Ford's former girlfriend Violet Hunt, whom she 'did not recognise but instantly disliked'.

During this time, Dorothea deepened her friendship with Joseph and Jessie Conrad. In her diary, she recorded visiting their home in Kent in October. As usual, she was immediately made to feel welcome by Jessie. Dorothea came to count the Conrads among her dearest friends, although there were long periods between visits, especially as Joseph now rarely travelled, even to London. Over the years, she had also become a favourite with one of their sons, John. Conrad met Dorothea at Canterbury, and they motored out to Bishopsbourne 'feeling happy'. Conrad took her 'all round the nice formal garden and the lawn with their splendid old trees and then round the house'. A poem from this period called 'The Cherry Tree' is unusually upbeat:

Shall I be troubled if beauty fade
And your harvest fade too?
If promise trick us and life be false— ?
For the beauty is true.
And Nature wasting a million lives
Knows that Life wins at length.
I send my roots through the deep sweet loam
And rejoice in my strength.[6]

She wrote that she did not need to record much in her diary about the visit because it was so memorable, and much later Dorothea still recalled her long conversations with Conrad about writing, including the need for characters in fiction to 'act as would a real person of their particular psychological make-up'. On one occasion, Conrad tried to describe to her the 'living death' that can follow when love and desire cannot be consummated. He then laughed and suggested she was too young to know of such things. Even though she was in her thirties, Conrad's advancing age – he was now in his sixties – made him think of her as younger than she was. She hinted that she had her own experience of unrequited love, although she did not elaborate.

Dorothea's return to Australia was drawing near. She was sad to leave the Conrad family, but hoped to return to England soon. She couldn't know it would be the last time she saw Joseph, whose generosity to her had been enduring even as his reputation as one of the greatest English-language writers grew. She would always be grateful for the friendship of this literary genius and his kind wife, who sent Dorothea a photo of her family as a keepsake.

The lead up to Christmas was thrilling amid the snow-covered landscape of London as Dorothea prepared to return to Australia. 'I had been expecting for some time to feel an awful wrench of farewell but so far it held off.' She began the long process of calling on various people to say goodbye, and caught a train to take a last walk through 'the glory of the snowy wood' just outside of London. She marvelled at the fact that the Christmas cards, with their scenes of a winter wonderland, were so true to life here in England. It had been an exhilarating trip, but soon she would gladly return to her sunburnt country.

Chapter 15

The Literary Life

Dorothea boarded the *Ormonde* to return to Australia in February 1921. 'Plenty of nice girls on board but no thrills. Or perhaps I was in the wrong mood?' she wrote in her diary. Soon after she and Eric arrived back in Sydney, the *Daily Telegraph* published an article which described their trip in great detail. The fact that Dorothea's year-long sojourn was deemed newsworthy enough to run on page six of a metropolitan newspaper gives an insight into the extent of her celebrity and the voyeuristic interest in her extravagant lifestyle. Dorothea had been interviewed at home at Rosemont in Woollahra, and the reporter's prose became a little overwrought in capturing her subject: 'Slight and lissom in her soft jade green gown, moving and speaking with the ease of someone accustomed to the gentle graces of a cultured world; a little fragile-looking but vivid in her strong personality, with the clear kind eyes of the poet – eyes of gold and bramble dew.' Dorothea told the reporter that she had not written a great deal while away – but after all, the reporter concluded, 'to write of life, one has to live, and for an author it profits much to rest awhile, seeing and knowing the breadth and length of the great world and its ever-varying men and women'.[1]

The changing postwar world had a profound influence on women artists of the 1920s, and those in the Sydney clique were no exception. Upper-class women had played new roles during the war – including fundraising or organising care packages – and this had given them new skills and new opportunities for networking. There was greater independence and camaraderie as women banded together in the absence of men, to counter grief and fear. Working-class women had to fill the gaps in the workforce, but many also embraced the opportunity to explore creative pursuits. The wider arts community was changing too. There were new opportunities for women writers, as well as a burgeoning amateur theatre scene, which was supported and teased out in the parlours of society homes, and all of this contributed to a growing fellowship among women.

Dorothea and Ruth were now very much a part of the literary scene, although they were not as strident as some of their sisters, as they did not need to write to earn a living. While Dorothea's social status kept her at arms-length from the 'jobbing' writers, the new willingness of women to network through literary groups and through theatrical circles brought her into contact with many of her well-known contemporaries. A more modern world allowed for unconventional domestic arrangements and reciprocal mentoring, with women writers and artists coming together in salons and drawing rooms across Sydney. Women from different backgrounds were rolling up their sleeves to fight for better pay and better recognition. In her thesis, 'Cultivating the Arts', academic Jane Hunt wrote about the mutual support women writers gave each other during this period, focusing on a network of predominantly Sydney-based novelists, playwrights, poets and journalists. The group included acclaimed poet, essayist and social crusader Mary Gilmore; bohemian and writer Dulcie Deamer; journalist Connie Stephens; and poets Alys Hungerford, Lala Fisher, Zora Cross, Dora Moore, Dorothea and Ruth.[2] These were the literary stars of the day and, collectively, their contribution to the wider literary culture was formidable.

Hunt wrote that Mackellar and Bedford's less than warm relationships with other writers probably reflected social differences rather than any lack of respect. 'Mackellar was well known and respected as a poet. Yet, she could record in her diary the pleasure of an afternoon spent writing verse. She could write for leisure, not for the odd extra payment that might result from the publication of a poem. Indeed, she could languish all day in bed reading books and daydreaming.'[3]

Hunt speculated about the relationship between Dorothea and Ruth. She wondered how their mutual support in literary pursuits could be recognised in the collaboration of other women writers, writing 'it is possible to see in their acting out of plays the extension of the psychological comfort of friendship to ... the mutual provision of an encouraging environment in which to develop as writers. Their acting out of plays may be taken as a little more serious than the light self-entertainment of two young women from affluent circumstances. It provided a supportive forum for the threshing out of their ideas and absorption of the work of others'.[4]

Mary Gilmore was particularly influential. She was a prolific writer, having edited the Women's Page in the journal *The Australian Worker* for decades, as well as writing poetry, but it was her unwavering support of other writers and her generosity with time and advice that set her apart. Having come from a working-class background, Gilmore was sympathetic to the struggles of women writers trying to find work to sustain themselves or juggling the demands of husbands and children, but she was equally supportive of Dorothea and Ruth with their more comfortable circumstances, believing in the importance of the sisterhood that crossed class lines. She often held a small salon in her *Worker* office on a Friday afternoon, attracting all sorts of literary types, experienced and aspiring, for drinks and conversation. Her vibrant personality would dominate the room. She was known for her no-fuss fashion sense, and often sported shapeless shift dresses in grey or brown and a nondescript felt hat. She was a tall, imposing woman sometimes described, unkindly, as 'mannish', but her ability to engage her audience, whether in a group or one-on-one, was her great skill and she addressed everyone regardless of status with great enthusiasm.[5]

Dorothea was well known and respected as a poet among her peers, but she had the luxury of spending long days writing and rewriting her verse. She had less in common with professional writers and was more inclined to spend time with writers from her own class, such as Ethel Turner. Ethel lived in affluent Mosman, was the wife of a judge and was part of Sydney's upper class: 'she, like Mackellar, appeared to have remained emotionally unattached to the city-based fellowship.'[6] They moved in similar social circles, but the friendship between Dorothea and Ethel went beyond their circumstances, with a genuine admiration growing between the two women. In a diary entry on 12 July 1921, Ethel wrote of her affection for her fellow writer: 'Dorothea Mackellar for lunch this afternoon –

a sincere pleasure. There ought to be more such spirits in the world. I had the feeling of touching fine porcelain after a course of handling pottery.'[7]

Another player during this period was feminist and playwright Marguerite Dale, who held salons in her home where writers and dramatists could socialise. She was the driving force behind the Tuesday Club, which echoed London's Tomorrow Club in inviting guest speakers from literary circles to address the forum. Prior to 1923, many local playwriting efforts were workshopped in private in the manner of Dorothea and Ruth's acting sessions, as there were limited opportunities for public readings. Now, informal recitals in parlours of the well-heeled literary community, as well as the rise of small independent theatre companies, allowed the practices of playwriting and acting to flourish. This eventually led to the formation of the Community Playhouse, housed in St Peter's Church Hall in Darlinghurst, where Ruth would later stage several of her plays.

Poet Dora Moore played a key role in highlighting new plays with well-patronised soirees. An article in the Sydney journal *Woman's World* reflected the desire for less snobbery in the promotion of the arts:

> The literary and artistic evenings are much more enjoyable. There is less of the stuffiness of the upper four hundred social gatherings about them, and the play-reading or verse-reading stimulates gossip and conversation. Mrs Dora Moore – she is better known as Dora Wilcox, poetess – has started enjoyable first Saturdays at her home . . . and there is good intellectual fare without any hint of superior highbrowism.[8]

Dorothea's interest in the theatre scene did not distract her from her poetry, however, and in 1923 her third poetry collection, *Dreamharbour and Other Verses*, was published by Longmans, Green & Co. in London. This showed some growth in her writing, both from a stylistic point of view and in her choice of subjects. The poems reflected her world travels and included Spanish and Italian translations. As such, they were less self-consciously Australian and more introspective. The book was divided into four sections: 'Dreams and Pictures', 'Songs and Jingles', 'Translations' and 'Moods and Masks'. In a review in *The Bulletin*, praise was less effusive than for her work in previous collections and – rather incredibly – she was still being referred to as a 'girl' at the age of thirty-eight:

> All poems in this Sydney girl's latest collection have charm; many tremble on a narrow marge between pensive wistfulness and the abyss of deep feeling, 'Flower of Youth', for instance, and 'In a Fair Garden'. They are full of colour and are written with the nicest choice of words; the imagery is clear cut and the lines are polished – there is not a slovenly phrase in the book.[9]

In November of that year, a journalist identified only by the initials 'G.I.' recounted sitting at a dinner in New York with eighty other Australians, including the federal Minister for Home and Territories, Senator George Pearce. The journalist was likely Guy Innes, one-time editor-in-chief of the Melbourne *Herald*, who was working out of London at the time. Senator Pearce lead the group of Australians as they rose to their feet to cheer the recitation of Dorothea's 'best-known patriotic poem', 'My Country'. It showed the poem's powerful ability to deeply affect people, and confirmed it had seeped into the national consciousness unlike any other Australian literary offering.[10]

Ironically, a review of *Dreamharbour* in New York's *Evening Post* appeared in April the following year, confusing Dorothea's nationality – calling her English – but delightfully positioning her as a citizen of the world. According to the article, she was variously resident in Surabaya, Java, Sydney, Singapore, Wahroonga, Anuradhapura, Kurrumbede, Cornwall, Kent, Oxfordshire, London, the Barrier Reef and the Namoi River. Unusually, the review elevated a woman's singular point of view and acknowledged qualities that had been forged through centuries of oppression:

> Miss Mackellar's poems have tenderness, an unschooled grace, and a singing quality purely feminine. To the peculiarly feminine we find added imagination which has for its kernel the self-consciousness that follows upon ages of enforced suppression. This is authentic woman's poetry and there are few finer adaptations in modern poetry than several folk songs by Miss Mackellar.[11]

A literary organisation which remained active throughout the decade was the Australian branch of the English Association. Formed in 1923 with strong links to the University of Sydney, the group boasted Ruth as secretary, Mary Gilmore as vice-president, and it increasingly called on Dorothea, Dora Moore and others to present their poetry or to talk about other writers.

In one presentation, Dorothea delivered an essay titled 'Not Understood', which discussed the development of language and how the changing use of words can obscure meaning. Her struggle with modernism was its requirement for earthy realism rather than the elevation of everyday life. She wrote: 'Realism as generally used, namely as the depiction of squalid or dismal scenes, is a maimed word. Horrible things do happen. So do beautiful things. Therefore, it must be as realistic to describe beauty as anything else.'[12]

In 1924, Dorothea and Ruth were actively involved in forming a Sydney chapter of the Zonta Club, an international group designed to encourage networking and support for businesswomen across all industries. A letter to Ruth in April that year from the president of the Zonta Club of New York, Rosalie Morton, urged her to continue to work towards the organisation of a local chapter and noted the receipt of some Australian books. 'I gave the president of the New York Board of the League, Dorothea Mackellar's book of poems and Mrs Aeneas Gunn's *We of the Never-Never* as samples of Australian women's contribution to literature and everyone was very interested.'[13]

Correspondence suggests the pair established the first Sydney Zonta Club that year, with Ruth as secretary and a number of other high-profile women on board. There is no mention of its inaugural meeting in Australian newspapers, but the club was referred to in the *Daily Telegraph* in 1924 as one among several 'clubs of business and professional women hurrying to overtake the men'.[14] Dorothea and Ruth invited numerous women of business, as well as those of professional, public, philanthropic or intellectual standing to join. The founders received acceptances from a wide range of women: Dr Constance D'Arcy, an obstetrician and gynaecologist, who later was made a Dame and became the first woman Deputy-Chancellor of the University of Sydney; artist Thea Proctor; adventurer and mountain climber Olive Kelso King; Bush Book Club secretary Beulah Bolton; portrait photographer Judith Fletcher; charity worker Phoebe Ellen Wesche; Society of Women Writers founding member Agnes Mowle; and journalist Connie Stephens. In a letter to the New York club drafted in her diary, Dorothea outlined some of the obstacles facing her in attracting women to the Sydney chapter, including a rule which stipulated members must be spending at least sixty per cent of their time engaged in their particular business or profession:

> Here comparatively few women are engaged in businesses or professions and so we cannot yet be strict about the 60 per cent rule. I for instance, much as I should like to devote that proportion of my time to writing verse, am at present, owing to family ties, quite unable to do so. When the club is in full tide, I mean to resign in favour of someone better qualified but just now nobody seems able to find any woman who has both the time, qualification and necessary enthusiasm for Zonta.

In September, a letter responding to Dorothea urged her to stay the course. 'Please do not talk of resigning from the club. You are exactly the type of person necessary to its success.' The club continued to gather numerous high-profile women during the following decade before being abandoned in 1935.

As her parents aged, Dorothea took on more responsibility for the running of the household, the organisation of social activities and answering correspondence for her father. Nevertheless, she continued to write poetry during this period and her poems were published in a variety of newspapers and journals, attracting a loyal audience of readers who followed her career. In August 1924, the *Sydney Morning Herald* printed a poem called 'An Unsociable Song', which spoke of the places in nature where it was possible to find solace in being alone.

> I am lucky who can fly
> To kingdoms of my own,
> With a picked and perfect friend
> Or, better still, alone.[15]

But in 1925, rather than finding herself in the solitude of the country, Dorothea realised a lifelong dream by treading the boards publicly, with a role in a play by Alice Gerstenberg called *Overtones: A Play in One Act* at Sydney's Playbox Theatre under the direction of Duncan Macdougall. It was described in a newspaper article as 'an ultramodern satire on hypocrisy. Throughout the piece a number of persons carry out the action of the plot, but on the stage are other ghostly figures like mocking shadows revealing the true motives and thoughts of the pretenders.'[16] Perhaps her father's advancing dementia gave Dorothea the courage to appear on the stage without fear of his disapproval. A Melbourne newspaper previewed the play with a breathless description of Dorothea's physical attributes. 'The picturesque poetess with the red gold hair ... has a distinct talent for dramatic work, and her lithe, sinuous form, exquisite colouring and musical speaking voice are big assets on the stage.'[17] Another review in Sydney's *World News* reported that Dorothea's appearance on the bill was a drawcard for the audience: 'Perhaps one of the reasons for the little theatre being crowded is the appearance of our noted woman poet, Miss Dorothea Mackellar, as a performer in the curtain-raiser, *Overtones*, which reveals in her a possession of stagecraft and a fine acting intelligence.'[18] Despite these accolades, her career on the stage was short-lived; perhaps it did not provide the satisfaction Dorothea had dreamed it would, or it may have been that her 'nerves' simply made the performances too stressful. Whatever the case, her first tilt at stage fame would also be her last.

It was also in 1925 that a very famous Australian came into the Mackellars' lives. Swimming legend Andrew 'Boy' Charlton came to Gunnedah, the year after his gold-medal triumph in the 1,500 metres at the Paris Olympics. He worked for several years as a jackaroo at Kurrumbede, living in a small workers' hut on the property. The reluctant hero trained in a popular swimming hole in the Namoi River near Cohen's Bridge, and with only the river as his training pool, he beat Japanese champion Katsuo Takaishi in world record time over 880 yards at Sydney's Domain Baths in 1927.

During this period, Dorothea's long-held affection for nature, and in particular trees, led her to enter the public debate about conservation, emerging as an early environmentalist, writing numerous newspaper columns condemning the ad hoc clearing of trees. She recognised a particular Sydney pastime of cutting down trees to maximise views – a habit which still plagues the suburbs, especially when water views are at stake. In an article headlined 'Trees: Oppressed People' in the *Sydney Morning Herald*,

Dorothea complained that trees were despised, neglected and misunderstood in Australia and pleaded for greater appreciation of native species. 'It may be an unconscious memory of pioneering days which makes us fell trees so recklessly on any pretext or none ... many of us sweep away trees indiscriminately in order to see a view which owed more than half its beauty to being seen through their screen.' She believed Australians made the mistake of preferring introduced species because they failed to see the beauty in their own natives, including the tea tree:

> It has its strong leaves, lettuce-green when they break from the bud, and like Indian jade in their maturity, and its profusion of lacy white stars. It is true that the stars fall as they fade and make a soft brown praying-carpet under the boughs; trees have been murdered for less.[19]

Dorothea was busy in the cultural and political life of the city she loved. But her parents were elderly and infirm, she was now forty, and the idea of marriage was fading. It was with a renewed sense of purpose, and perhaps a little resignation, that she committed herself to friendship and artistic pursuits.

Chapter 16

Sorrow and Sanctuary

Dorothea was to experience a year of great highs and lows in 1926. She would publish a fourth collection of poetry, and she would lose her beloved father. January began with little fanfare. The *Sydney Morning Herald* welcomed the New Year with a list of the privileges the citizens of Australia enjoyed, pondering how far the young nation had come in the past hundred years. With a population passing one million, Sydney was the 'queen city of a great dominion' whose good fortune was greater than the people of any other country in the world. As was typical of the period, the newspaper ignored the hardships faced by Indigenous and non-white Australians, smugly applauding a predominantly Anglo Australia that had 'no colour problem': 'We are free from the anxieties which afflict other nations. Poverty in the European sense of the term does not exist here. We have no unassimilable racial element, no colour problem, no serious unemployment. We have a continent to fashion as we will, and a healthy, vigorous people to address itself to the inspiring task.'[1]

Dorothea had been working assiduously towards the release of her new collection of poetry. Published by Angus & Robertson, *Fancy Dress* was highly anticipated by a public who still considered Dorothea one of their greatest poets. After publication, an article in the *Sunday Times* was somewhat cool in its critique, claiming the poems were not great soulful verses worthy of her skills, but speculating that her best work was yet to come: 'She gives us the idea of ever seeking for the unattainable, groping for something we cannot find. Her soul is a blind thing, striving vainly to snatch at the gems of verse scattered abroad. So, we have her to be proud of and esteem as one of our poets to come.'[2]

The death of her beloved father Charles on 14 July, aged eighty-one, was a huge loss. He had only officially retired the previous year, but his dementia had taken hold, and, towards the end, the family had made the decision to physically restrain him to ensure he was not a danger to himself. It was an undignified end for an extraordinary man. The obituaries that appeared in newspapers in Australia and overseas were extravagant in their praise of a man who had served the public in his capacity as physician, politician and statesman. Presiding at his funeral, first at Rosemont and then at Waverley Cemetery, Canon William Langley of St Andrew's Cathedral said Sir Charles 'would be remembered as a man who had served his country well. He had realised that the fundamental problem of the State was the problem of the child. His work on behalf of the children had been a great one – a lasting one also – and they would realise, perhaps even more fully in the future what the citizen really owed to him.'[3] The *Medical Journal of Australia* obituary was full of admiration:

Courage, determination to fight for a righteous cause, wide vision and sound judgement and unequalled honesty of purpose, these were the attributes that made Charles Kinnaird Mackellar a great man. His eminence was as a sociologist, but throughout his public life his actions and aspirations were tinctured by his medical knowledge and by his understanding of human beings.[4]

The *Sydney Morning Herald* described him as 'one of the most prominent of Australian public men. He has left behind him a record of work that has placed the people of this State and Commonwealth under a lasting debt of gratitude to him. Apart from that, his pleasant personality and gentle nature endeared him to a wide circle of friends.'[5]

On 18 July 1926, Dorothea received a sympathy letter from Brother Wilbred – a teacher at St Joseph's College, Hunters Hill – an acquaintance of hers who was a great supporter of Australian literature and Australian writers. He described visiting the location of Charles's final resting place at Waverley Cemetery:

> The grave is beautifully situated within the sound of what always seems to be the eternal requiem the waves are chanting for the dead, on the rocky keyboard below that wonderful graveyard. I always fancy when I find myself alone in this strangely beautiful place of rest that I can see the souls of the dead from this high sloping ground overlooking the sea, watching season on season, age after age for the first flush of the Great Dawn, sweeping over that blue rim of water, and to hear the trumpet peal of the Angels calling them to rise again.

Although Charles's later work saw him embracing some of the dangerous tenets of eugenics which are objectionable today, it is impossible to ignore his considerable achievements. He improved the lives of women through progressive legislation and was responsible for groundbreaking programs in the area of paediatric mental health. For Dorothea, he was a doting father who was protective of her but also gave his only daughter an unusual amount of freedom for a woman of that time. The lack of grandchildren from any of his offspring would likely have been a disappointment to Charles and Marion, and particularly sad for a man who spent so much of his life working to improve the care of vulnerable children.

In the aftermath of her father's death, Dorothea was again looking for an opportunity to escape the city and find refuge in the bush. The previous year, she had purchased three blocks of land at Lovett Bay at Pittwater on Sydney's northern beaches, an area she had visited many times. The property had more than ten acres of land, with a waterfront stretch of more than 250 yards, and was a short boat trip from Church Point. She engaged renowned architect William Hardy Wilson to design her a summer house, which she would call Tarrangaua – possibly an Indigenous word meaning high, rough hill, although the etymology is unclear.[6] Hardy Wilson designed a four-bedroom brick bungalow with a colonnaded verandah, and construction took place over the summer of 1925–1926. The property was later described by author Susan Duncan in her memoir *The House at Salvation Creek* as 'a solid, quietly authoritative house – stately even – made of bricks and terracotta tiles and surrounded on three sides by a gracious verandah'.[7]

When Tarrangaua was finished, Dorothea and Ruth enjoyed spending time at the idyllic waterfront setting. They loved going to Newport to swim in the surf and, later, Dorothea described picking billy cans of ripe blackberries and taking some home to be made into jam. As Howley wrote: 'This was in the days when Palm Beach was what its name implies, with palms growing to the edge of the sand.'[8]

Dorothea, who was now forty-one, single and wealthy, enjoyed having a retreat of her own. She was able to leave her mother for longer periods to be cared for by the staff they still retained, including a housekeeper, a cook and a driver. She was grateful for her own space, for solitude and for nature, enabling her to read and write and swim and walk. She continued to meet her literary and charitable commitments, but she loved to withdraw to Tarrangaua, which was surrounded by bushland with towering native trees and an abundance of flora and fauna. The house at Pittwater was adjacent to the home of Dr Donald Fraser, a prominent psychologist and family friend to Dorothea. It was the perfect place to call her own.

Her reputation was continuing to grow and there was rarely an article about Australian literature and, in particular, Australian poetry, that did not include Dorothea. Often, she was the only woman mentioned in the company of the best-known male Australian poets of the first hundred years of the country's literary history: Adam Lindsay Gordon, Henry Kendall, George Essex Evans, Henry Lawson, Banjo Paterson, Will Ogilvie and C.J. Dennis. Including her in this group, an article in July quoted Dorothea's poem 'In a Southern Garden', claiming she caught 'colour from the moonbeams, dancing on the waters of the harbour, and heard the heartbeat of the earth':

When the tall bamboos are clicking to the restless little breeze,
And bats begin their jerky skimming flight,

And the creamy scented blossoms of the dark pittosporum trees,
Grow sweeter with the coming of the night.[9]

In January 1927, further reviews of *Fancy Dress* were published and the comparison of her later work with her most famous poem continued. An article in *The Queenslander* suggested her latest effort was uneven:

> Her poem 'My Country' is known, or ought to be known by every Australian schoolboy, but that is but one of her many gems. All are not of the same high standard as some of her earlier verse, but there is not a poem in the book that any lover of poetry would say could have been omitted from a Dorothea Mackellar collection.[10]

A profile published in the *Daily Telegraph* in March 1927 described her life at Rosemont, and foreshadowed the stalling of Dorothea's literary career. The author of the article commented that the poet's time was now taken up with 'family concerns' and she was 'content, with the exception of odd verse publications, to leave writing for the time being in the background'.[11] At forty-one, she could have rightly expected to have several decades of writing left. She was not quite over the hill yet. And while her mother was dependent on her, she was not without home help.

At the time of the journalist's visit, Dorothea was busy packing for her next trip to England. Her mother was accompanying her, and they intended to be away for a year or more, remaining in England until the autumn, and then going south to Italy. Before leaving for Europe, Dorothea consulted an astrologer, eager to look for new beginnings. The note provided by the astrologer after a reading of her horoscope described her, unsurprisingly, in general terms. It touched on aspects of her personality that purported to explain her creative energy, her desire for autonomy and escape, her fears and self-doubt. It alluded to her 'ragged nerves', and the soothing effect time spent communing with nature had on her. A prediction of a marriage blossoming was oddly specific: 'Marriage under ideal conditions awaits you in Rangoon or Calcutta. Both places show up with brilliant success and such wonderfully bright conditions. Make for India as soon as you like, it's the right spot for you alright and holds all that life calls sweet in the realm of social success and romance.'[12] Whether Dorothea was seeking guidance on her romantic life is unclear, but what the horoscope foretold was not to be. She did not heed the advice to travel to India, and instead continued with her plans to go back to England with her mother.

Dorothea and Marion left Sydney on 22 March 1927, on a hot muggy day, aboard the ship *Cathay*. On the following day, Dorothea wrote that there was a stiff southerly and the empty *Cathay* tossed like a cork. Two days later they reached Hobart in 'a cloud of comely seagulls, wings black tipped with feet of coral', and spent a couple of days entertaining friends both on and off the ship. Dorothea was excited to see 'one of the best rainbows in my large collection. Triple, amazingly. In the first bow there were seven clear colors, in the second five and a broad tri-color band on the outside. Sails indescribably limpid greens and mauves'.

On Sunday, the ship reached Melbourne in the midst of a grey wintry wind, and by the time they were leaving two days later Dorothea was already feeling ill. 'The ship was crammed even more tightly with noisy flower laden people than it had been in Sydney. Heaps of new passengers. Two slim pale small pretty girls . . . among others,' she wrote. On 30 March, the ship reached Adelaide and then sailed on to Fremantle. Dorothea had caught a cold and went to bed for the next two days.

Back in Sydney, Ruth had her own illness to deal with. On 31 March, she had checked into St Vincent's Private Hospital in Sydney to undergo a hysterectomy, waiting until Dorothea was at sea before writing to her, wanting to spare her the worry of the surgery. She addressed her affectionately as 'My Darling Polly', a pet name for her and short for the exuberant and optimistic Pollyanna of Eleanor Porter's 1913 eponymous novel. By now Ruth was in her mid-forties and the option of having children had passed her by. The lack of understanding surrounding women's health was apparent in Ruth's explanation: 'It means the removal of the uterus, but nothing else, and they both swore it makes no difference to one's mental development – removing everything might in a quite young woman but not as things are.' She wrote again on 9 April, sending the letter ahead to London, her casual tone undermining the seriousness of the surgery and her ill health:

> My dearest Polly, they don't know how I got through my life to date. Won't it be lovely if I really should be strong now? Only I'm afraid I'll get fat. I could do with a kiss or two from my Polly Ann, I could, and I shall miss your visits frightfully from now on, but all the same I'm glad you're missing this.

In a letter on 12 April, Ruth bemoaned the fact that she had not felt well enough to think about the lives of their play people, but she hoped to 'have a little turn with them all this week'.

When the Mackellars reached Colombo, Sri Lanka, Dorothea and her mother went for a long, peaceful drive 'through the colored streets with poincianas in their glory and everything green as a salad and hot as a curry. Smell of coconut oil, anise, vanilla and humanity. I do like it,' Dorothea wrote. Back on the boat, she noted that a younger crowd had joined the ship, which was a pleasant distraction. 'There are many nice young creatures on board, Doreen Hordern [of the Hordern retail family] in particular, and Jean Anderson, an 18-year-old cousin of the Horderns, is as pretty as any magazine cover that was ever painted. They are very nice to me, all of them, but they make me feel like the Hag of Beare – older than the world.' After sailing on to Egypt, Dorothea wrote of a musical encounter which beautifully demonstrated her sensitive, romantic nature, but also the intense interest others seemed to find in her. She told the story of a man from Port Sudan who came on board whenever a ship docked to take advantage of its grand piano:

> I listened to an hour or more and the music called and deepened, questioned and begged. Also, I called myself a self-conscious middle-aged idiot and walked out towards the forward stairs and bed. The music stopped in two rather abrupt chords and a swift step followed. I didn't look round 'til the young voice said, 'Oh aren't you going to say goodnight?' So, we had a brief conversation since it is a mistake not to be human and its name was Boxall. A curious little episode. He must have been very lonely – but I'm not his sort . . .

By Tuesday 26 April, the ship had reached the Mediterranean Sea on its way to Marseille. They slid past Crete and it was evening when they approached Sicily, and by the following Monday they had reached Algiers, where Dorothea and Marion went ashore:

> It's rather a lovely city piled up white and cubical from the water's edge. We simply drove round and up the hill, not going into the carpet factory or any of the other places where passengers were congregating. The Old Town was fascinating with alluring views down steep narrow flights of stairs, onyx with sun and shade – the garments of the people, mainly white, but there was a good deal of dull orange with occasional patches of emerald green. Most satisfying against all white houses with faded green shutters.

At last, on Friday 6 May, the *Cathay* sailed into Plymouth and Dorothea revealed in her diary her enduring attachment to the country in which she had spent so much of her time. 'England came nearer and nearer and it was so lovely, so lovable, so utterly unlike any other country in the world that I found myself crying.' It was late afternoon when they landed, and stiflingly hot. After they had finished with customs they went directly to their hotel and afterwards wandered the streets, where they saw warships moored in the harbour and black against the sunset,

> and the memorials to the officers and men from these parts who lost their lives in the war. A huge and simple thing with low bronze reliefs round the base and a staggering, heartrending total of names. There were people walking with dogs, there were sailors with girls filling every corner of the sheltered lookouts and entirely unabashed. It's something to do with salt in the blood. There was a lovely young moon.

The next day they took the train to London, where they met Mac and Enid, who had arrived ahead of them and accompanied the new arrivals to their accommodation at the Welbeck Palace Hotel. Dorothea had lost her voice, so she went directly to her room: 'laid on my bed in brilliant sunshine and tried to realise being in London again'. Soon after, she and Marion moved to more long-term accommodation in a flat which had a view of Kensington Gardens.

Dorothea planned to attend the PEN Club conference in Brussels in June of that year at the invitation of PEN's founder, novelist Catherine Dawson Scott. Founded in London in 1921, its charter enshrined the belief that literature should be shared among nations regardless of political or international conflicts. Members supported freedom of expression and were committed to opposing race, class and national hatreds. They believed works of art and libraries should be untouchable even in wartime. Its first president was novelist John Galsworthy, and early members included literary heavyweights J.M. Barrie, G.K. Chesterton, Rebecca West, Robert Frost, H.G. Wells, Joseph Conrad and George Bernard Shaw. Dorothea hoped to establish a branch of PEN in Australia when she returned. Dawson Scott was well connected, having earlier formed the Tomorrow Club. She invited literary agents and editors to the weekly gathering to give young writers the opportunity to network.

Around this time, Dorothea came under friendly fire in the form of a series of ambivalent reviews by her contemporary, Zora Cross. Cross was a poet who had published a book of love sonnets in 1917 which were sensationally erotic for the times. She and Dorothea were known to each other and moved in the same circles, even if it could not be said that they were close friends. On 9 March 1927, Cross wrote a review under the pen name Bernice May, her middle names. She observed that 'one is always more or less rewarded when one reads any verse written by Miss Mackellar, even though sometimes the matter is slight and the treatment loose' – a statement that must have stung.[13] Later the same year, Cross doubled down when writing an article for the *Australian Women's Mirror*. The review was based on an interview conducted via letters between the two women, and began pleasantly enough:

> 'I was born at Rose Bay and one of my first memories was the South Head lighthouse fingering through the blue dark.' So writes Dorothea Mackellar to me from distant London recalling perhaps her very earliest recollection of Sydney, the city about which she has so often written with such wealth of lovely colour . . . I do not think that even Henry Lawson saw Australia in truer colour than Dorothea Mackellar . . . Several books have been published by her, but none that gave lovers of poetry quite the same thrill as the first little book. Australia, waiting for so long to find one who loved and saw her in all the browns and blues and golds and greens of her shimmering beauty, had got what she wanted at last, a singer who understood, and a woman.[14]

Cross then described how she was permitted to look into an old exercise book from Dorothea's schooldays – 'a precious possession held by a dear friend', presumably Ruth, although she is not named. It was crammed with beautiful verses.

'Why did she never publish these?' Cross asked.

'Oh, but she had many, many,' replied the friend. 'She just gave me this because I wanted it.'[15]

Cross quoted a letter from Dorothea in which she explained that writing had always been part of her life and poetry the most important form of all: 'Poetry was there from the beginning, and poetry appeared at an early age. I hope no one takes my fiction seriously because it was only done for fun; and my published novels must on no account be regarded as serious work.' But such remarks apparently irked Cross, who felt that her fellow poet lacked ambition, and had not made the best use of her skills – especially considering her talent, and the experience she had in travelling the world. 'With the material she had at her fingertips, I wonder why Miss Mackellar does not take fiction seriously. But the muse is an exquisite companion at her side, and one would not like to disturb it,' she wrote. 'I remember turning to a friend once after reading "Burning Off", one of the finest bush poems she had written, and saying, "This writer lived this"'. Cross's article was full of slightly backhanded praise, and had the sum effect of pronouncing Dorothea, in modern terminology, a 'one-hit wonder'. Cross wrote that Dorothea had influenced Australian poetry 'a good deal', but she also reproduced another critic's comment: that 'My Country' would hand Dorothea down to posterity as 'a one-poem singer'.

And there it was: the judgement Dorothea had been battling since the poem was first published in 1908. She loved that 'My Country' had been embraced by most Australians and, after the war, had become an anthem for the nation. It had afforded her great affection and recognition and made her a household name. And yet it constrained her. She could not move on from it no matter how hard she tried. Every poem she wrote was measured against it. Every emotion poured onto the page paled in comparison, according to critics, with the passion she had conjured in her original ode to the unique Australian landscape. Dorothea might have been poised to embark on one of the most productive periods of her writing career; she had fewer family responsibilities following the death of her father and she had a retreat at Lovett Bay which gave her all the seclusion and access to nature she craved. But in her early forties, having weathered the storm of early adulation, the societal pressure for upper-class women to spurn a career in favour of marriage, and a world war which changed people's perception of women writers, she could not seem to harness the creative energy she might otherwise have found in her new circumstances. Her health issues continued and were increasingly kept at bay with medication – and brandy.

In November 1927, Mac, who had returned to Australia, wrote to his sister in London, commenting on eleven months of 'dire' drought conditions in Gunnedah. He was optimistic that recent rain might provide enough grazing for the sheep before the lease on extra land for feed was finished. However, frustration with farm life in the middle of an extended drought was evident:

> There have been a great number of property sales in this district, mostly to Southerners, during the past year or so and very few of the old hands are left. And if one of these Victorian millionaires comes smelling round, with the bags

of money, the big cigar and the watch chain, which we see pictured in the Bolshie newspapers, I know another property that is likely to change hands too.
Your loving brother,
Mac.

And if such missives caused Dorothea to long for her homeland, it was clear that Australia was also feeling the absence of its pre-eminent woman poet. On 12 November, a small article appeared in the *Telegraph* in Brisbane commenting on Dorothea's continued stay in England:

> Miss Dorothea Mackellar, whose verses on Australia have placed her amongst the poets of her native land is at present living in England. A daughter of the late Sir Charles Mackellar, she has the gentle spiritual personality of some poetess of mid-Victorian days. Unhurried by the stress of modern life, happy circumstances place her in a position to write when she feels inclined. Several English newspapers have favourably commented on her Australian verse.[16]

But the poet had no intention of returning just yet. The year 1928 saw Dorothea and her mother continuing their extended European sojourn, which would last almost three years. Perhaps Charles's death the year before had left such a huge void that the distraction of travel was a welcome balm. While travelling alone through northern Europe, Dorothea received news from her mother in London that Eric had married after what appeared to have been a whirlwind romance. Neither of them had heard of his new wife, Ann, but letters soon arrived from Australia explaining she was a barmaid who, no doubt, had made Eric's acquaintance at one of his many long days and nights drinking in hotels. Both women were stunned. Eric had always been unlucky in love, but they were happy to concede that he might find some happiness with this woman, and they may even have been a little relieved that someone else might bear some responsibility for his wellbeing.

By March, Marion had joined Dorothea in Italy, enjoying a day trip to Tivoli, outside Rome. 'San Antonio is a dear old monastery with one of the loveliest views in the world,' Dorothea wrote. Named after Saint Antonio of Padua, the house was built over a Roman villa believed to have belonged to the poet Horace from about 60 BC. The windows looked over a deep ravine with a thunderous waterfall on the other side. In a golden sunset, they arrived in Perugia, a rose-red city of Etruscan walls. When they awoke the next day and looked out from the 'eyrie' in their hotel, everything was covered with snow. That day, Dorothea and Marion motored to Assisi through the gentle Umbrian landscape. They first visited Santa Maria Degli Angeli, just outside the town, the mother church of the Franciscan order. 'Indeed, we are *molto, molto felici* for we tread where San Francisco's feet have trod – and this in the very place where the order was born.' They walked through the dusk to the Quarter of the Ivory Gate, where a piazza with a 'mad, little, black, steep medieval street twists down, overlooked by sinister houses – the street of the witches! Not one, but a coven?' Dorothea wondered in her diary.

On a Sunday drive several days later, they travelled across Tuscany – through masses of spring flowers, including buttercups and hyacinths – to Siena. Dorothea wrote: 'We loved it and its narrow streets with wrought iron rings in the great palace walls and our own palatial rooms looking out over such a roofscape.' Eventually, they moved on to San Gimignano, 'the city of thirteen fair towers', where they wandered over the noble, beautiful Palazzo Comunale, also known as the Sala di Dante – poet and philosopher Dante Alighieri had once stood there and made a speech to the people in the square below.

In the following week they journeyed on to Florence and then to Milan. The beautiful scenery was juxtaposed against a 'tense hush' in the city where an act of shocking political violence had just been committed. That day, there had been an attempt to assassinate King Victor Emmanuel III. The bomb, placed in a lamppost, was exploded by 'clockwork'. It was reported that seventeen people – mostly women and children – were killed, but the king was ten minutes late 'delayed by the cheering crowds'. At the same time, Prime Minister Benito Mussolini also had a narrow escape from death. A powerful bomb was discovered on a railway line near Como, over which Mussolini was due to pass on his return to Rome.[17]

Dorothea's diary described a frenetic but fabulous few weeks travelling from Milan to Lake Como and on to Lugano and Lucerne in Switzerland and then to Paris, where the finest glassmaker of the day could tempt a tired Dorothea into shopping: 'Mother was inclined for galleries and I wasn't up to them. But we did go to Lalique's shop.' By the end of April – with their suitcases presumably stuffed with holiday purchases – the women were back in London.

A letter from Ruth – who was staying at the Magellan hotel in Paris, but soon to arrive in London herself – anticipated their reunion:

Oh, my darling Polly, aren't I just excited too! I've been writing letters on meeting you all day and when I came up after dinner . . . there was yours poked under the door. I haven't got you any present, my Pussy! As I didn't know what to get when you've just been to all these places yourself. You'll only get me.

Chapter 17

Of Kings and Trolls

Taking a series of small planes, Dorothea flew to Norway up the west coast of continental Europe, an incredibly brave journey considering the precarious safety of the fledgling aviation industry. On the novel experience of flying, Dorothea wrote: 'Cars looked as small as ladybirds and it was marvellous that one could still distinguish chickens. There are discreet little paper bags for air sickness, also maps (very thoughtful) and cotton wool pads.' She was attending a meeting of the International PEN club in June 1928, still intending to form an Australian chapter. Flying first to Calais and then up the coast of Belgium, she landed at Rotterdam, before journeying on to Amsterdam. Dorothea finally arrived in Oslo in the late afternoon, and English writer and PEN co-founder Catherine 'Sappho' Dawson Scott turned up at her hotel. Sappho had earned her pet name after publishing a poem of the same name in 1889. She came and sat with Dorothea and they talked into the evening.

The northern air seemed to agree with Dorothea, and she found she could manage with very little sleep. She went motoring by fjords and through lovely birch woods and lunched or dined with 'pleasant people in fascinating houses'. On Monday, Dorothea and other representatives from PEN had an audience with Norway's King Haakon VII: 'It was interesting to notice people's reactions. I, being Australian went up first with America and South Africa who spent the whole time explaining that they were not impressed, bless their anxious republican hearts.' Later that evening, there was a party with bonfires at the fjord's edge in a rambling garden. 'Millions of sparks floating up to a powder blue sky. It never got dark all night,' Dorothea wrote. In a museum, they saw the gold and jewels that belonged to the Viking Queen who had been buried in a ship. 'And most luxurious of all, her wheeled carriage! Delicately carved, walrus ivory and jewels from Byzantine.'

The PEN group left several days later on a train trip to Lillehammer and the open-air museum town of Maihuagen, where people had 'put on their beautiful old costumes and were inhabiting the old houses', in the manner, Dorothea noted, of Henrik Ibsen's plays. The players staged a wedding and, as the bride and groom came out of the door of the one hundred-year-old church with a fiddler playing old, delicate folk music, the scene was so beautiful that Dorothea wept. The wedding party and its followers wound along the upper path below the tall birch trees and were reflected in the lake. The bride in her gold wreath and all the following throng were hand in hand. They dined at the parsonage and went up the hill 'through soft silver-blue dark'. The birch log fires were lit and smoke curled through the roof holes, and there was folk dancing and soft singing. Dorothea was sitting next to a Norwegian woman, Dagmar Kirkwood, who was married to an American. Dorothea commented that it was an environment where one might see a troll, her imagination fired by the evocative scenes they had witnessed all day: 'I've never seen one,' Kirkwood said seriously, 'but my mother did when she was a little girl.' She then relayed an astonishing story:

> Mother was staying with an aunt on the mountain when she was about 10. It was a lonely house – only one path led to it and that went to the village. And one day a strange old woman came in. My mother's aunt wanted her to take something, if it was only a cup of milk, for it is a custom in this country, not to let anyone go from the house without eating or drinking. But the old woman wouldn't. She would only mutter 'No, no there is trouble in this house.' And my aunt said, 'Then where will you go? It is far to the village.' And the old woman said, 'I go back to my own people in the mountains.' When she turned to go, mother saw that she had a tail.

'Had a what?' Dorothea gasped.

'A tail. A short, thick tail,' the woman confirmed, continuing, 'So they knew all wasn't quite right. And she didn't go down the road at all, she went straight into the thick woods and on to the mountains.'

Back in Oslo, far from the woods and tales of trolls, Dorothea attended a dinner in the Queen's Restaurant looking out over the fjord. 'The midsummer evening was full of light and colour rather like Sydney Harbour on an autumn afternoon, ferryboats criss-crossing, rowing eights in scarlet and white flashing past over the green water; and in the distance, on a wooded slope, pleasant pale houses gilded in the late sun's rays.' She described her dinner companions with journalistic flair:

> Sappho Scott, 60, novelist, peasant housewife (as she says) with a strong dash of gypsy. Barbra Ring, novelist, rather younger, white haired with a worn, pink face and gay, blue eyes acquainted with tears … an atmosphere of youth unquenched. [Pieter] Boutens, an old Dutch poet like a sick, white eagle and Hermon Ould, playwright; dark, friendly, sensitive and unattached.

Early the next morning, Dorothea left for Stockholm. 'Sweden, at first sight isn't so romantic-looking as Norway, flat but full of lakes and birch woods. The wooden farmhouses black or dark red. They must look rather lovely in the snow.' She had arrived in time for Midsummer Eve. There was dancing around a maypole with people in the costumes of various provinces. The horses and the bonnets of the cars in the town were decorated with birch boughs. She described crossing one of the bridges and realising that Stockholm was 'as shot through with the sea as Sydney and much more bridges'.

By 1 July, Dorothea had flown back to London, but was reliving the discomfort of the trip in her diaries: 'Nine hours flying against a strong head wind, a forced landing and a struggle home by train and boat and train with hours of waiting and surly people and no food for twenty-two hours except one cup of coffee.' Ruth came to visit in the afternoon for her birthday. 'It turned heavenly

hot, hot enough to wear thin dresses in the street without a coat. We went to some theatre and saw various friends and lovers,' Dorothea wrote. Meanwhile, Eric and his new wife, Ann, were on their way to London. When they arrived later that month, Dorothea heartily approved of her brother's new bride: 'Ann is a dear and utterly lovable.'

Dorothea continued sending poetry to newspapers and journals, and some of her poems were even picked up in other countries, including 'The Waiting Life', which was published by the *Cape Argus* in South Africa in July of that year. Her global reach and popularity in English-speaking countries was quite extraordinary. That poem does not appear in any of her collections, but it does appear in one of her manuscript verse books from some years earlier. It is prescient, considering her growing creative paralysis and her continued, somewhat frenetic need for distraction:

Since it befell, with work and strife
I had not time to live my life;
I turned away from it until
Work should be done and strife be still.
My hands and head for use are free,
Nor does my own life worry me,
But docile as a spaniel waits
Until this present stress abates.
Tranquil it breathes, and waits, I know,
With all its joy contained. But oh,
I hope when I have time to play
My life will not have run away![1]

Perhaps in hope of finding such 'time to play', Dorothea left for a trip to Scotland in August. She set off after breakfast in a chauffeur-driven car, visiting the towns of Trossachs, on the fringe of the Scottish Highlands, and Stirling and Perth. 'Stirling's beautiful lion-like on its hill, grey against the pale sky. A wonderful castle and a fascinating old church that has been split in two for 300 years. Some want to unite it again.' Another day was spent at Dunblane, before travelling down to Edinburgh. Her family ties to Scotland remained as strong as she had expressed them in her poem, 'Another Heritage', which detailed her attachment to the land and her ancestors only three generations earlier:

> Not long ago,
> Only three lives ago—
> It is too little for a soul's forgetting.
> Mountain and sea
> Are magic food to me
> Since I have known them in another setting.[2]

Not able to stay away from that 'grim and lovely land', Dorothea made a second visit to Scotland in October, this time to stay with Meg and Hugh Scarlett, who had moved there. She was thrilled to be travelling through the night in a storm while she felt safe and luxurious in her train carriage. It was still pouring with rain when she reached Inverloch, where her friends welcomed her warmly. 'The surroundings also are most beautiful, right under Ben Nevis who wears a perpetual, though shifting, snow cap. And there's an exquisite view to the northwest over the loch towards the mountains of Skye.'

Back in London, Dorothea had much to distract her. She was looking forward to seeing her friend Mela Koehler, who she described as being 'very attractive and one wanted to see a lot of her'. Mela was an Austrian artist Dorothea had met before the war and she remained a faithful pen pal. She worked as a freelance artist designing whimsical postcards and fashion illustrations which would eventually be coveted by collectors. She was delightful company but frequently asked both Dorothea and Ruth for money when unable to sell her designs, or when her husband could not work, apparently suffering from depression. Dorothea often donated clothes she no longer wore to Mela, and she and Ruth were her patrons for many years. On this occasion, Mela spent an evening sketching Dorothea after promising Ruth she would complete a portrait of her. 'It was a nice month full of friends but agitating,' Dorothea wrote. Ruth was subsidising their friend's visit to England, and Dorothea was lending her assistance too, as a letter from Mela reveals:

What an exciting thing, Ruth told me I may stay another week more in London. Isn't that lovely! Oh, I have to meet some more people. What fun! Dorothea, I have got another news from Ruth – now I know – you have not only made me such beautiful presents you were helping Ruth to let Mela coming over in a most generous way.

Several months later, Mela would write to Dorothea from Vienna, explaining just how vital their support had been. She had illustrated Ruth's poetry collection for children, *Fairies and Fancies*, which was to be published that year, and their collaboration had come to an end. The shocking letter revealed Mela had earlier been contemplating suicide before Ruth and Dorothea intervened with financial support:

> Now I can confess just before Ruth wrote I can come over, I wished to make an end with me. You all have now some rights on me. You have recreated Mela Kohler. I came to think how very strange it seems that in the very last moment some mysterious hand has time for one of the millions of souls, to find friends to help and gives you and Ruth the parts of leading ladies.

Undoubtedly, Dorothea would have been touched by the young woman's words, for she herself knew the importance of friendship and support for a woman leading an artistic life.

One November evening, she drove through 'a thick yellow fog' on her way to attend a PEN dinner in celebration of the Russian writer Leo Tolstoy. She found the event amusing and was surprised to find herself at the 'A' table. 'I suspect it was because Hermon Ould knew I understood French,' she surmised. She kept up with the literary crowd as the year drew rapidly to a close, and soon Dorothea was enjoying the festive season with 'last shopping in ever more feverishly Christmassy streets'. She and Marion went to church on Christmas Day and had dinner with Eric, Ann and Ruth. Eric and Ann were soon leaving for Europe, and she hated saying goodbye.

Her diary at this time mentions a suitor named Charles, although his name is recorded in code, despite the fact that she was now a grown woman of forty-three years old – surely there was no longer a need to be secretive? And yet, she admits to consistently omitting any mention of Charles 'over the past few months and yet he is such a dear and I am seeing a lot of him and taking comfort from his great outspokenness. For once I did say the right thing at the right time and there has been no more trouble'. Perhaps she was being more forthright about not wanting to commit to a long-term relationship, having learned the consequences from her experiences with earlier suitors. In any case, it seemed that Dorothea was now firmly committed to the single life.

∾

In January 1929, Dorothea and Marion were on the move again, leaving from Southampton for a cruise around the Caribbean. Dorothea complained that the *Athenia*, a large ship, was 'crammed' and though there were 'many pleasant people' aboard, she confessed: 'I feel that I dislike the whole human race'. On Wednesday 30 January, the ship made port at Barbados:

> Barbados is low and windswept and surprisingly pale at first sight, the grass not sunburnt as in an Australian summer, but sun-bleached. You land in launches and the first sight that strikes you is black women moving with a long free stride, carrying trays of yellow bananas or bundles of washing or even small paper parcels, the size of oranges on their heads. Some of the older ones wear vivid bandannas knotted about the said heads, and, beautifully, this fashion suits them. Many wear white handkerchiefs but the young girls do their best to be standardized in long waisted frocks, pink cotton stockings and floppy hats.

They drove through Bridgetown and out to the Marine Hotel past bungalows with pink-washed walls and covered with crimson bougainvillea. She described the houses as 'weathered wooden boxes with open shutters (no glass in the windows, naturally) and innumerable babies all, like their parents, with outstretched palms'. She wrote plainly about what she saw, but without any self-consciousness about how her privilege set her apart from the scenes of poverty that she encountered only as a detached observer.

By dawn the next day, the ship was sliding through the Bocas del Dragón, or 'Dragon's Mouths', a series of straits separating islands with tall, jagged mountains approaching Trinidad. Once ashore, Dorothea and Marion motored slowly towards Santa Cruz Mountain, alongside one huge plantation of cocoa and rubber. Dorothea described the colour of the cocoa pods as varying from shades of green through orange to crimson, bright magenta and pink. They went to the Queensland Hotel and visited the markets. 'I bought some Japanese parasols for Mother because she minds the sun and changed a five-pound note for fat gold American double eagles.'

After arriving in Jamaica and going ashore, Dorothea and Marion walked in the gardens and lunched in an open dining room with no walls. Then away across the mountains and up to the hill station of Newcastle, where they stopped at a cigarette factory. Dorothea described watching machines rolling out cigarettes like 'long white worms at 400 a minute, chopping them quick as thought and spilling the imperfect ones in the waste with ruthless intelligence and then the allied cigar factory' with its 'barrels of scented tobacco, and heaps of leaf and they gave us souvenir cigars'.

Next stop was Nassau in the Bahamas, where the water was 'that enchanting opal colour that coral lends it – aquamarine and pale emerald'. Dorothea and Marion sailed out to the sea gardens in glass-bottomed boats 'poised like sea birds all about the harbour'. She saw the ocean floor beneath her, 'sown with golden clumps and mauve and lilac fans of coral, coloured fish dart through, and blue and orange angel fish, striped ones, blue and silver, spotted and barred with vermillion and azure'. Afterwards, they took lunch at the New Colonial Hotel, where they enjoyed the view of the sea from the terrace: 'There are many wrecks. It's easy to imagine pirates here,' she wrote.

The ship carrying Dorothea and Marion arrived back at Southampton on a bitterly cold February day with the ground, as they disembarked, covered in snow. Marion was feeling a little under the weather, but when they made it back to their hotel, she and Dorothea found a large pile of letters waiting for them. As Dorothea eagerly read news from home, she heard a little sound from her mother, who then came stumbling towards her. There was a letter from a family friend bringing the shocking news that Eric's new bride, Ann, had died in Paris from heart failure.

'Oh, my poor boy!' Marion exclaimed. They read on to discover that Eric had already left aboard the *Orama* from Toulon to make his way home to Australia. It was too late to overtake him except by air to Port Said, but Marion wasn't well enough to travel and Dorothea could not leave her mother. They made the agonising decision to stay, and let Eric make the long journey home on his own. The women could not believe the tragic misfortune

Eric had suffered after finally finding some happiness. And they feared his grief could have a devastating effect on him.

A week later, Marion was well enough to take a shorter trip, and the women left for Vevey, Switzerland, where they ensconced themselves in the Hotel des Trois Couronnes. 'Mother has withstood the shock wonderfully and shows no sign of collapse,' Dorothea reported. Ruth arrived in Switzerland the following Tuesday night and the next day, Marion drove with her daughter to Montreux, and dropped her at the Beau Rivage where Ruth was staying. 'Plumface', as Dorothea had dubbed the chauffeur, drove Marion on to the Rhone Valley while she sat with 'Borge' – one of several nicknames she had for Ruth. Next morning, all three went for a drive through Bex and on to St Maurice, through the valley, 'over old bridges and green rushing glacier water, through little old towns, all with their wash places in the street underneath houses and steep lipped roofs and gay shutters painted in wriggly stripes of green and white or white, blue and orange'. The next few days were filled with gentle walks and Dorothea bought little pots of purple and gold crocuses for Marion, hoping to cheer her up. They sat on the terrace and watched the seagulls on the lake and the fish that quivered in the shallows:

> [For] days I thought them a mat of close growing dark green water weed. Thick, thick, thick and apparently about four inches deep. Through them weave silver gleams of a slightly larger fish with the effect of light glinting on a polished surface. If it is not the little dark ones showing a silver belly occasionally . . . Men sit patiently along the landing stages with rods and childish lines at frequent intervals. They draw these up with a silver tiddler attached but they never catch a

little dark mystery nor do the swans and coots and terns and greedy squealing gulls take any notice of them.

On 13 March, the two women called for Ruth and drove up the mountains, through pine forests and across great valleys, to Gruyere. Snow was piled high on the roadside and streams had only just melted. They drove through several little old towns, 'walled and twisty and the chalets grow more and more charming in the villages and beyond. Never have I seen shingling done in such exquisite delicate patterns on the roofs and gable ends. Even the wood-stacks were piled in patterned symmetry'.

By now it was Easter, and the weather was starting to improve. Dorothea described feeling less on edge as she slowly dealt with the shock of Ann's death. 'Ruth comes often but we don't go far afield. Beautiful pansies coming out in the hotel garden and the fat Swiss children beginning to discard their coats.' On Sunday 7 April, Ruth arrived at the hotel and she and Dorothea talked while the latter packed to continue her European tour with her mother, leaving her friend to return to London. 'I don't know if it's a good move but someone has to make the move . . . nerves,' Dorothea confided to her diary.

The next day, Dorothea and Marion travelled by train to Avignon in the Provence region of France. While Marion rested, Dorothea explored the town on foot, first walking along the Rue de la Republique, then to the Palace of the Popes beyond. 'Through grim medieval houses and near palaces of a squalid magnificence to the ramparts . . . the 14th century massiveness of the walls and southern, southern, southern men playing bowls in every dusty open space.' Over the next few days they visited Arles, Les Baux and St Remy before driving across the salt plains of the Camargue to Saintes-Maries-de-la-Mer, and a short distance further where 'the ancient city of Aigues Mortes appeared exquisite and melancholy in her perfection above the dead waters'.

That month, her poem 'Psyche's Wings' was published in the *Sydney Morning Herald*. It would be the last time any of her unpublished poems appeared in a newspaper or journal, although she continued to write poetry over the next decade and many of her older poems were reprinted. The inexorable rise of modernism was beginning to render her verses somewhat old-fashioned, even as she reached for greater naturalism and a certain degree of cynicism in poems like 'Psyche's Wings':

Prize them and love them, but never touch,
The moth-wing silver spoils if you clutch,
But still the test of loving's the giving,
And when you've learnt that you've earned your living
Earned your place as a small link shaking,
In the endless chain of our human making.
Lucky, if 'ere the soul has woken
The mind's not jaded, the heart broken.[3]

To a large extent, she had moved on from landscapes and whimsical mysticism and was in a more philosophical mood, still trying to make sense of the world and her place in it.

Dorothea and Marion were back in London in May 1929, and Dorothea and Ruth had just spent a week together. The intensity of their relationship as related in Ruth's letter – written the day after they parted – is undeniable:

> I hated getting out of the car and saying goodbye to you yesterday ... Thank you very, very much, my blessed Polly, for giving me such a lovely week. Apart from the joy of all the things we saw, the joy of being with you alone made the trip worthwhile!!! And it wasn't 'apart from' either, it was two joys inseparable and enhancing each other. I loved being with you, and our little acts, and all the things we saw. We'll never forget the apple trees. I love my little Worcester bowl what you gave me. A lot of love, from Borge.

The letter illuminates both the romantic sweep of their relationship in her 'hating to say goodbye', and the everyday intimacy embodied by the gift of 'the little Worcester bowl'. And, above all else, it expressed the joy of being together, 'inseparable and enhancing each other', as they would for many years to come.

Chapter 18

A Changed Country

When the *Otranto* left London for Sydney in early January 1930, Dorothea had mixed feelings about returning home after three years abroad. Her friend, Mela Koehler, had written to her in sympathy, saying: 'Poor darling Dorothea, I can imagine how you are feeling, leaving your heart, your poor suffering heart in England. You are strong, God help you and bless you and make life easier for your delicate soul.' Whether Mela's letter referred to another possible love interest or simply her sadness at leaving England itself remains unclear, but it must have been with a heavy heart that she boarded the ship.

Also onboard was Australian novelist and Nobel laureate in-the-making Patrick White. Just seventeen at the time, White was returning to Australia after an unhappy four years at Cheltenham College on the proviso he work on a farm in the Snowy Mountains that belonged to a friend of his father.[1] Although the youth was ostensibly in the care of the ship's purser, he was largely left to his own devices.

White would later tell his biographer David Marr that he regularly walked the ship's deck, a routine which he later gave to the protagonist of his novel *The Twyborn Affair*: 'It was his habit to walk the deck before its holy-stoning ... For miles he tramped up and down and around the corner. He would like to have thought it was exorcism whereas it was repetition: he was accompanied by the same dun-coloured, laden figures returning to the front line ...'[2] Aboard the *Otranto*, White pictured himself returning to the freedom and sensuality of childhood as described in his memoir, *Flaws in the Glass*; riding 'bare-back through girth-high tussock, stripping leeches from my body after a swim in a muddy creek, my solitary mooning through a forest of dripping sassafras towards the sound of the waterfall'.[3]

White also recalled being anxious to meet Dorothea: 'My Country' had captured his 'homesick imagination'.[4] A meeting was arranged, but White was less than impressed: 'She was drifting about in veils, pissed', he later told Marr.[5] Despite Eric's disastrous journey a decade earlier, when his incessant intoxication had caused mayhem for other passengers and much embarrassment for his sister, it seems that Dorothea, at times, also drank alcohol to excess, and this caught young White's attention.

Some years later, however, as a sign of mutual respect, White would write to Dorothea from aboard the RMS *Niagara*, off Auckland, thanking her for sending him a book plate – a fashionable literary gift of the times. He returned the favour by sending her one of his, along with an explanation of the illustration: 'Pleasure is embodied in the form of the Nymph and here we have pursuit of her by Man – the faun – while the Temple of Wisdom and Learning falls into decay through neglect.'

While White's star would continue to rise in the literary firmament, Dorothea's was showing the first signs of decline.

But in 1930, the reportedly 'pissed' Dorothea could perhaps be forgiven for hitting the bottle: she was sailing home to a country changed dramatically by the Wall Street Crash of the year before, and already sliding into the economic disaster yet to be named the Great Depression. Ahead of industrial unrest and the mass unemployment to come, the country was already facing coal strikes and a slump in wool prices. A *Canberra Times* editorial was pessimistic about the state of politics in New South Wales, stating that 'an election will take place in which the people will have to decide between a weak government who is endeavouring to do the best according to its lights, and an unruly and unimpressive opposition which is not deserving of popular confidence'.[6] Later in the year, as the Depression took hold, the National-Country Party coalition government was defeated by the Labor Party, led by colourful political figure Jack Lang.

Dorothea's return from her three-year trip overseas was considered notable by the national media, with numerous articles marking her arrival. The *Evening News* reported: 'Miss Mackellar said the sight of Sydney Harbor cheered her, and when the *Otranto* entered the Heads and she saw the foreshores bathed in the early sunlight, she confessed that she wanted to cry.'[7]

A lengthy puff piece on Dorothea's return also appeared in *The Sun*, waxing lyrical on the poet's refined appearance and future plans:

> She is a symphony in tortoiseshell, from her shingled head to her wide-open tawny eyes which hold yours for a fleeting

moment ... Her frock is golden, and she wears a magnificent waist-length string of graduated oval amber beads in tones ranging from gold to dark brown. That is a picture of Dorothea Mackellar home again in Sydney after three years abroad, and anxious to be off to her little cottage at Pittwater which she has thought of so often while away. Her winging thoughts clamour to be put on paper. 'I'm dying to get to work again,' she says. 'But I need quiet. At present ... my brain is simmering like a boiling kettle. And I don't know what will come out of that simmering.'[8]

Meanwhile, Ruth had been experiencing a particularly creative period of her own, with an article from the previous year noting she had lately contributed to *Punch* magazine and was 'now at work on a play, a novel and a volume of verse'.[9] Her book *Fairies and Fancies* had been published in late 1929 and was reviewed in a number of Australian newspapers, including the Hobart *Mercury*:

> Her rhymes are delicate and express the instinctive feeling of the child. She wanders in thought in and out of the world of reality and the result is very much like the untidy mind of the child, little bits of fairyland, little bits of life, mixed with little bits of everything under the sun.[10]

An article in *The Sun* a year later described how Ruth and her cousin Janet Stephen had visited Mela in Vienna and hatched the plan for the artist to illustrate Ruth's book of verses. It described the friendship formed between the women in a pension in Paris prior to the Great War and how thrilled they were to be reacquainted nearly two decades later:

> Then came Miss Koehler's visit to England, filled with many consultations with the poetess and her publishers. English flowers she knew not; so days were spent in the country fields, fields where she was able to make sketches of flowers and ferns and take specimens home for reference.[11]

Both Ruth and Dorothea's literary efforts remained noteworthy during this period, and another newspaper report mentioned that they were working together on a new novel, though it was never published – its title and subject matter lost to time.[12] It is possible it was the unpublished *Unbroken*, which had begun its life as a play appearing in Dorothea's notebooks. She wrote in her diary that she was adapting it as a manuscript for a novel, but there was no mention of a collaboration with Ruth, and no manuscript for it exists amongst her personal papers.

While Ruth's success over the years had been more modest than Dorothea's, she had been consistently writing articles, books, plays, poetry and lyrics as well as the two earlier novels co-written with her literary friend. Ruth had been a precocious child, with her first book – *Rhymes by Ruth* – published in 1896 when she was just fourteen years old. The same year, she had also written a play called *Pears' Soap* for a Benevolent Society Concert which was set to music. The *Daily Telegraph* described it as a 'laughable and bright little piece' which introduced the characters from the Pears advertising posters of the time:

The words of the play are all set to well-known airs and a dance and tableau were introduced in the last act, showing the Dirty Boy, Bubbles, the Pedlar etc. The play begins with a princess being disconsolate for the loss of a talisman, stolen by a witch. The Prince offers to search for it and after killing the witch (which is a capital scene) a spirit brings him the talisman which he finds is a cake of Pears' soap.[13]

It was the theatre and her experience in writing plays that was to come to the fore in Ruth's creative life at the start of the 1930s. Playwright and theatre producer Carrie Kelly, later Tennant, had launched the Community Playhouse in Darlinghurst in 1929 with the express purpose of nurturing the writing and production of Australian plays. She organised a monthly Australian authors' night where plays could be read or acted:

> It attracted an audience large enough to fill every seat in the little theatre. Two plays appeared on the programme, both by Miss Ruth Bedford; and Miss Bedford herself took part in the readings. One entitled *Postman's Knock* was in a lighter vein and the other, called *Fear*, developed a subtle psychological situation in sensitive and well-balanced blank verse.[14]

As Ruth waited for Dorothea to make her return to Sydney, she wrote to her about the reading of her plays at the Community Playhouse and how much she longed to see her friend:

> There was, surprisingly, quite a large audience, only nine of them my friends. The readers themselves liked the second play and want to act it. I think we'll do the play in May if

the theatre exists so long. Darling Polly, when am I going to see you? I don't like to be hanging about on your doormat, because presumably all your own family will be there, so I think I'd better just be at home with my hat ready and you riffle me up when you want me to come.

These Community Playhouse performances were a taste of things to come, with Ruth going on to produce many plays, including radio plays with the then Australian Broadcasting Commission. Only a year after her debut at the Community Playhouse, she was being celebrated for writing her first thriller, *Murder Next Door?*, a theatrical experience 'packed full of bloodshed, mystery and mirth':

> So powerful is the comic element, that members of the cast who are working hard to have it ready for a season at the Community Playhouse on May 26 still become hysterical at rehearsals . . . So exciting is the solving of the mystery that patrons are to be asked that on no account to disclose the solution to their friends who will be visiting the theatre.[15]

And while Ruth's theatrical career was gathering speed, Dorothea was in high demand as a guest speaker at various literary soirees and – while a somewhat reluctant public performer as she grew older – she held forth on a range of literary subjects that were close to her heart. She delivered speeches to admiring audiences, including a passionate plea against a proposed tax on international books, in which she concluded, 'and at this moment Australia decides to cut herself off from the rest of the world by taxing books which is to say by taxing the free flow of ideas'.[16]

In another piece, entitled 'The Art of Reading', she praised her friend Joseph Conrad:

> Some find him hard to read. Many others, some of them much more simple-minded, find him not only easy but glorious. There is a special place in Purgatory for those who lie about their preferences for snobbish reasons. If you don't like a really fine writer it is not your fault but your serious loss.[17]

Yet another essay found among her personal papers expressed her frustration at the portrayal of women in literature by male authors, whom she felt presented their female characters 'clad in some soft clinging stuff'. She went on to say that 'the man's heroine in general would be more convincing to women if male authors would not always speak of her as a thing apart. She suffers, as her living sisters do, from the fact that "man" is the term for the race as well as for a male member of it'.[18]

These essays – many of which were given as speeches – were never published as a collection, though they were reported on in the newspapers and several survive in her notebooks and papers. They reveal the depth of her love for and knowledge of literature, her repudiation of intellectual snobbery, and even her fledgeling feminism, offering up a surprisingly rich portrait of the poet's mind.

The founding of the Sydney chapter of PEN in 1931 was another mark of her literary activism. The club, which Dorothea formed with the help of Ethel Turner and Mary Gilmore, was a networking opportunity for writers across Sydney during the years of the Depression when work had dried up in many areas of the literary profession alongside high unemployment across the board. The first meeting in August was celebrated in *The Bulletin* as a triumph, bringing together Sydney's men and women of letters: 'First of all, everybody talked a little and when the proper matey atmosphere had been created, dinner was served.' Poet, University of Sydney professor of English literature and librarian John Le Gay Brereton was elected president, Dorothea vice-president and Ruth secretary. Dorothea and Ruth were credited with being the driving force behind the club, however the announcement in *The Bulletin* focused on what the writers were wearing. 'Dorothea draped herself in a Sappho-like scarf that had a deep gold border, while Marjorie Quinn's coat wore a collar (or so it seemed) of red geranium petals. The Barnard-Eldershaw alliance wore evening garments befitting successful novelists.' Marjorie Barnard and Flora Eldershaw had a creative relationship similar to that of Dorothea and Ruth, and they collaborated on several novels. *The Bulletin* article continued: 'Most of the men came in tweeds, but the glad-rag sex, no matter how poetic, turned up in marcel, earrings and the whirling chiffons of the moment.' (The 'marcel' was the deep soft wave made in hair with a heated curling rod, a popular hairstyle of the period.) Writers Mary Gilmore, Dora Moore and Ethel Turner showed their support for Sydney's newest club and 'all the male literary lions and lion cubs roared approval, pianissimo of course'.[19]

Despite the Depression, Sydney literary life continued to thrive, and Dorothea turned her poet's eye on her home city. Her comments on the nearly finished Harbour Bridge were astute as well as appreciative: 'Sydney is a place of lovely surprises. You never knew when you looked down a street whether you would see tall masts or green trees at the other end, and I now find as I cross Pitt Street suddenly, I get a thrilling glimpse of the bridge.

Sydney will one day realise the great beauty which that maze of iron and steel has given to the city.'[20]

Dorothea watched the final years of construction with great interest. In March 1932, the bridge's official opening took place with much fanfare – and controversy, after a protester rode forward and cut the ribbon before the official ceremony began. The ribbon was quickly retied and cut by the Premier ahead of jubilant celebrations. As reported in the *Sydney Morning Herald*:

> With pageantry unsurpassed probably in the Southern Hemisphere, with clash of cymbals and music, from many bands, with deafening noise of sirens of overseas and small steamers and the hum of aeroplanes, with a procession of floats decorated with millions of choice blooms, with the sound of guns, of cheering and of whistles from city factories, the great occasion was celebrated by thousands upon thousands of citizens who crowded every point of vantage, and a brilliant and memorable pageant unfolded itself before the vast concourse. Sydney Harbour itself presented a sight unique in its history.[21]

∽

Dorothea's beloved mother Marion suffered a stroke in 1933, and died soon after. Dorothea was again plunged into grief, so deeply reliant was she on the love and affection of her mother. The three remaining Mackellar siblings chose a quieter life than the prominent society role of their parents. Rosemont at Woollahra was sold and Dorothea bought Cintra, a more modest late nineteenth-century two-storey home at Darling Point. For the rest of her life, she divided her time between Cintra and Tarrangaua, her retreat on Pittwater. Some years later, in 1939, with neither Mac nor Eric in a position to manage the farm, the Mackellar property Kurrumbede at Gunnedah was sold. Mac's health – compromised during the war – was deteriorating, and Eric's alcoholism continued. Dorothea, too, was developing a dependency on alcohol as well as the opiates that had long been prescribed for her 'nerves'.

Increasingly withdrawn at the relatively young age of fifty-four, Dorothea was the subject of much concern from her friends. Ethel Turner hoped that 1939 would be 'happier and calmer' for her:

> I imagined that you had come to quieter waters for the last year or so (and you were looking so well it was easy to think so) but Ruth Bedford says no, you still have a choppy sea to contend with and the infinitude of caring for many others. Ah well, it's life, isn't it? There is no freedom, no peace anywhere, anywhere. Nothing to do but make believe we like it. I don't know why I am writing this – I think it was just that so warm a wave went washing to you from me the other night I had to say something. So, count that it just takes my real love to you.

While Dorothea was slowly disengaging from public life, Ruth was still very active in the literary world, travelling to Buenos Aries, Argentina in 1936 for an International PEN convention. She recalled the event in an article for the *Sydney Morning Herald*, describing Buenos Aires as a 'great city', where representatives from forty nations had gathered 'to compare notes, to argue, to make or renew friendships, to see, hear and remember all they can of these crowded hours and impressions of places and people'.²²

※

Dorothea had her own battles to fight on the home front during the war years. She and Mac had to battle to keep Eric from hurting himself. He had been living at the Coogee Bay Hotel with a manservant, a Mr Speight, who was charged with getting him up the stairs to bed each night and ensuring some food was eaten. Eric was also in and out of hospital. His accountant, Mr E.A. Holden, who was only ever referred to in correspondence by his initials, had taken it upon himself to manage Eric's affairs. He was trying to gain access to Eric's inheritance to purchase a home for himself and his wife, supposedly with the aim of looking after Eric there.

Dorothea's neighbour at Lovett Bay, the eminent psychologist Dr Donald Fraser, acted as an adviser on Eric's wellbeing. Mr Holden was known to throw his weight around and issue threats to the family. On one occasion, Dr Fraser took notes during a conversation with Holden to accurately inform the family of his intentions. Dr Fraser said it was a comparatively simple matter to take notes on Holden's conversation as it was his habit to repeat everything at least twice and sometimes from twelve to twenty times! According to a letter Dorothea received from Dr Fraser, Holden complained endlessly about having to look after Eric, telling the doctor:

> I have to be everything to him. Every day I take him home with me at night to keep him out of the pubs, and every day

I am pestered by the same thing: to get him out of hospital. In my opinion he will outlive his brother and sister. Anyway, they care nothing about him. Our heart aches for him and as his income is now in excess of Dorothea's, I am determined he will have the benefit of it.

Dr Fraser's notes reveal that Holden's fixation with Eric's 'fortune' was matched by his paranoia in relation to the Mackellars' machinations over inheritance. 'I do not want it to be all left to the Bucklands [their cousins] in London,' Holden complained. His alleged control over Mac – who 'will do exactly what I wish him to. I have him where I want him' – was allegedly bought with 50,000 pounds of Eric's money. Holden had already started making plans to buy a house in Eric's name, despite having no authority to do so. 'We will get a home within easy distance for you to visit . . . Eric will have a bit of a garden to rest in and help to keep him from the continual rounds of worrying me.' With delusions of grandeur, a more unpleasant character than this puffed-up accountant would have been hard to find: 'Remember,' he reportedly told Fraser, 'I am practically monarch of all I survey. Between you and I, I can do and *do* do what I like.'

Holden also expressed concern that Eric would be committed to a mental asylum, presumably robbing him of his easy pay cheque, but Dr Fraser assured Dorothea there was no need to institutionalise Eric against his will. Dorothea could be seen, at times, as fragile, but when it came to her family she was indefatigable and stepped up to defend Eric from the increasingly rapacious Mr Holden. She made it clear in a series of letters that she would not consent to Eric being 'placed in a home where he would be under some restraint and would not enjoy his full personal freedom of action in relation to the conduct of his own affairs'. Dorothea consulted a lawyer and forwarded a legal letter to Holden with the advice that it was unlikely he would be able to act against the wishes of the family. In a telephone conversation with Holden, Dorothea was given certain assurances which were later broken, and it became evident he was playing Mac and Dorothea against each other. Further, he was trying to convince others that Dorothea did not have Eric's best interest at heart: 'It's my belief that she is jealous of my influence over the patient. Keep him away from her as much as you possibly can. Her influence is entirely bad. She intends to put him into an institution in order to take him out of my control.' Dorothea continued to protect Eric throughout his life, and he was never committed to a psychiatric facility, although his alcoholism caused much misery for himself and those around him.

Dorothea also had her own problems. In July 1939, the nation's newspapers carried a curious story with headlines including 'Two Swoon in Sydney Beauty Salon', telling the story of a hairdresser and her client who were found unconscious. At first it was thought they were suffering from gas poisoning, but later it was concluded that their collapse had been caused by ill health. The women were named as Mrs Madeline Elliott of Darlinghurst, 'proprietress' of the salon, and Miss Dorothea Mackellar, 'poetess', of Darling Point: 'It is believed that while Mrs Elliott was treating Miss Mackellar she swooned and fell unconscious on the floor, and that the shock of her sudden collapse affected Miss Mackellar so badly that she also swooned.'[23] Not only was this strange mishap considered worth reporting, but it was also followed up in the *Australian Women's Weekly*: 'A few days previously Miss Mackellar had received an anti-tetanus injection after having been bitten by her pet dog. Her medical adviser said she was not a good subject for anti-tetanus serum, and this may have contributed to her collapse in the beauty parlour.'[24] While her poetry was no longer being published, Dorothea's fainting fit was still deemed newsworthy.

With ill health plaguing her, a literary career that seemed to be behind her, and the first signs of World War Two looming on the horizon, Dorothea increasingly withdrew to the peace and comfort of her sanctuary, Tarrangaua.

Chapter 19

Out of Reach

Dorothea's time at Lovett Bay was a great comfort to her in later life. It represented a refuge from the city, a place to commune with nature and the satisfaction of having built a home for herself. She enjoyed a certain independence she had never felt when her parents were alive. Dorothea was a well-known figure in the local community, even if she was considered something of an eccentric, and was frequently seen making the crossing from Church Point by boat – there was no road access. For a time during the war, however, Dorothea had not actually been able to access the house, after her boat was requisitioned by the navy: '[a]t Pittwater, naval defence registered all boats to select some of them for auxiliary patrol boats,' writes historian Keith Amos. 'It isn't certain where Dorothea's launch ended up, however it was definitely seconded; and as a result Dorothea couldn't use Tarrangaua until wartime restrictions were lifted in 1944.'[1] It was an isolated little spot, but for Dorothea, that was likely a good deal of its charm.

Author Susan Duncan, who later lived at Tarrangaua, described the idyllic setting in her book *The House at Salvation Creek*:

> From a distance it is still as a painting. Up close, it teems with life. The bush never rests, not even at night when you hear the heavy drumbeat of wallabies on their age-old tracks, or the scream of a barking owl. And all around, always, there is the faint chorus of the water.[2]

The area was also home to many creative types, including the famous Australian actor Chips Rafferty and his wife Quentin, who moved to Lovett Bay in 1947 and were part of the eclectic bohemian arts community that thrived in a setting of natural beauty not far from the city.

Australian novelist Di Morrissey also grew up in the area, and found much inspiration there. Morrissey describes Lovett Bay as 'an early hippy artist hangout . . . it is the most beautiful place . . . a series of linked bays with a national park behind it. You had to get the little ferry from Church Point.'[3] She recalls going exploring when she was only seven years old and finding herself at Tarrangaua, where she encountered the rather formidable Dorothea in her garden.

'What do you think you are doing?' Dorothea asked. Thinking quickly, she replied that she was searching for fairies.

'How terribly splendid,' Dorothea said, 'I'll help you look.'

Later, Dorothea invited the young girl into her home, and Morrissey remembered being overwhelmed by her library and the sheer number of books. She explained to Dorothea that her family was poor and she didn't own many books, so she made up stories in her head to entertain herself. Dorothea then urged the girl to 'put your stories in a book one day for other people to enjoy'.⁴ Morrisey said she was always going to be a writer because the idea was Dorothea's gift to her:

> It wasn't until I got to High School and studied 'My Country' – I thought, 'Oh, that's the old witch that used to live down the end of the bay'. Everyone told me she was a witch and not to bother her as she wore long black skirts and was still very rather Victorian – but she was the warmest loveliest witch.⁵

This was not the first time Dorothea had been cast in the role of the witch. An article from 1930 had wondered if, 'with her quick darting eyes, and her elusive personality, Dorothea Mackellar with all the Celt in her, might be a witch herself'.⁶ The idea would have amused Dorothea, given her fascination with witches. And it was true that she had some decidedly unusual habits – the locals still relay anecdotes about Dorothea skinny dipping in the bay, naked except for a red swimming cap. Her dedication to ocean swimming did not appear to diminish as she aged.

Aside from her steadfast relationship with Ruth, romance continued to prove elusive for Dorothea, although she referenced a love interest in her diary in the early 1940s, using her long-neglected secret code to record the new turn of events. It appeared there was a considerable age difference between her and the mysterious romantic interest, the opposite of her doomed relationship with the much older Robin Dods some decades earlier. She wrote:

So, we were made for each other?
Bad staffwork then, that Fate
Should fashion me so much too soon
And you such years too late!⁷

While these years were sparse creatively, Dorothea enjoyed her community, her interactions with schoolchildren as the education curriculum continued to include her poetry, and freedom from most family duties – although Eric continued to cause great anxiety. The daylight hours were filled with walks in the bush, swimming or boating, picnics or community art exhibitions, but the night brought a sense of dread. Dorothea's insomnia was both a consequence and a cause of her depression. In *My Heart, My Country*, Adrienne Howley pieced together the way Dorothea filled those long nights when alone at Tarrangaua:

> Often the sound of the gramophone and low singing came from the big sitting room, then the chink of a decanter against a glass; the sound of two bare feet, dancing, perhaps stumbling a little; the swish of soft garments falling to the floor; and then, last of all, dry, heart-wrenching sobs stifled behind trembling hands. Later still, a silent figure wandered amongst the trees or by the water, till the first lighting of the eastern sky ended the sorrow of the night.⁸

The last poem recorded in her verse books was an entry in 1942. At fifty-seven, Dorothea was not old, but there was a sense of exhaustion and a deep resignation creeping into her life and her poetry:

From the Sky,
Through the Flames,
To the Sea,
All Earth gone.
Vale.⁹

～

Dorothea's younger brother, Mac, died in 1943, having never fully recovered his health after the Great War. His death was announced in the Gunnedah *Independent*:

> Although it was known that Mr Mackellar had been in poor health for some time, the news of his death came as a shock. He had recently made business visits to Gunnedah, leaving from the last on Sunday week . . . [He] served in the last war as an officer in the British Life Guards and while in the fighting line was gassed and suffered serious after-effects during his after life.¹⁰

Eric had a stroke soon after, and was moved to Dorothea's home, Cintra, where he lived as a semi-invalid until he died after a second stroke in 1950. Losing her brothers, and particularly Eric, was a blow for Dorothea. There were many sympathy cards, all remembering Eric fondly despite his 'troubles'. One came from Dorothea's cousin Clare Faithfull in England: 'Eric was always so dear to us all and so lovable. This sad passing takes me back to the happy days at Dunara and the wonderful homelife there. I am feeling so unhappy and my comfort is to think of them now all together again, dear Eric loved them so dearly and

I always thought he was never quite the same after Keith's sad and brave death.'

Dorothea wrote to her friend Meg Scarlett, now Lady Abinger, in Scotland to tell her the news and received a condolence letter in reply: 'My sympathy goes out to you too. I had not heard of your loss. Oh, those happy days so long ago.' Dorothea had outlived them all, and in one generation the immediate Mackellar line had ceased with no offspring to inherit their wealth or carry the family name. Dorothea's overseas trips had ceased following the death of her mother over a decade earlier, although friends and family in the United Kingdom, and particularly Meg Scarlett, continued to urge her to visit them.

Dorothea's health continued to decline and she lived as something of a recluse for the next decade, with her lifelong friend Dorothy Macmillan, known as 'Fethers,' becoming her live-in companion at Tarrangaua. Fethers had lost her husband in World War I and her son in World War II, and was grateful to find a home with Dorothea, even if at times it meant playing nurse to the ageing poet.

In the mid-1950s, Dorothea stopped travelling to Lovett Bay altogether, no longer having the energy or the physical strength to visit her beloved home. The property was not easy to access, with an hour-long drive from Sydney, followed by a ferry or boat trip to Lovett Bay from Church Point, and then a long trek up the steep and rough track to the house. A letter to Helen Rankin, president of the Australian Fellowship of Writers, in September 1952, gives an insight into Dorothea's state of mind and physical limitations. At the age of sixty-seven, she found that she no longer had the energy for socialising, and apologised to Rankin for being unable to attend a luncheon:

As I think Miss Bedford told you, I have had a great deal of illness for many years and have been forced into leading a very quiet life. Will you accept this small cheque on behalf of the Society as a sign of my good wishes? I did write one more than a year ago but was not well enough to complete the letter and my accountant has this week written to ask why it was not presented.[11]

As the letter suggests, Ruth was still an integral part of Dorothea's life, and knew all the particulars of her travails. Visiting when she could, Ruth also continued to travel and was working on a new literary project. In 1954, Ruth published a biography of her grandfather and New South Wales Supreme Court Justice, Sir Alfred Stephen, called *Think of Stephen*. The book was sponsored by the Commonwealth Literary Fund and received favourable reviews. In response to the book, Ruth received a letter of praise and an invitation to lunch from Australian Nobel laureate Patrick White.[12] Later, in a radio interview in 1961, she spoke about how the biography came to be:

When he died, the diaries and letters of his [second] wife, which were tremendously interesting and detailed, the diaries most faithfully kept over all her married life, came to me, and I realised that I had to make a book of them.[13]

Ruth died only two years later in 1963, one month shy of her eighty-first birthday. She had remained a true and loyal friend to Dorothea until the end, and it is impossible not to believe that she was the great love of Dorothea's life. Although the true depth of their relationship may not have been understood by their friends and family, it left an indelible mark on both their lives and their literary works.

In September of 1962, Dorothea had been approached by the principal of a Sydney school, then called the Manly Girls' Domestic Home Science School, now Mackellar Girls High School, inviting her to be patron of the school, which would take her name. She apologised to the principal, Mrs Rosenthal, for not responding sooner but turned down the role on the basis she was not well enough to be useful: 'An interest should be practical, don't you agree?' she wrote. 'I am sorry not to be able to attend Speech Day, but though I expect to be able to go for a short drive sometime this week, I'm not yet strong enough for anything more than that.' She was delighted that one of the students was planning to recite 'Colour' at Speech Day. 'It is the best thing I ever wrote,' she said.[14]

Unable to enjoy such rewards as more involvement in the school would undoubtedly have offered, Dorothea's later years were spent in and out of hospital with various illnesses, her life now spent in reflection, clinging to powerful memories, and often returning to the bush in her mind, if not in reality. This had always been Dorothea's refuge, and was captured in her poem 'Peaceful Voices', published in 1926:

> I fortunate, I knew a refuge,
> When the strained spirit tires
> Of town's metallic symphony,
> Of wheels and horns and wires.
>
> Where through the golden empty stillness,
> Cool-flowing voices speak.
> The alto of the waterfall,
> The treble of the creek.

From far, beyond the headland's shoulder,
Southeasters bring to me
Reminder of earth's wanderings,
The strong voice of the sea.

I happy, in a leafy fortress,
Listen to hidden birds
And small waves of a hidden tide,
Mingling their lovely words.[15]

Although not a great deal is known about her at this time, her cousin Jennifer Stiller recalled meeting an elderly Dorothea when she was a child in the 1950s and '60s:

> My memories of Dorothea are that of a young person. It was during a visit to Sydney, to meet up with various family members, that we were invited to meet with my third cousin. Such a special treat. She was resting in hospital, propped up with pillows, with personal items and shelves of books decorating her room. I was probably around twelve years of age, and so, was full of wonder and excitement at meeting with such a much loved and talked about member of my family. Dorothea certainly didn't disappoint my expectations. She had a very theatrical way of telling a story, with her soft expressive mouth and big brown eyes which seemed to add to that extra intrigue. Our visit seemed to give her so much joy and energy. Her many remembered family and life stories flowed backward and forth all afternoon. All too soon it was time to leave, but not without a treasured book, a gift, tucked under my arm. There were many other visits to her

Darling Point Home where even a simple lunch invitation took on unexpected special moments to remember. There were the gleaming silver serving trays, the polished timber panelling, the floor-to-ceiling timber bookshelves filled with books all with in this beautiful much-loved home, harking back to long forgotten days. There was always a sense of warmth, and a welcoming engagement from Dorothea, when we were together.[16]

In 1967, a friend and admirer of Dorothea's, Gordon Williamson, who was a frequent visitor at Cintra, wrote to the state government to request recognition of her contribution to Australia's literary canon. He wrote of 'the widespread joy the epic "My Country" has imparted to incalculable numbers' and the 'deep sense of appreciation and gratitude' the Australian people felt for the poet 'who has awakened in them, and in all of us, patriotic sentiments'.[17] The powers that be must have agreed, because Dorothea was awarded an Order of the British Empire (OBE) in the 1968 New Year's honours. She was said to have commented in her usual droll way, that it was 'a bit late'.

Not long after this 'late' triumph, Dorothea suffered a series of slight strokes and, although not incapacitated, she was growing weaker. She remained at home at Cintra with Fethers as a companion and with nursing care around the clock. But after a fall which left her with a broken ankle, she returned to the Scottish Hospital, Paddington, originally known as The Terraces, where she had spent time in 1911. It was here that she suffered another stroke, and on 14 January 1968, died peacefully in her sleep. Her nurse and biographer, Adrienne Howley, described the scene when she arrived at the hospital to find that Dorothea had passed away: 'She lay there looking so peaceful, almost happy, when our work was done. I scattered flowers on the sheet that covered her and around her face. That proud and generous heart was still at last.'[18]

Dorothea had outlived all those she most loved, her last years had been difficult, and yet, as Howley wrote, 'she had never inflicted her miseries on those around her but kept them locked in her heart, only to be released in her poems'.[19] The funeral service was held at St Mark's Anglican Church, Darling Point. She was cremated and placed next to Keith in the family plot at Waverley Cemetery beneath that heart-rending epitaph, 'His sister'. Dorothea left an estate worth more than $1.5 million, which included some small provisions for loyal staff members, godchildren and friends, while the rest went to her cousins Charles ('Mac') Dredge and Kathleen Elkin, since there were no direct descendants of the four Mackellar children. In a letter to a friend, writer Pixie O'Harris wrote of Dorothea:

> [S]he was a lady born. Her manner was not formal and yet not friendly – a kindly reserve, the interest of gentility. Evidently a beautiful girl when young – there was some romance which didn't eventuate. Being the only daughter, it looks as though Dorothea had not gone out in the world much, although she had travelled a great deal. She was also very protected.[20]

O'Harris attended her funeral service but felt it did not reflect the contribution Dorothea had made to Australian literary life:

The minister mouthed her verses to his own great delight – and to my shame. I am sure Dorothea turned in her coffin. The followers or leaders were schoolgirls, young and beautiful and bashfully conscious of their position. They led the way out of the church preceding the coffin. They had come from the school that bears her name. All the rest of the mourners appeared to be relations or old retainers. On her coffin were the delicate pink roses that she loved. I thought of Dorothea as a flower – a hot-house bloom – growing in an atmosphere of protection – which is so unlike her verse 'My Country': that verse was a moment of freedom, a longing for more than she found in her life.[21]

The poem had been Dorothea's great joy but also a burden, and in its stark comparisons between Australia's 'beauty' and its 'terror' also seemed to capture the dualities of her life, like two sides of a coin. She was both the humble country girl and the sophisticated city dweller and world traveller; a woman who longed for love, but struggled with her sexuality and found it hard to commit to those who came in and out of her life; and ultimately, an ambitious poet who first courted extraordinary fame and then shrank from it.

The poem brought her recognition on three continents and the kind of national acclaim later reserved for celebrities – her utterances, social engagements and travel plans detailed endlessly in newspapers across the country. It also left her increasingly self-conscious and vulnerable, dreading the attention and the inevitable pressure to produce something even more triumphant.

Those who wrote in tribute to the poet after her death claimed it would be a great pity if everything Dorothea wrote was to be overshadowed by the one poem for which she was famous. Poet Dorothy Green – whose own verses appeared under her maiden name, Dorothy Auchterlonie – told the *Canberra Times* that Dorothea's other poems deserved to be better known:

> There was a most unusual fantasy in her work and this is especially noticeable in her translations of poems from the Spanish. These are both passionate and grim and show a totally different side of the poet who wrote 'I love a sunburnt country'. We tend to think of her as a landscape poet but she was much more than that, her work is full of colour and light.[22]

Others felt differently. Poet and academic Professor Tom Inglis Moore, who remembered Dorothea from the days when they were both members of the PEN Club in Sydney as a 'charming, reticent and dignified woman, widely travelled and a most interesting dinner table companion', remarked that he felt 'My Country' 'quite deserves its fame and popularity. It has a warmth of feeling about it and some very good expression,' he told the *Canberra Times*.[23] Moore also included the poem in the two-volume anthology, *Poetry in Australia* (1964), feeling that the poet had earned her place there.

Journalist and poet Marjorie Quinn was astute in noting that although Dorothea's urge to write may have faded in her later life, her poems still shone brightly:

> Dorothea was not, like many writers, forced by circumstances, economic or otherwise, to make writing her life work. She was left with all that was needed for material comfort. The inspiration, the incentive to write, that bright flame which

had illuminated her early verses so that they stole the hearts of many, died down, but her poems have their own life. They will not easily be forgotten.[24]

So unforgettable was Dorothea's most famed poem that, according to *The Oxford Companion to Australian History*, several phrases from 'My Country' including 'the wide brown land' and 'a sunburnt country' had entered the national lexicon. The *Companion* also notes that 'My Country' had become familiar to generations of Australian schoolchildren, having featured in the Australian school curriculum for most of the century. And yet, in summarising the poet's contribution to Australian literature, the authors of the *Companion* could not help but repeat the old barb that haunted Dorothea; that her poetry 'confirmed her delight in nature as well as her facility at verse translations, but for many Australians she remains the author of one famous poem'.[25]

Dorothea continued to be honoured in various forms long after her death. A plaque installed in Chiswick Gardens on Ocean Street, Woollahra in 1992 by the local council reads:

In these ordered gardens we remember with affection a great admirer of Australian nature whose 'love was otherwise'. Dorothea Mackellar OBE (1885–1968) author of the poem 'My Country' who lived nearby at Rosemont in Ocean Street.

It includes the first two verses of the poem.

She also became the first Australian woman writer to be recognised by the United Nations Educational, Scientific and Cultural Organisation in 2017, when the only known manuscript of 'My Country' was included on the Australian Memory of the World register. Her notebook 'Verses 1907–1908', which includes the poem, became the first Australian literary work to be added to the register.

In 2022, the state government announced Dorothea would be honoured, again in the Woollahra Municipality, with one of its 'Blue Plaques', which recognise notable citizens of New South Wales and their contribution to society and to history. The program is modelled on the London Blue Plaque scheme, which has been operating since 1866 and installs plaques on buildings where famous Londoners lived and worked.

Dorothea was also remembered in the places she spent some of her happiest years. In 2022, her beloved Kurrumbede homestead near Gunnedah was heritage-listed by the state government in a bid to protect it from encroaching mining operations after the house and the land surrounding it were bought by a mining company in 2010. The town of Gunnedah in NSW claims Dorothea Mackellar for its own, with a bronze sculpture of her on horseback in the centre of the town. The Dorothea Mackellar Memorial Society, based in Gunnedah, continues to administer an annual eponymous poetry competition, a fitting legacy which boasts more than 7,000 entries. The nearby Paterson Valley Historical Society has various items on display in its museum celebrating Dorothea's connection to Torryburn, the family's first property, and the greening of the fields after drought.

In a 1982 review in the *Canberra Times* of a later selection of her verse, *My Country and Other Poems*, Ralph Elliott pointed to Dorothea's omission from recent anthologies of Australian poetry and from Geoffrey Dutton's critical *The Literature of Australia* (1964). But much like the earlier pronouncements of Dorothea's contemporary Zora Cross, Elliott conceded that poets were generally remembered by their best poems, not by their worst. In the end, he was sympathetic to the place Dorothea held in Australian literary history because of *that* poem:

> Dorothea Mackellar deserves to be remembered by a few more besides 'My Country', the one poem that has ensured her lasting renown, at least in that sunburnt country which it describes so vividly, with its 'stark white ring-barked forests,' its 'pitiless blue sky,' its 'flood and fire and famine'. An occasional image lingers in the memory: 'An opal-hearted country' in the same poem, possibly an echo of Christopher Brennan; or in 'Colour', 'that unearthly/clear shining after rain'; or in 'The Tryst', 'Autumn, the gentle one, comes north again, to a land too hotly kissed.'[26]

There was an elitism that crept into criticism of Dorothea's poetry in the second half of the twentieth century, as if popular verse – despite capturing the hearts and minds of so many Australians – was ultimately without merit. Yet many of her poems, besides 'My Country', stand the test of time and exemplify her true craft, including 'Night on the Plains':

Out here on the plain-land at night
   There is no sound, not a sigh;
And nothing is moving now
   But scornful stars in the sky:

    The night is too great for my heart,
      It flutters and halts and trips,
    The terrible mirth of the stars
      Has slain my song on my lips.[27]

This exquisite poem is reminiscent of the words of Gustave Flaubert, who 'longed to move the stars to pity'. It demonstrates both technical prowess and emotional intelligence, but also references the struggles that eventually silenced Dorothea's voice.

In an article in the *Sydney Morning Herald* in 1965, Dorothea described the images of the breaking of the drought which later would be poured into 'My Country'. She recalled her astonishment when people wrote to her and said, 'they understood exactly what I meant, but they did not have the words for it'.

Always her own worst critic, she told the interviewer that she did not consider she had 'written a line of real poetry in her life'. Her own conclusion about the reason 'My Country' was so successful was suitably straightforward, 'it was a statement of fact – and it was sincere'. She said that, over the years, many people thought she had died because 'people in hard covers should be dead like Shakespeare. When I was young a lot of people loved their country, but it was not fashionable to do so. There was a certain snobbishness which I jumped on with both feet'.[28]

The impact of Dorothea Mackellar's literary legacy might best be summed up by an article in the *Australian Women's Weekly* in 1939. The journalist recounted reading an item about Dorothea in a newspaper while on a train, when a girl sitting beside him and peeping over his shoulder gave a tiny gasp of excitement.

'Is that Dorothea Mackellar?' she asked, referring to the news item.

'Do you know her?' he enquired.

'Of course,' she replied. 'Everybody does.'

'And that is true,' the journalist noted, reminiscing about encountering her poem 'My Country' for the first time:

Remember the lines in our schoolbooks? 'I love a sunburnt country'. I can remember how they thrilled me when as a little country kid I first read them hidden among English poems about the wolds of Kent and the cliffs of Dover that I had never seen. The lines sang in my head like a melody. Here was something I knew. From my desk in the schoolhouse, I could see out into the paddocks across the shimmering heat haze to the purple mountains on the far horizons. Yes, the wide brown land for me. The words seemed like an act of faith in Australia.[29]

The journalist's words predicted the place the poem would hold in the history of the nation. 'My Country' acknowledged the struggle that several generations of Australians had faced in deciding which country deserved their loyalty. Dorothea, the journalist argued, helped Australians 'to a love of the wide brown land . . . the happy land that has swept to even a broader destiny than Dorothea Mackellar ever dreamed of when she wrote those beautiful lines'.[30] The article pointed to a nation's inferiority complex, due in part to the work of Australian poets who had come before and had written mostly about the nation's harshness; its conflicts and disasters, convicts, bushfires and drought. If such poetry made Australians critical of their country, Dorothea's restored their faith:

But here was a woman making melody out of the melancholy landscape. The straggly old bush paddocks and the tired gum trees had a new significance for me from that day. Here was a thrilling message for Australians . . . a melody of our own land which had caught some of the blazing vitality of our country.[31]

Dorothea had rendered the Australian landscape lovely in all its extremes; mysterious and mercurial. And in doing so she had shown her fellow Australians how to love their homeland on its own terms. The words of the critic E.D. echo this sentiment, and remain just as true as when they were written more than a century ago:

> She is the first real Australian patriot; she is the first genuine Australian songster. This is not merely because her subjects are Australian but because she sings as if she were singing *of* her own *to* her own and because all real Australians across the whole of Australia will hear an echo in their own hearts when they hear her sing.[32]

Dorothea herself was pragmatic, understated and self-deprecating to the end: 'I have written from the heart, from imagination, from experience, some amount of verse. All I can say of "My Country" is that I wrote it with sincerity.'

Dorothea had imagined death long before she met with it. In her poem 'Tests', she painted the end of life in beautiful words that beckoned and tumbled like the ocean, evoking the siren call of the sea, which she had so often answered.

> whisper to me of dawn
> over the sandhills; say
> 'The surf is good today',
> (green hollow glassy waves rushing upon the beach)—
> if I stir not nor smile, I shall be out of reach.[33]

Acknowledgements

Thank you to the family of Dorothea Mackellar for giving me the opportunity to write her biography with access to her closed papers at the Mitchell Library, particularly her cousin Jennifer Stiller whose vision for her life story was the inspiration for this project. Thank you to Jennifer's daughter, my friend Lyndal Hughes, for reaching out to me and having faith that I could do Dorothea justice.

Many thanks to my supervisor at the University of Sydney's School of Literature, Art and Media, Associate Professor Peter Kirkpatrick, whose patience, encouragement, brilliant insight and expert knowledge were invaluable during the writing of the thesis which was the basis for the book.

Thank you to Val Anderson from the Paterson Historical Society who hosted my trip to the Paterson Valley, helped organise tours of the former Mackellar homestead, Torryburn, and the Paterson Court House Museum, and whose publication *The Dorothea Mackellar 'My Country' Paterson Valley Connection* was a welcome resource. I am grateful to Pip Murray, President of the Dorothea Mackellar Memorial Society for organising my trip to Gunnedah to see the Mackellar homestead, Kurrumbede. During a period of extended drought in the region, she was a generous host, accommodating me at her home and providing a wealth of knowledge about the Mackellar family's connection to the region. Thank you to Byron Patching for hosting me at Tarrangaua on Pittwater, and to Dr Keith Amos whose recent monograph *Dorothea Mackellar at Pittwater* was another great resource.

In 2021, I was delighted to receive the Abbie Clancy Award from the Society of Women Writers NSW for my abstract 'Dorothea Mackellar: Whose Country?' on the exegetical essay as part of this thesis. It was an honour to be recognised in the great company of those who have gone before.

Much gratitude to my former publisher Fiona Henderson who championed the book from the beginning, my former editor Katie Stackhouse who guided me through the first drafts and to the dedicated team at Simon & Schuster Australia including passionate publisher Michelle Swainson, brilliant editor Lizzie King and marketing supremo Anna O'Grady. Thank you to my literary agent Pippa Masson at Curtis Brown.

Finally, to my husband Mark Waugh and my sons Mac and Finn, for their constant love and support.

Notes

All uncited quotations come from the diaries and personal correspondence of Dorothea Mackellar, which can be found in the Mackellar Family Papers at the Mitchell Library in Sydney. Dorothea's diaries from 1910–1918 are available in abridged and edited form in *I Love A Sunburnt Country: The Diaries of Dorothea Mackellar*, edited by Jyoti Brunsdon and published in 1990 by Angus & Robertson.

CHAPTER 1
1. Adrienne Howley, *My Heart, My Country* (St Lucia: University of Queensland Press, 1989), pp. 29–30.
2. Dorothea Mackellar, 'In a Southern Garden', *The Poems of Dorothea Mackellar*, edited by C.K.M Dredge and B.K. Elkins (Adelaide: Rigby, 1971), p. 27.
3. Dorothea Mackellar, 'Settlers', *The Poems of Dorothea Mackellar*, p. 12.
4. Howley, *My Heart*, p. 28.
5. Howley, *My Heart*, p. 32.
6. Howley, *My Heart*, p. 43.
7. Howley, *My Heart*, pp. 42–43.

CHAPTER 2
1. Adrienne Howley, *My Heart, My Country* (St Lucia: University of Queensland Press, 1989) p. 16.
2. Dorothea Mackellar, 'Heritage', *The Poems of Dorothea Mackellar*, edited by C.K.M Dredge and B.K. Elkins (Adelaide: Rigby, 1971), p. 107.
3. Dorothea Mackellar, 'Another Heritage', *The Poems*, p. 124.
4. Howley, *My Heart, My Country*, p. 40.

CHAPTER 3
1. Val Anderson, 'The Dorothea Mackellar Paterson Valley Connection', Record of an exhibition held for Heritage Week, 1996 at Paterson Court House Museum, p. 9.
2. Craig Wilcox, 'Our Other Unknown Soldier', *Australian Army Journal*, Vol. 3, No. 2, p. 158.
3. Wilcox, 'Our Other Unknown Soldier', p. 161.
4. 'The Death of Lieutenant Mackellar', *Sydney Morning Herald*, 28 August 1900, p. 5.
5. 'The Death of Lieutenant Mackellar', p. 5.
6. 'The Death of Lieutenant Mackellar', p. 5.
7. 'Lieutenant Mackellar's Death', *The Australian Star* [Sydney], 17 July 1900, p. 6.
8. 'A Promising Career Cut Short', *Sydney Morning Herald*, 17 July 1900, p. 5.
9. 'Military Church Parade', *Sydney Morning Herald*, 6 August 1900, p. 3.
10. Dorothea Mackellar, 'When It Comes', *The Poems of Dorothea Mackellar*, edited by C.K.M Dredge and B.K. Elkins (Adelaide: Rigby, 1971), p. 19.
11. Adrienne Howley, *My Heart, My Country* (St Lucia: University of Queensland Press, 1989), p. 63.
12. 'Memorial to Lieutenant Mackellar', *Sydney Morning Herald*, 13 July 1903, p. 8.
13. 'Memorial to Lieutenant Mackellar', p. 8.

CHAPTER 4
1. Louise Mack, *An Australian Girl in London* (London: T Fisher Unwin, 1902), pp. 129–130.
2. Mack, *Australian Girl*, p. 131.
3. Dorothea Mackellar, 'Drought Time', 1902 verse book, MLMSS 1959, Box 16, Mackellar Family Papers, Mitchell Library, Sydney.
4. Dorothea Mackellar, 'Settlers', *The Poems of Dorothea Mackellar*, edited by C.K.M Dredge and B.K. Elkins (Adelaide: Rigby, 1971), pp. 12–13.

5   Dorothea Mackellar, 'In the Plague Year', *The Poems*, p. 104.
6   Dorothea Mackellar, 'The Tearless Girl', *The Poems*, p. 104.
7   Adrienne Howley, *My Heart, My Country* (St Lucia: University of Queensland Press, 1989), p. 84.
8   Howley, *My Heart,* p. 85.
9   Dorothea Mackellar, 'Another Heritage', *The Poems*, p. 50.
10   Howley, *My Heart,* p. 87.
11   'Personal', *Sydney Morning Herald,* 1 February 1905, p. 7.
12   Martha Vicinus, *Intimate Friends: Women Who Loved Women, 1778-1928* (Chicago: University of Chicago Press, 2004), p. 34.
13   Dorothea Mackellar, 'To Her', 1904 notebook, MLMSS 1959, Box 18, Mackellar Family Papers, Mitchell Library, Sydney.
14   Dorothea Mackellar, 'The Wolves Pursuing,' *The Poems*, p. 144.
15   Dorothea Mackellar, untitled poem, 1904 notebook, MLMSS 1959, Box 18, Mackellar Family Papers, Mitchell Library, Sydney.
16   Jane Connors, 'Bedford, Ruth Marjory (1882–1963)', *Australian Dictionary of Biography*, National Centre of Biography, Australian National University, accessed 15 May 2023, http://adb.anu.edu.au/biography/bedford-ruth-marjory-9468/text16655
17   'Return of a Sydney Authoress', *Daily Telegraph* [Sydney], 23 January 1914, p. 11.
18   Ruth Bedford, Interview by Hazel De Berg, 15 September 1961, The Hazel De Berg Collection, Australian National Library, Canberra.

CHAPTER 5

1   Lorraine Hickman, 'It's a Woman's Country Too', *Women's Weekly*, 7 May 1975, p. 57.
2   Adrienne Howley, *My Heart, My Country* (St Lucia: University of Queensland Press, 1989), p. 78.
3   Ruth Bedford, 'Dear Land of Mine', *The Lone Hand*, Vol. 10, No. 57, 1 January 1912, p. 22.
4   '1885', *Evening News* [Sydney], 1 January 1886, p. 4.
5   'The Season in New South Wales', *Town and Country Journal* [Sydney], 15 January 1908, p. 8.
6   'The Hunter River Flood', *Sydney Mail*, 4 March 1908, p. 602.
7   'After the Rains', *Sydney Mail*, 4 March 1908, p. 584.
8   Dorothea Mackellar, notes on an interview with Mrs Owen, 4 September 1908, MLMSS 1959, Box 2, Mackellar Family Papers, Mitchell Library, Sydney.

9   Jessie Owen to Marion Mackellar, 15 September 1908, MSS 1959, Box 2, Mackellar Family Papers, Mitchell Library, Sydney.
10 Jessie Owen to Marion Mackellar, 26 September 1908, ML MSS 1959, Box 2, Mackellar Family Papers, Mitchell Library, Sydney.
11 'Hurrah for Australia!', *Sydney Stock and Station Journal*, 20 November 1908, p. 2.
12 Howley, *My Heart,* p. 101.
13 'Miss Dorothea Mackellar', *Sydney Mail*, 24 May 1911, p. 18.
14 Dorothea Mackellar, 'Australia', *The Australasian* [Melbourne], 29 April 1911, p. 56.
15 Stephanie Trigg, 'Introduction', *Medievalism and the Gothic in Australian Culture* (Carlton: Melbourne University Press, 2005), p. xvii.
16 'Core of My Heart – My Country', *Sydney Mail*, 21 October 1908, p. 1044.
17 Peter Kirkpatrick, 'New Words Come Tripping Slowly: Poetry, Popular Culture and Modernity, 1890–1950', *Cambridge History of Australian Literature,* edited by Peter Kirkpatrick (Cambridge University Press, 2009), p. 199.
18 'With the Guns', *Daily Mail* [Brisbane], 8 March 1919, p. 12.

CHAPTER 6
1   'Books in the Bush', *Sydney Morning Herald*, 7 April 1910, p. 8.
2   Ida Poore, *Recollections of an Admiral's Wife* (Smith Elder and Co, London, 1916), p. 233.
3   Dorothea Mackellar, 'Recollections of the Ancient Mariner', *Sunday Times* [Sydney], 19 December 1909, p. 7.
4   Dorothea Mackellar, 'The Lie', *The Australasian* [Melbourne], 9 September 1916, p. 41.
5   'Hyde Park', Dictionary of Sydney, accessed 15 April 2023, https://dictionaryofsydney.org/entry/hyde_park
6   Clair Wright, 'Birth of a nation: How Australia empowering women taught the world a lesson', *The Conversation*, 10 February 2016, http://theconversation.com/birth-of-a-nation-how-australia-empowering-women-taught-the-world-a-lesson-52492
7   Wright, 'Birth of a nation'.
8   'Grace Palotta', Austlit: Discover Australian Stories, https://www-austlit-edu-au.ezproxy1.library.usyd.edu.au/austlit/page/A29000, accessed 1 August 2021.
9   'Review: "A Viennese Romance"', *Tasmanian News*, 11 January 1907, p. 6.

10 Sylvia Martin, 'These Walls of Flesh: The Problem of the Body in the Romantic Friendship/Lesbianism Debate', *Historical Reflections*, Vol. 20, No. 2 (1994), pp. 243–266.
11 'Lord Chelmsford's Degree', *Sydney Morning Herald*, 2 May 1910, p. 7.

CHAPTER 7
1 'Ladies in Council Chambers', *Daily Telegraph* [Sydney], 12 July 1910, p. 2.
2 R.J. Riddel, 'Robert Smith (Robin) Dods (1868-1920)', *Australian Dictionary of Biography*, National Centre of Biography, Australian National University, http://adb.anu.edu.au/biography/dods-robert-smith-robin-5991/text10227. Accessed 20 May 2019.
3 Adrienne Howley, *My Heart, My Country* (St Lucia: University of Queensland Press, 1989), pp. 104–105.
4 Riddel, 'Robert Smith (Robin) Dods'.
5 'Woman's World', *Brisbane Courier*, 10 August 1910, p. 7.
6 Rudyard Kipling, 'The Eggshell', *Songs from Books* (London: Macmillan and Co, London, 1913), p. 254.
7 'Gossip for Women', *The Week* [Brisbane], 14 October 1910, p. 7.

CHAPTER 8
1 Marcus Clarke, 'Country Leisure', *The Queenslander* [Brisbane], 4 September 1875, p. 14. This article later formed the basis for Clarke's preface to *Poems of the Late Adam Lindsay Gordon* (1876), in which form it is best known.
2 Dorothea Mackellar, 'Burning Off', *The Poems of Dorothea Mackellar*, edited by C.K.M Dredge and B.K. Elkins (Adelaide: Rigby, 1971), p. 16.
3 Ida Poore to Ruth Bedford, quoted in *I Love a Sunburnt Country: The Diaries of Dorothea Mackellar* by Dorothea Mackellar, edited by Jyoti Brunsdon (North Ryde: Angus & Robertson, 1990), p. 26.
4 'A Book of Australian Verse', *Sydney Morning Herald*, 13 May 1911, p. 10.
5 'An Australian Poetess', *Daily Telegraph* [Sydney], 20 May 1911, p. 6.
6 Marjorie Quinn, *The Years that the Locust Hath Eaten: The Memoirs of Marjorie Quinn* (Melbourne: Arcadia, 2011), pp. 64–65.
7 Quinn, *The Years*, pp. 64–65.
8 Archibald T. Strong, 'The Closed Door and Other Verses', *The Herald* [Melbourne], 8 June 1911, p. 7.
9 Dorothea Mackellar, 'The Other Woman's Word', *The Poems*, p. 172.
10 'Eric Mackellar's Hard Riding', *Daily Telegraph* [Sydney], 28 June 1911, p. 15.

11 E.E.D [possibly Enid Durham], newspaper clipping from *Commonweal*, 1 November 1911, ML MSS 1959, Box 19, Mackellar Family Papers, Mitchell Library, Sydney.
12 Karl Pearson, *The Life, Letters, and Labours of Francis Galton* (London: Cambridge University Press, 1914), p. 291.

CHAPTER 9

1 'A New Steamer for the Orient Line Service to Australia', *Geelong Advertiser*, 23 December 1911, p. 7.
2 'Cruising in 1910', P and O Heritage, https://www.poheritage.com/the-collection/exhibitions/po-in-1910-a-decade-in-time/Item?ID=29508. Accessed 5 August 2021.
3 Ruth Bedford to Rex Barrett, 4 March 1912, MLMSS 777, Box 12, Stephens Family (Sir Alfred Stephens) Papers, Mitchell Library, Sydney.
4 Bedford to Rex Barrett.
5 Newspaper clippings, 1912 commonplace book, ML MSS 1959, Box 11, Mackellar Family Papers, Mitchell Library, Sydney.
6 'A Fine Australian Novel', *Daily Telegraph* [Sydney], 6 July 1912, p. 6.
7 'The Little Blue Devil', *Sydney Morning Herald*, 8 June 1912, p. 4.
8 Joseph Conrad, 'To H.H. Champion', *The Collected Letters of Joseph Conrad*, Vol. 5, edited by Frederick R. Karl and Laurence Davies (Cambridge: University Press, 1996), p. 50.
9 'Joseph Conrad in Australia', *Kalgoorlie Miner*, 5 June 1942, p. 2.
10 John Stape, *The Several Lives of Joseph Conrad* (London: Bond Street Books, 2007), p. 175.
11 Karl Pearson, *The Life, Letters, and Labours of Francis Galton* (London: Cambridge University Press, 1914), p. 291.
12 'First International Eugenics Congress', *The British Medical Journal*, 3 August 1912, pp. 253–255.
13 Clyde Chitty, *Eugenics, Race, and Intelligence in Education* (London: Continuum Publishing, 2007), p. 38.
14 'Sir Charles Mackellar: A Trip to Germany', *Sydney Morning Herald*, 12 October 1912, p. 5.
15 Gossip [Robert McMillan], 'The Little Blue Devil', *Sydney Stock and Station Journal*, 16 August 1912, p. 4.
16 'An Australian in London,' *Sydney Stock and Station Journal*, 25 February 1913, p. 3.
17 Dorothea Mackellar and Ruth Bedford, *Two's Company* (London: Alston Rivers, 1914), p. 5.

CHAPTER 10

1. 'Miss Tittell Brune', *Sunday Times* [Sydney], 30 March 1913, p. 26.
2. Leann Richards, 'Minnie Tittell Brune', History of Australian Theatre Archive, https://hatarchive506333279.wordpress.com/minnie-tittell-brune/, accessed 5 August 2021.
3. Dorothea Mackellar and Ruth Bedford, *Two's Company*, (London: Alston Rivers, 1914), p. 54.
4. Newspaper clippings, 1930, ML MSS 1959, Box 16, Mackellar Family Papers, Mitchell Library, Sydney.
5. 'Literary', *Critic*, 25 June 1913, p. 8.
6. 'Patrick R. Chalmers', Read & Co. Books, https://www.readandcobooks.co.uk/book-author/patrick-r-chalmers/, accessed 31 July 2021.
7. Adrienne Matzenik [Howley], 'Dorothea Mackellar: A Memoir', *The Poems of Dorothea Mackellar*, edited by C.K.M. Dredge and B.K. Elkin, (Adelaide: Rigby, 1971), p. iv.
8. Patrick R. Chalmers, 'Roundabouts and Swings', *Green Days and Blue Days* (London: Maunsel and Company Ltd, 1912), p. 18.
9. Imelda Palmer, 'Enid Derham (1882–1941)', *Australian Dictionary of Biography*, National Centre of Biography, Australian National University, https://adb.anu.edu.au/biography/derham-enid-5960/text10169. Accessed 5 August 2021.
10. 'A New Australian Poet', *The Register* [Adelaide], 14 December 1912, p. 4.
11. Arundel del Re, quoted in *Harold Monro and the Poetry Bookshop* by Joy Grant (London: Routledge and Kegan Paul, 1967), p. 78.
12. Edward Marsh, 'Prefatory Note', *Georgian Poetry, 1911–1912* (London: The Poetry Bookshop, 1913).
13. Robert H. Ross, *The Georgian Revolt: Rise and Fall of a Poetic Ideal 1910 to 1922* (London: Faber and Faber, 1967), p. 82.
14. Dorothea Mackellar, 'Wind and Rain', *The Poems*, p. 96.
15. Adrienne Howley, *My Heart, My Country* (St Lucia: University of Queensland Press, 1989), p. 111.

CHAPTER 11

1. Ethel Turner, *The Diaries of Ethel Turner*, edited by Philippa Poole (London: Ure Smith, 1979), p. 244.
2. 'Women in Poetry', *Sydney Stock and Station Journal*, 29 May 1914, p. 2.
3. 'Women in Poetry', p. 2.

4   Dorothea Mackellar, 'To Norman Lindsay on an Old Grievance', quoted in *I Love a Sunburnt Country: The Diaries of Dorothea Mackellar*, edited by Jyoti Brunsdon (North Ryde: Angus & Robertson, 1990), p. 195.
5   Matthew S. Seligmann, 'War Lord in Training: Churchill and the Royal Navy during the First World War', winstonchurchill.org, https://winstonchurchill.org/publications/finest-hour/finest-hour-182/war-lord-in-training-churchill-and-the-royal-navy-during-the-first-world-war/. Accessed 6 January 2020.
6   'The New Year's Promise', *Sydney Morning Herald*, 1 January 1915, p. 6.
7   'Dorothea Mackellar', *Daily Telegraph* [Sydney], 2 January 1915, p. 6.
8   'The Witch-Maid', *Sydney Morning Herald*, 9 January 1915, p. 8.
9   Dorothea Mackellar, 'Encounter', *The Poems of Dorothea Mackellar*, edited by C.K.M Dredge and B.K. Elkins (Adelaide: Rigby, 1971), p. 76.
10 'War Verses', *Sydney Morning Herald*, 30 July 1915, p. 7.
11 Dorothea Mackellar, 'On Kelly's Ridge', 1915 Diary, ML MSS 1959, Box 10, Mackellar Family Papers, Mitchell Library, Sydney.
12 Dorothea Mackellar, 'Flower of Youth', *The Poems*, p. 88.

CHAPTER 12

1   'The Lure of the Bush', *The Argus*, 19 October 1918, p. 6.
2   'Our Poets', *Sunday Times*, 18 June 1916, p. 18.
3   'Poetry in War Time', *Sydney Morning Herald*, 5 July 1916, p. 7.
4   'Mr Hughes's Speech', *Sydney Morning Herald*, 7 October 1916, p. 17.
5   'Mr Hughes's Speech', p. 17.
6   'Faint Heart and Tender Heart', *Sydney Morning Herald*, 25 October 1916, p. 5.
7   Barry York, 'The Sydney Twelve: Treason, Conspiracy and Conscription in Australia in 1916', Museum of Australian Democracy, https://www.moadoph.gov.au/blog/the-sydney-twelve-treason-conspiracy-and-conscription-in-australia-1916/#, accessed 6 November 2019.
8   Dorothea Mackellar, 'Town and Country', *The Poems of Dorothea Mackellar*, edited by C.K.M Dredge and B.K. Elkins (Adelaide: Rigby, 1971), p. 61.
9   Susan Sheridan, *Along the Faultlines: Sex, Race and Nation in Australian Women's Writing 1880s–1930s* (St Leonards: Allen and Unwin, 1995), p. 112.
10 Frank Farrell, 'Socialism, Internationalism and the Australian Labour Movement', *Labour*, No. 15 (Spring, 1985), pp. 125–144.
11 'The Feeble-minded', *Sydney Morning Herald*, 4 November 1917, p. 9.

CHAPTER 13

1. Adrienne Howley, *My Heart, My Country* (St Lucia: University of Queensland Press, 1989), p. 134.
2. Dorothea Mackellar, 'The Youthful Sheila', quoted in *I Love a Sunburnt Country: The Diaries of Dorothea Mackellar*, edited by Jyoti Brunsdon (North Ryde: Angus & Robertson, 1990), p. 194.
3. 'Peace and Victory', *Sydney Morning Herald*, 12 November 1918, p. 6.
4. 'Influenza Campaign', *Sydney Morning Herald*, 30 January 1919, p. 6.
5. Bertram Stevens, 'Australian Writers', *The Herald* [Melbourne], 1 November 1919, p. 10.
6. Stevens, 'Australian Writers', p. 10.
7. Stevens, 'Australian Writers', p. 10.
8. Robert H. Ross, *The Georgian Revolt: Rise and Fall of a Poetic Ideal 1910 to 1922* (London: Faber and Faber, 1967), p. 210.
9. 'Motion Pictures', *Sydney Morning Herald*, 3 September 1919, p. 11.

CHAPTER 14

1. Dorothea Mackellar, 'Whitsunday Passage', *The Poems of Dorothea Mackellar*, edited by C.K.M Dredge and B.K. Elkins (Adelaide: Rigby, 1971), p. 68.
2. 'Society Wedding', *Sydney Morning Herald*, 11 April 1920, p. 2.
3. Dorothea Mackellar, 'Vestal, 1920', *The Poems*, p. 71.
4. 'The Danish Pavilion,' Overstrand Parish Council, https://www.overstrandparishcouncil.org.uk/our-village/danish-pavilion/, accessed 21 July 2021.
5. Dorothea Mackellar, 'I Will Not Think Her Foundered', *The Poems*, p. 75.
6. Dorothea Mackellar, 'The Cherry Tree', *The Poems*, p. 73.

CHAPTER 15

1. 'Home Again: Miss Dorothea Mackellar's Travels', *Daily Telegraph* [Sydney], 4 February 1921, p. 6.
2. J.E. Hunt, *Cultivating the Arts*, Doctoral Thesis, Macquarie University, 2001, p. 167.
3. Hunt, *Cultivating the Arts*, pp. 187–188.
4. Hunt, *Cultivating the Arts*, p. 188.
5. Marjorie Quinn, *The Years that the Locust Hath Eaten: The Memoirs of Marjorie Quinn* (Melbourne: Arcadia 2011), p. 155.
6. Hunt, *Cultivating the Arts*, p. 167.
7. Ethel Turner, *The Diaries of Ethel Turner*, edited by Philippa Poole (London: Ure Smith, 1979), p. 257.

8   Susan Mary Waterford, 'PEN Portraits of Some Sydney Women', *Woman's World*, quoted in Hunt, *Cultivating the Arts*, p. 193.
9   'A Satchel of Books', *The Bulletin* [Sydney], Vol. 44, No. 2289, 27 December 1923, p. 5.
10 '*Dream Harbour*: Miss Mackellar's Verses', *The Herald* [Melbourne], 10 November 1923, p. 16.
11 Review of *Dreamharbour*, 1923 notebook, ML MSS 1959, Box 19, Mackellar Family Papers, Mitchell Library, Sydney.
12 Newspaper clippings, 1930, ML MSS 1959, Box 16, Mackellar Family Papers, Mitchell Library, Sydney.
13 Rosalie Morton to Ruth Bedford, April 1924, ML MSS 1959, Box 8, Mackellar Family Papers, Mitchell Library, Sydney.
14 'What the World Is Thinking', *Daily Telegraph* [Sydney], 17 May 1924, p. 14.
15 'An Unsociable Song', *Sydney Morning Herald*, 16 August 1924, p. 11.
16 'The New Drama in Sydney', *Table Talk*, 23 April 1925, p. 14.
17 'The New Drama in Sydney', p. 14.
18 'Poetess at Actress', *World News*, 9 May 1925, p. 9.
19 Dorothea Mackellar, 'Trees: An Oppressed People', *Sydney Morning Herald*, 15 August 1925, p. 11.

CHAPTER 16

1   'New Year', *Sydney Morning Herald*, 1 January 1926, p. 4.
2   'Dorothea Mackellar', *Sunday Times*, 6 June 1926, p. 3.
3   'Late Sir Charles Mackellar', *Sydney Morning Herald*, 16 July 1926, p. 12.
4   'Charles Kinnaird Mackellar', *The Medical Journal of Australia*, Vol. 2, No. 6, 7 August 1926, p. 196.
5   'Notable Citizen', *Sydney Morning Herald*, 15 July 1926, p. 12.
6   Keith Amos, *Dorothea Mackellar at Pittwater* (Cromer: Amos, 2020), p. 11.
7   Susan Duncan, *The House at Salvation Creek*, eBook edition (Random House, 2008).
8   Adrienne Howley, *My Heart, My Country* (St Lucia: University of Queensland Press, 1989), p. 134.
9   'Australian Poetry', *The Register* [Adelaide], 3 July 1926, p. 5.
10 'Dorothea Mackellar', *The Queenslander* [Brisbane], 29 January, 1927, p. 8.
11 'Poetess and Novelist', *Daily Telegraph* [Sydney], 10 March, 1927, p. 5.
12 Horoscope reading, 1927, ML MSS 1959, Box 9, Mackellar Family Papers, Mitchell Library, Sydney.

13 Bernice May, 'Fancy Dress', *Australian Worker*, 9 March 1927, p. 13.
14 Bernice May, 'Dorothea Mackellar', *Australian Women's Mirror*, Vol. 3, No. 49, 1 November 1927, p. 11.
15 May, 'Dorothea Mackellar', p. 11.
16 'Gossip from Sydney', *Telegraph*, 12 November 1927, p. 19.
17 'Attempt to Assassinate Mussolini', *Daily Telegraph* [Sydney], 13 April 1928, p. 4.

CHAPTER 17

1 Newspaper clippings, 1928, ML MSS 1959, Box 19, Mackellar Family Papers, Mitchell Library, Sydney.
2 Dorothea Mackellar, 'Another Heritage', *The Poems of Dorothea Mackellar*, edited by C.K.M Dredge and B.K. Elkins (Adelaide: Rigby, 1971), p. 124.
3 Dorothea Mackellar, 'Psyche's Wings', *Sydney Morning Herald*, 6 April 1929, p. 13.

CHAPTER 18

1 Elizabeth Webby, 'Patrick Victor White (Paddy) (1912–1990)', *Australian Dictionary of Biography*, National Centre for Biography, Australian National University, https://adb.anu.edu.au/biography/white-patrick-victor-paddy-14925. Accessed 1 June 2023.
2 David Marr, *Patrick White: A Life* (North Sydney: Random House, 1991), pp. 82–3.
3 Patrick White, *Flaws in the Glass* (New York: Penguin, 1983), p. 14.
4 Marr, *Patrick White: A Life*, pp. 82–3.
5 Marr, *Patrick White: A Life*, pp. 82–3.
6 'Australia in 1930', *Canberra Times*, 1 January 1930, p. 4.
7 'Poetess Home: "Wanted to Cry"', *Evening News* [Sydney], 13 February 1930, p. 13.
8 'A Poetess at Home', *The Sun* [Sydney], 23 February 1930, p. 6.
9 'Australians Abroad', *The Australasian* [Melbourne], 9 February 1929, p. 15.
10 'The World of Books,' *The Mercury* [Hobart], 22 November 1929, p. 3.
11 'Pre-War Friendship', *The Sun* [Sydney], 26 January 1930, p. 35.
12 'Chatter', *North Western Courier* [Narrabri], 12 December 1929, p. 1.
13 'Social', *Daily Telegraph* [Sydney], 19 December 1896, p. 14.
14 'Community Playhouse', *Sydney Morning Herald*, 30 January 1930, p. 15.
15 'Ruth Bedford Writes First Thriller', *The Sun* [Sydney], 17 May 1931, p. 35.

16 Dorothea Mackellar, quoted in 'Book Snobs', *The Sun* [Sydney], 29 August 1930, p. 10.
17 Dorothea Mackellar, 'The Art of Reading', 1930 notebook, ML MSS 1959, Box 16, Mackellar Family Papers, Mitchell Library, Sydney.
18
19 Newspaper clipping from *The Bulletin,* 12 August 1931, ML MSS 1959, Box 11, Mackellar Family Papers, Mitchell Library, Sydney.
20 'A Poetess at Home', *The Sun* [Sydney], 23 February 1930, p. 6.
21 'Sydney Harbour Bridge', *Sydney Morning Herald*, 21 March 1932, p. 4.
22 Ruth Bedford, 'The PEN Club', *Sydney Morning Herald*, 7 December 1936, p. 8.
23 'Two Swoon in Sydney Beauty Salon', *The Examiner*, 14 July 1939, p. 7.
24 Michael Sheridan, 'She Sang of Our Own Wide Brown Land', *Australian Women's Weekly*, 22 July 1939, p. 12.

CHAPTER 19

1 Keith Amos, *Dorothea Mackellar at Pittwater* (Cromer: Amos, 2020), p. 26.
2 Susan Duncan, *The House at Salvation Creek*, eBook edition (Random House, 2008).
3 Di Morrissey, 'Tragedy on Lovett Bay', Interview by Sarah Kanowski, *Conversations,* ABC Radio, 31 October 2019.
4 Di Morrissey, Interview by Deborah FitzGerald, 10 September 2022.
5 Morrissey, 'Tragedy on Lovett Bay'.
6 'A Poetess at Home', *The Sun* [Sydney], 23 February 1930, p. 6.
7 Dorothea Mackellar, untitled poem, 1940 verse book, ML MSS 1959, Box 18, Mackellar Family Papers, Mitchell Library, Sydney.
8 Adrienne Howley, *My Heart, My Country* (St Lucia: University of Queensland Press, 1989), p. 181.
9 Dorothea Mackellar, untitled poem, 1942 verse book, ML MSS 1959, Box 18, Mackellar Family Papers, Mitchell Library, Sydney.
10 'Malcolm Mackellar (1889–1943)', Obituaries Australia, National Centre of Biography, Australian National University, http://oa.anu.edu.au/obituary/mackellar-malcolm-19659/text30980. Accessed 22 September 2020.
11 Dorothea Mackellar to Helen Rankin, quoted in *Dorothea Mackellar at Pittwater* by Keith Amos (Cromer: Amos, 2020), p. 28.
12 Jane Connors, 'Bedford, Ruth Marjory (1882–1963)', *Australian Dictionary of Biography*, National Centre for Biography, Australian National University, https://adb.anu.edu.au/biography/bedford-ruth-marjory-9468, accessed 9 January 2023.

13 Ruth Bedford, interview by Hazel De Berg, The Hazel De Berg Collection, Australian National Library, 15 September 1961.
14 Dorothea Mackellar to Principal Rosenthal, quoted in *Dorothea Mackellar at Pittwater*, p. 28.
15 Dorothea Mackellar, 'Peaceful Voices', *Sydney Morning Herald*, 6 February 1926, p. 11.
16 Jennifer Stiller, written recollection, 19 January 2023.
17 Pixie O'Harris, quoted in *Dorothea Mackellar at Pittwater* by Keith Amos (Cromer: Amos, 2020), p. 34.
18 Howley, *My Heart*, p. 204.
19 Howley, *My Heart*, p. 204.
20 Pixie O'Harris, quoted in *Dorothea Mackellar at Pittwater*, p. 16.
21 Pixie O'Harris, quoted in *Dorothea Mackellar at Pittwater*, p. 34.
22 'Almost a Signature', *Canberra Times*, 16 January 1968, p. 9.
23 'Almost a Signature', p. 9.
24 Marjorie Quinn, *The Years that the Locust Hath Eaten: The Memoirs of Marjorie Quinn* (Melbourne: Arcadia 2011), p. 65.
25 K. Torney, 'Mackellar, (Isobel Marion) Dorothea', *The Oxford Companion to Australian History*, edited by Graeme Davison, John Hirst, and Stuart Macintyre, eBook edition (Oxford University Press, 2003).
26 'Poet of a Sunburnt Country Reassessed', *Canberra Times*, 21 August 1982, p. 13.
27 Dorothea Mackellar, 'Night on the Plains', *The Poems of Dorothea Mackellar*, edited by C.K.M Dredge and B.K. Elkins (Adelaide: Rigby, 1971), p. 28.
28 'Why I wrote "My Country"', *Sydney Morning Herald*, 12 March 1965, https://www.smh.com.au/national/from-the-archives-1965-why-i-wrote-my-country-20200306-p547k9.html
29 Michael Sheridan, 'She Sang of Our Own Wide Brown Land', *Australian Women's Weekly*, 22 July 1939, p. 12.
30 Sheridan, 'She Sang', p. 12.
31 Sheridan, 'She Sang', p. 12.
32 E.E.D. [possibly Enid Durham], newspaper clipping from *Commonweal*, 1 November 1911, ML MSS 1959, Box 19, Mackellar Family Papers, Mitchell Library, Sydney.
33 Dorothea Mackellar, 'Tests', *The Poems*, p. 180.

The stark white ringbarked
                    forests
All tragic 'neath the moon,
The sapphire-misted moun-
                    : tains
The hot gold rush of noon,
Green tangle of the brushes
Where lithe lianas coil
And orchid-laden tree-
                    ferns
Smother the crimson soil

Core of my heart, my coun-
                    : try —
Her pitiless blue sky,
When sick at heart, around
                    us
We see the cattle die ...
And then the grey clouds
                    gather
And we can bless again,
The drumming of an army,
The steady, soaking rain.